LABORATORY Manual

PHYSICS

CBSE Class XII

Author
Sayonika Jana

Name...

Class........................ **Section**........................ **Roll No**........................

School...

arihant
SUCCESS AND NOTHING LESS
Arihant Prakashan (School Division Series)

Arihant Prakashan (School Division Series)

All Rights Reserved

卐 © Publisher

No part of this publication may be re-produced, stored in a retrieval system or by any means, electronic mechanical, photocopying, recording, scanning, web or otherwise without the written permission of the publisher. Arihant has obtained all the information in this book from the sources believed to be reliable and true. However, Arihant or its editors or authors or illustrators don't take any responsibility for the absolute accuracy of any information published, and the damage or loss suffered thereupon.

All disputes subject to Meerut (UP) jurisdiction only.

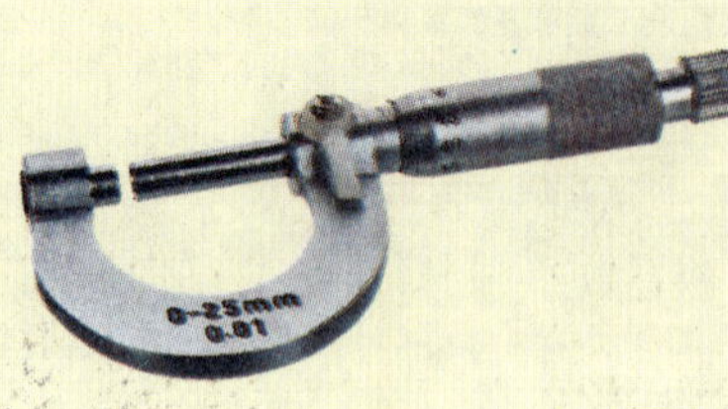

卐 Administrative & Production Offices

Regd. Office
'Ramchhaya' 4577/15, Agarwal Road, Darya Ganj, New Delhi -110002
Tele: 011- 47630600, 43518550; Fax: 011- 23280316

Head Office
Kalindi, TP Nagar, Meerut (UP) - 250002, Tel: 0121-7156203, 7156204

卐 Sales & Support Offices
Agra, Ahmedabad, Bengaluru, Bareilly, Chennai, Delhi, Guwahati, Hyderabad, Jaipur, Jhansi, Kolkata, Lucknow, Nagpur & Pune

卐 Price : ₹375.00

卐 PO No :TXT-59-T070108-3-26

Published by Arihant Publications (India) Ltd.

For further information about the books from Arihant, log on to **www.arihantbooks.com** or email to **info@arihantbooks.com**

Follow us on    

Contents

SECTION B

Experiments

Activities

Suggested Investigatory Projects

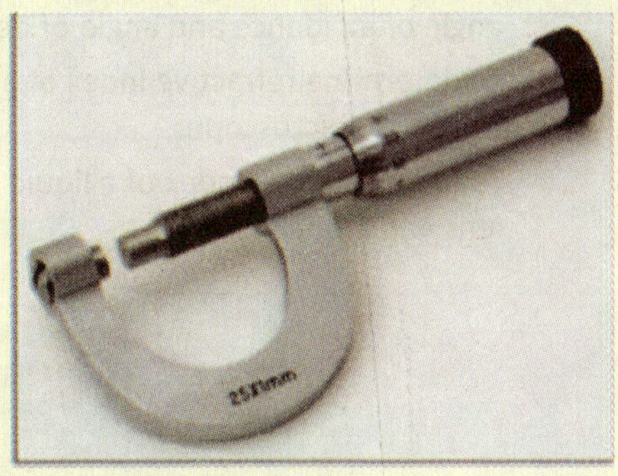

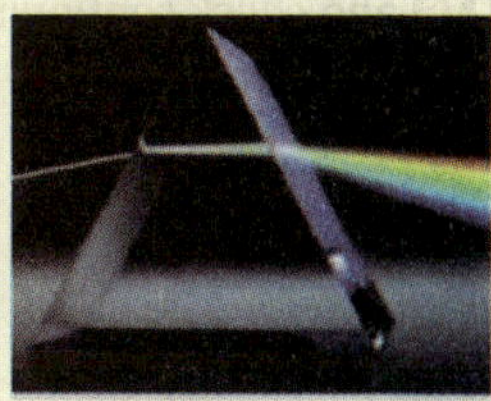

Syllabus

SECTION A

Experiments

1. To determine resistivity of two/three wires by plotting a graph for potential difference *versus* current.
2. To find resistance of a given wire/standard resistor using meter bridge.
3. To verify the laws of combination (series) of resistances using a meter bridge.

   Or

   To verify the laws of combination (parallel) of resistances using a meter bridge.
4. To determine resistance of a galvanometer by half-deflection method and to find its figure of merit.
5. To convert the given galvanometer (of known resistance and figure of merit) into a voltmeter of desired range and to verify the same.

   Or

   To convert the given galvanometer (of known resistance and figure of merit) into an ammeter of desired range and to verify the same.
6. To find the frequency of AC mains with a sonometer.

Activities

1. To measure the resistance and impedance of an inductor with or without iron core.
2. To measure resistance, voltage (AC/DC), current (AC) and check continuity of a given circuit using multimeter.
3. To assemble a household circuit comprising three bulbs, three (ON/OFF) switches, a fuse and a power source.
4. To assemble the components of a given electrical circuit.
5. To study the variation in potential drop with length of a wire for a steady current.
6. To draw the diagram of a given open circuit comprising at least a battery, resistor/rheostat, key, ammeter and voltmeter. Mark the components that are not connected in proper order and correct the circuit and also the circuit diagram.

SECTION B

Experiments

1. To find the value of v for different values of u in case of a concave mirror and to find the focal length.
2. To find the focal length of a convex mirror, using a convex lens.
3. To find the focal length of a convex lens by plotting graphs between u and v or between $1/u$ and $1/v$.
4. To find the focal length of a concave lens, using a convex lens.
5. To determine angle of minimum deviation for a given prism by plotting a graph between angle of incidence and angle of deviation.
6. To determine refractive index of a glass slab using a travelling microscope.
7. To find refractive index of a liquid by using convex lens and plane mirror.

8. To find the refractive index of a liquid using a concave mirror and a plane mirror.
9. To draw the *I-V* characteristic curve for a *p-n* junction diode in forward and reverse bias.

Activities

1. To identify a diode, an LED, a resistor and a capacitor from a mixed collection of such items.
2. Use of multimeter to see the unidirectional flow of current in case of a diode and an LED and check whether a given electronic component (e.g., diode) is in working order.
3. To study effect of intensity of light (by varying distance of the source) on an LDR.
4. To observe refraction and lateral deviation of a beam of light incident obliquely on a glass slab.
5. To observe diffraction of light due to a thin slit.
6. To study the nature and size of the image formed by a (i) convex lens or (ii) concave mirror, on a screen by using a candle and a screen (for different distances of the candle from the lens/mirror).
7. To obtain a lens combination with the specified focal length by using two lenses from the given set of lenses.

SUGGESTED INVESTIGATORY PROJECTS

1. To study various factors on which the internal resistance/EMF of a cell depends.
2. To study the variations in current flowing in a circuit containing an LDR because of a variation in (a) the power of the incandescent lamp, used to 'illuminate' the LDR (keeping all the lamps at a fixed distance). (b) the distance of a incandescent lamp (of fixed power) used to 'illuminate' the LDR.
3. To find the refractive indices of (a) water (b) oil (transparent) using a plane mirror, an equi convex lens (made from a glass of known refractive index) and an adjustable object needle.
4. To investigate the relation between the ratio of (i) output and input voltage and (ii) number of turns in the secondary coil and primary coil of a self-designed transformer.
5. To investigate the dependence of the angle of deviation on the angle of incidence using a hollow prism filled one by one, with different transparent fluids.
6. To estimate the charge induced on each one of the two identical Styrofoam (or pith) balls suspended in a vertical plane by making use of Coulomb's law.
7. To study the factor on which the self-inductance of a coil depends by observing the effect of this coil, when put in series with a resistor/bulb in a circuit fed up by an AC source of adjustable frequency.
8. To study the earth's magnetic field using a compass needle-bar magnet by plotting magnetic field lines and tangent galvanometer.

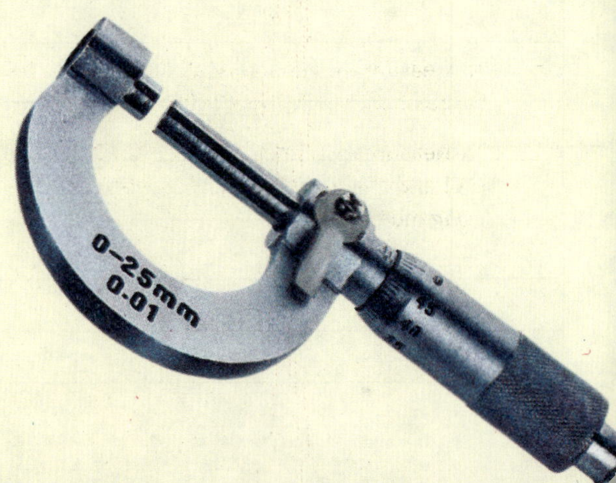

INDEX

S.No.	Name of the Experiment	Page No.	Date	Remarks

S.No.	Name of the Experiment	Page No.	Date	Remarks

INDEX

S.No.	Name of the Experiment	Page No.	Date	Remarks

LABORATORY Manual

PHYSICS

CERTIFICATE

This is to certify that Activities & Projects recorded in this Practical Notebook have been performed by ______________________
(Student's name)

of __________ of ______________________________
(Class/Section) (School name)

during academic session ____________________

....	....	....
Examiner Signature	Principal Signature (with school stamp)	Teacher Signature

General Introduction of Practical Work

Physics, a study of the basic laws of nature and their manifestation in the various natural phenomena, raises our eagerness and helps us to utilise this understanding to make our life interesting. As we know that all branches of science needs the experimental verification. The main purpose of laboratory experiments in physics is to verify the concepts, laws, principles and hypothesis related to physical phenomena.

From the past few centuries, the inventions and the discoveries made by the great scientists have resulted in the immense growth of physics. It implies that performing experiment once by our own hands in the physics laboratory generates the feeling of direct involvement with the generation of knowledge.

Attaining the data in the form of a result or a conclusion helps in boosting up the scientific temper, logical thinking, sense of self confidence, patience and develops the spirit of inquisitiveness and analytical skills. Eventually, it can be said that **the concepts of learner are made more stronger with the help of experimental physics**.

Objectives of Practical Work

Practical work is the basic foundation for the development and growth of science. The main objective of experimentation in science is to confirm the feasibility of a process which we study theoretically. The practical work in physics involves **learning by doing**. It clarifies the concepts and hence lays the seed for enquiry. Careful and stepwise observations of sequences during an experiment or activity facilitate personal investigation as well as small group or team learning. Thus, **practical work enhances the basic learning skills**.

Scientific Method To Perform The Experiments

The experiments should be performed in a systematic manner to get an accurate result. It may be proceed as:

(i) **Aim** The main aim of the experiment and the concept on which it is based should be very clear to the learner.

(ii) **Apparatus** The apparatus required during the experiment should be collected and their functioning should be clear to the learner.

(iii) **Theory/Principle** Most of the experiments are based on principles. They should be very clear to the learner.

(iv) **Experimentation** Study and follow the correct procedure for carrying out the experiment.

(v) **Observation** Record the observations, i.e. what the learner observed while doing the experiments. If possible, record the observations in a tabular form.

(vi) **Hypothesis** The learner should analyse the observations carefully to give a logical reasoning to explain them.

(vii) **Verification** Apply the hypothesis to other similar experiments in order to make a decision what you observed is correct or not.

(viii) **Predictions** To find new phenomena by changing variables (quantities) involved in the study of main phenomenon.

(ix) **Modifications** From the past few decades, more new techniques have been introduced, thus the old methods and procedures of experimentation need to be modified.

Some General Guidelines To Perform Experiment

1. Prepare yourself first with the experiment which you are going to perform. The principle, objective of the experiment and procedure to be followed should be clear.
2. Carefully, read all the instructions because in each and every sentence, there is some meaning which should be understood by you at the same time.
3. If at any instant, any doubt arises in your mind, then clear it from your respective physics teacher else it will create a problem in between the experiment.
4. After this, start collecting the apparatus and material required for performing the experiment.
5. Each and every item of the working apparatus should be checked initially, else if it is found with some technical defect later on, then it will result in the wastage of your time. **A minute error can create a big inaccuracy.**
6. The apparatus should be handled carefully, mainly the small weights, nuts, screws etc.
7. The table surface on which you perform the experiment should be neat, clear and free from the unnecessary articles.
8. The apparatus should be wiped with the clean, wet cloth smeared with Vaseline.
9. Do not try to disfigure the wooden parts of the apparatus.
10. The apparatus should be arranged in proper order to avoid any damage (specially, in case of experiments). Any accidental damage or breakage of the apparatus should be immediately brought to notice of concerned teacher, otherwise, it may cause some accident.
11. While taking the observations, observe the reading two to three times correctly and note it down in your observation copy and get it checked and signed by your physics teachers. **Highly precise readings result in the accurate measurement.**
12. While recording the observations, do not forget to note down the units in which the measurements are made.
13. It is mandatory that atleast one reading should be checked and verified by the teacher in charge while performing the experiment.
14. The series of observations should always be taken and always try to record them in a tabular form as it is an effective way of representing the readings.
15. Every part of your effort should be made honestly and don't try to write the false observations in order to have an exact result. Always mention the result in proper SI unit. Wherever possible, the observations should be represented with the help of graph.
16. Before leaving the laboratory, you should get your book signed and the apparatus used are to be returned to the laboratory assistant.
17. Switch off all the power plugs, which are used in the experiment before leaving the laboratory. In case of any electric power related accident, switch off the main supply of the laboratory.

How to Record An Experiment?

A neat and systematic recording of the experiment in the laboratory notebook is very important for keeping an upto date record of the work which has been done in the laboratory. Infact, a proper record of the experimental results and conclusions is an indispensable part of scientific work. The laboratory notebook must be well maintained and protected from mechanical and chemical damage. It should be made checked regularly by the teacher.

The experiment should be recorded in the laboratory notebook under the following heads as:

Date......   Experiment No. ......   Page No. ......

Aim or Objective of the Experiment State clearly and precisely the objective of the experiment to be performed.

Apparatus and Materials Required Mention the name of the apparatus and materials to be used in the experiment clearly.

Description of Apparatus Including Measuring Devices Describe the apparatus and measuring devices used in the experiment.

Terms and Definitions State the important terms and definitions used in the experiment.

Theory or Principle Mention the concept on which the experiment is based in a very brief manner. Also, write the formula used explaining the symbols involved clearly.

Procedure Mention various steps in the experiment followed with precautions.

Diagrams Wherever required, draw the diagrams on the left hand side of the notebook.

Observations Record the observations or data in a tabular form as far as possible, neatly and without any overwriting.

Calculations and Plotting Graph (wherever desirable) For writing the calculations, substitute the observed value in the formula and do the computations systematically and neatly. Wherever is possible, use the graphical method for obtaining the result.

Result State the conclusions drawn from the experimental observations. If the result depends upon the conditions of temperature and pressure, mention these conditions also along with the result.

Precautions Mention the precautions observed during the course of setting an apparatus and the steps followed while performing the experiment.

Sources of Error Mention the possible sources of error while performing the experiment and are liable to affect the result.

Discussion Under this heading mention any special inferences or special difficulties faced during the experimentation.

These may include points for making the experiment more accurate and for better understanding of the basic principle involved.

Experimental Errors

Every measurement is done with the help of some instruments. While making the measurement, some uncertainty gets introduced in the measurement. As a result, the measured value is always some what different from the actual or true value. This is called **error** which is equal to the difference between the true value and the measured value of the quantity. It is a fact that **there is no measurement without errors**. But the errors occurred during the experiment can be minimised upto a certain extent after knowing about them.

Different Types Of Errors

1. Systematic Errors

The errors which tend to occur in one direction, either positive or negative, are called systematic errors. We can eliminate such errors once we know the rule which governs them. These errors are of following types:

(a) **Instrumental Errors** These errors occur due to inbuilt defect of the measuring instrument. This error can be detected by measuring a physical quantity with two different instruments of the same type or by measuring the same physical quantity by two different methods.

(b) **Imperfection in Experimental Technique** These errors occur due to the limitations of the experimental arrangement. Such errors cannot be eliminated altogether but necessary corrections can be applied for them.

(c) **Imperfection in Procedure** These errors occur due to the imperfection in experimental technique. e.g. to determine the temperature of a human body, a thermometer placed under armpit will always give a temperature lower than the actual value of the body temperature.

(d) **Personal Errors** These errors arise due to inexperience of the observer, such as lack of proper setting of the proper apparatus, reading an instrument without setting it properly, taking observations without observing proper precautions etc. e.g. If we keep our eye to read the scale in inclination, then **parallax error** will occur.

(e) **Errors due to External Causes** The external conditions such as changes in temperature, pressure, humidity, wind velocity etc., during the experiment may systematically affect the measurement.

2. Random Errors

The random errors are the errors which occur irregularly. They are random with respect to the sign and size. The random errors are sometimes called the **chance errors**.

They may arise due to random and unpredictable variations in experimental conditions, i.e. temperature, pressure, voltage supply, vibration, etc. These errors can be minimised by repeating the observation a large number of times and taking arithmetic mean of all the observations. The accuracy of measurement is related to the systematic errors but its precision is related to the random errors, which include least count error also.

Least Count Error

The smallest value that can be measured by a measuring instrument is called least count of the instrument.

e.g. A metre scale having graduations at 1 mm division scale spacing has a least count of 1 mm or 0.1 cm. Thus, in the measurement of length using a metre scale reliability is up to 1/10 cm, instruments of higher resolution and by improving experimental technique, we can reduce the least count errors.

Hence, **least count error is the error associated with the resolution of the instrument.**

Note The least count of an instrument is inversely proportional to the precision of the instrument.

Absolute Error, Relative Error and Percentage Error

Consider the values obtained in the several measurements be $x_1, x_2, ..., x_n$. The arithmetic mean of these values will be considered as the best possible value of the quantity.

$$x_{\text{mean}} = \frac{x_1 + x_2 + ... + x_n}{n} \quad \text{or} \quad x_{\text{mean}} = \frac{\sum_{i=1}^{n} x_i}{n}$$

These three errors (i.e. absolute, relative and percentage) are related with arithmetic mean of the measured values and are discussed below:

Absolute Error

It is the magnitude of the difference between the true (actual) value and individually measured value of the quantity.

$\therefore$ Absolute error $|\Delta a_i| = |\text{True value } (a_{\text{mean}}) - \text{measured value } (a_i)|$

The value of a physical quantity a is the arithmetic mean of all the absolute errors.

i.e. $$\Delta a_{\text{mean}} = \frac{|\Delta a_1| + |\Delta a_2| + ... + |\Delta a_n|}{n} = \frac{\sum_{i=1}^{n} |\Delta a_i|}{n}$$

For a single measurement, the value of the physical quantity may be in a range of $a_{\text{mean}} \pm \Delta a_{\text{mean}}$.

Relative Error

It is the ratio of the mean absolute error Δa_{mean} to the mean value a_{mean} of the physical quantity measured.

i.e. $$\text{Relative error} = \frac{\Delta a_{\text{mean}}}{a_{\text{mean}}}$$

Percentage Error

If the relative error is expressed in percent, it is called percentage error. Therefore,

$$\text{Percentage error} = \frac{\Delta a_{\text{mean}}}{a_{\text{mean}}} \times 100\%$$

Significant Figures

The digits that are known reliably plus the first uncertain digit are known as significant digits or significant figures.

e.g. when a measured distance is reported to be 374.5 cm, it has four significant figures 3, 7, 4 and 5. The digits 3, 7 and 4 are certain and reliable, while the digit 5 is uncertain. When time period of a simple pendulum is reported as 1.37 second it has three significant digits 1, 3, 7. The digits 1 and 3 are certain and reliable, while digit 7 is uncertain. Clearly, the digits beyond the significant digits reported in any result are superfluous.

The significant figures of the measured value should match with that of the error.

Rules for Counting Significant Figures

- All non-zero digits are significant.
  e.g. $x = 2356$ has 4 significant figures
- All zeros occurring between two non-zero digits are significant no matter where the decimal point is, if at all.
  e.g. $x = 1098$ has 4 significant figures,
  $x = 1.0709$ has 5 significant figures.
- If the number is less than one, the zero(s) on the right of the decimal point and to the left of first non-zero digit are not significant.
  e.g. In $\underline{0}.\underline{0}\,\underline{0}5804$, the underlined zeroes are not significant. The zero between 8 and 4 is significant. The number of significant figure is 4.
- In a number without a decimal point, the terminal or trailing zeroes are not significant.
- However, in a number with decimal point, the trailing zeroes are significant.
  e.g. $x = 3.600$ has four significant figures
  Similarly, $x = 0.0079000$ has five significant figures.
- Change of units does not change the number of significant figures in a measurement.
- The digit 0 conventionally put on the left of a decimal for a number less than 1 is never significant.
  e.g. $\underline{0}.3580$ has four significant digits. The underlined zero is not significant.
- The multiplying or dividing factors, which are neither rounded numbers nor numbers representing measured values, are exact. They have infinite number of significant digits as per the situation.

  e.g. radius $(r) = \dfrac{\text{diameter } (d)}{2}$ and circumference,

  $S = 2\pi r$, the factor 2 is an exact number. It can be written as 2.0, 2.00 or 2.000 as required.

Logarithms

Logarithm of a number to a given base is the index of the power to which the base must be raised to equal that number. If we relate a, x and N such that

$$a^x = N$$

then x is called the logarithm of N to the base a and is written as

$$x = \log_a N \quad \text{[read as log } N \text{ to the base } a]$$

If $2^6 = 64$, then the log of 64 to the base 2 is equal to 6.

$$\log_2 64 = 6$$

Generally to represent a number, we use logarithm to the base 10. Here, $\log 10 = 1$, $\log 100 = 2$ and so on.

Similarly, $10^4 = 10000$, log of 10000 to base 10 is equal to 4 or

$$\log_{10} 10000 = 4$$

Note Logarithm is of two types

(i) **Napierian**, in which the base is e. This is not used in general practice.

(ii) **Common**, in which base is 10. This is generally used in practice. Logarithm to base 10 is usually represented as log.

Properties Of Logarithm

1. $\log_a mn = \log_a m + \log_a n$
2. $\log_a \frac{m}{n} = \log_a m - \log_a n$
3. $\log_a m^n = n \log_a m$
4. $\log_e m = 2.303 \log_{10} m$

Common Logarithm

The logarithm of a number consists of two parts

1. integral part, called **characteristics**.
2. decimal or fractional part, called **mantissa**.

Note Characteristic may be either positive or negative but mantissa is always positive.

How to Find Characteristic of a Number?

The characteristics of a number depends on its magnitude and is determined by the position of the decimal point.

We use the following rules to find the characteristics of a number:

1. If the given number is greater than 1, its characteristic is positive. Count the number of digits to the left of decimal point. Subtract 1 from this number. This is the characteristics of the log of given number.

For example, Characteristic 1795.2 is 4 – 1 = 3

Characteristic 16.78 is 2 – 1 = 1

Characteristic of 17.943 is 2 – 1 = 1

2. If the given number is less than one, its characteristic is negative. It is put under the bar. Count the number of zeros immediately after the decimal point. Add 1 to this number. It gives us the characteristic of log of given number. For example,

   Characteristics of 0.7821 = – (0 + 1) = $\bar{1}$

   Characteristics of 0.0618 = – (1 + 1) = $\bar{2}$

How to Find Mantissa of a Number?

The value of mantissa depends upon the digits and their order. It is independent of the position of the decimal point. As long as the digits and their order is same, mantissa of numbers is same, whatever be the position of the decimal point.

The logarithm tables give the mantissa of a number only. They are usually meant for numbers consisting of four digits, and if a number contains more than four figures, it is rounded off to four figures after finding out the characteristic.

To determine the mantissa, the logarithm tables are used in the following manner.

1. In the given number, omit the decimal point and zeros in the beginning and at the end. e.g. In the number 0.001184, we have to look up the mantissa of 1184.
2. Take first two digits, i.e. 11 and locate it in the first vertical column of the four figure log table.
3. Go through the horizontal row beginning with 11 and look up the value under the column, headed by the fourth digit. i.e. 8 from the log table. We find this number as 0719.
4. Continue moving in the same horizontal row and note the number in small differences column, headed by the fourth digit. i.e. 4. This number is 15.
5. Add 15 to 0719. We get 0734

   ∴The mantissa = .0734

   Now, with the help of characteristic and mantissa, one can find the logarithm from the table.

Example 1 Find the logarithm of 132.4.

Sol. Step I ***Find the characteristic of 132.4.***

The number has 3 figures to the left of the decimal point.

Therefore, its characteristics is 3 – 1 = 2.

Step II ***Find the mantissa of 132.4.***

To determine mantissa, ignore the decimal point and look for 13 in the first vertical column in the logarithm table. For 2, look in the central topmost column. Proceed from 13 along a horizontal line towards the right and from 2 vertically downwards. The two lines meet at a point where number 1206 is written. This is the mantissa of 132.

Step III ***Looking up the figures just after the decimal point.***

Proceed further along the horizontal line in the logarithm table and look vertically below the figure 4 in mean difference column. You will find 13 there.

Thus, the mantissa of 1324 is 1206 +13 = 0.1219

Step IV ***Finding the final logarithm of 132.4.***

∴ Logarithm of 132.4 is 2.1219 i.e. log 132.4 = 2.1219

Example 2 Find the logarithm of 132400.

Sol. The characteristics of this number is 5. The mantissa is the same as in example 1,above. We can find the mantissa of only four significant figures, therefore, we neglect last two zeros.

$\therefore$ $\log 132400 = 5.1219$

Example 3 Find the logarithm of 0.00132422.

Sol. The characteristic of this number is $\bar{3}$, as there are only two zeros after the decimal point.

We can find the mantissa of only four significant numbers, therefore, we neglect the last two figures (22) and determine the mantissa of 1324 which is 1219.

$\therefore$ $\log 0.00132422 = \bar{3}.1219$

When the last figure of a number containing more than four significant figures is equal to or more than 5, the figure next to the left of it is raised by one and so on till we have only four significant figures. However, if the last figure is less than 5, then it is neglected as in the above example.

For example, if the number is 1324.57, the last figure is 7, therefore, we shall raise the next figure to 6 and since 6 is again more than 5, therefore, we shall raise the next figure to 5 and determine the logarithm of 1325.

Antilogarithm

The number whose logarithm is x, is called antilogarithm and is denoted by antilog x. Therefore, as log 2 = 0.3010, then antilog 0.3010 = 2

Example 4 Find the number whose logarithm is 1.7086 by using antilogarithms table.

Sol. Step I ***Identifying figures in the fractional part.***

1.7086

Characteristic Mantissa

In the fractional part, the first two figures from the left are 0.70, the third figure is 8 and the fourth figure is 6.

Step II ***Finding the number of mantissa .708.***

In antilogarithms table, first look in the vertical column for 0.70. In this horizontal row under the column headed by 8, we find the number 5105 at the intersection. This implies the number for mantissa 0.708 is 5105.

Step III ***Finding the number of mantissa .7086.***

Proceeding further along the horizontal line and under the mean difference column on the right under 6, we find the number 7 at the intersection. On adding 7 to 5105, we get 5112. Therefore, 5112 is the figure of which .7086 is the mantissa.

Step IV ***Putting the decimal according to the characteristic of the given number.***

The characteristic of number is 1, which is one more than the number of digits in the integral part of the required number.

Therefore, the number of digits in the integral part of required number = 1 + 1 = 2.

Step V ***Finding the final antilogarithm.***

Thus, the required number is 51.12, i.e. antilog 1.7086 = 51.12

Study of Graphs

A Graph is a pictorial way of representing relationships between various quantities, parameters, or measurable variables in nature. It basically summarizes how one variable called **dependent variable** changes if another variable called **independent variable** that is related to it also changes.

In any graph, the independent variable is represented along *X*-axis and the dependent variable is represented along *Y*-axis.

Plotting A Graph

Graphs are generally plotted on a graph paper ruled in millimeter or centimeter squares. The following steps should be followed by a learner while plotting a graph:

1. Identify the independent variable and dependent variable and represent them along *X*-axis and *Y*-axis, respectively.
2. The horizontal line represents the **abscissa** or *X*-axis and the vertical line represents the **ordinate** or *Y*-axis, intersecting at a point *O*, called the **origin**.
3. Find out the range of each of the variables and count the number of big square available to represent each, along the respective axes.
4. To choose the scale for plotting a graph, the smallest division on the graph paper should be ideally equal to the least count of measurement or the accuracy to which the particular parameter is known.
5. Choose (0, 0) as origin when the relation between variable begins from zero or it is desired to determine the zero position of one of the variables, if its actual determination is not possible. But in all the other situations, the origin can be represented by a round number nearest to but less than the smallest value of the corresponding variable.
6. The scale marking on each of the axis should not be crowded. Write the numbers at every fifth cm of the axis. Also, write the units of the physical quantity plotted. Give the scientific representations of the numbers i.e. write the number with the decimal point following the first digit and multiply the number by appropriate power of ten. Give a suitable caption of physical quantities involved below the plotted graph.
7. For drawing a graph, take at least six to seven readings extending equally over a wide range.
8. Plot the points for various pairs of corresponding values to two quantities and draw a small circle i.e. ⊙ or put a × around each of the plotted points. Along with the circle, two bars are also drawn such as ⊙̄. The distance between these two bars gives the **uncertainty in measurement**.

9. If the graph appears to be a straight line, draw a straight line passing exactly through most of the points and symmetrically through the rest. However, if graph does not appear to be a straight line, then draw a free hand smooth curve so that maximum number of points lie exactly on it.
10. Give the name of the graph at the top of the graph paper i.e. write the heading **Graph showing relation between** x (independent variable) **and** y (dependent variable).

Applications of Graph

1. The shape of the graph plotted for two quantities gives the idea about the relationship between those two quantities. Let say, if the graph is a straight line and passes through the origin, it may be represented by a relation $y = mx$. If the graph is a straight line having positive or negative intercepts on Y-axis, it is represented by $y = mx + c$.
2. The slope of the graph and its intercepts on the X or Y-axis give us the value of physical quantities.
3. The graph plotted between the two quantities helps us in identifying the accuracy in the experimental data.
4. We can find out the mean value easily from a large number of observations.

Determination of the Slope of a Straight Line

The slope of a straight line is determined by pointing the two values of a variable on Y-axis due to the corresponding two values of a variable on X-axis. If the change in two values on Y-axis is Δy while on X-axis is Δx, then, the slope of a straight line can be given as

$$\text{Slope, } m = \frac{\Delta y}{\Delta x}$$

We will get the positive slope when both Δy and Δx are of same sign as shown in Fig. (a). In the contrast to this, the slope will be negative if Δy is of opposite sign than that of Δx as shown in Fig. (b).

The slope of a given straight line has the same value for all points on the line i.e. $\Delta x = \Delta y$. It means that the change in x and the corresponding change in y will be same. Thus, for a given straight line, the slope is fixed as shown in Fig (c).

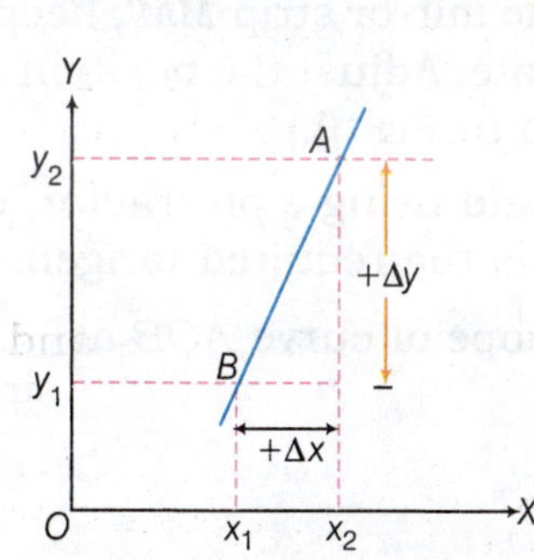

(a) Figure showing positive slope

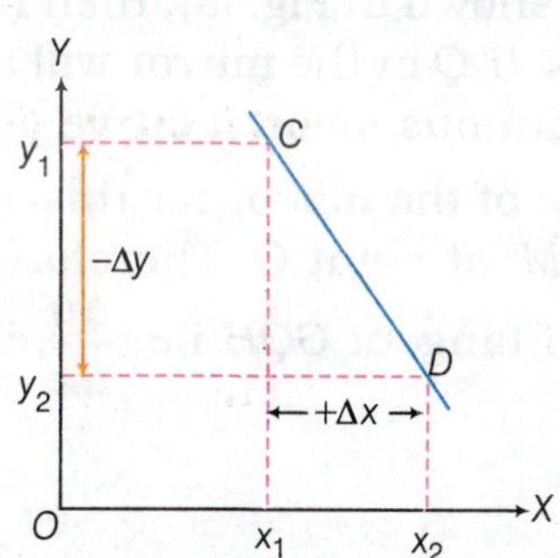

(b) Figure showing negative slope

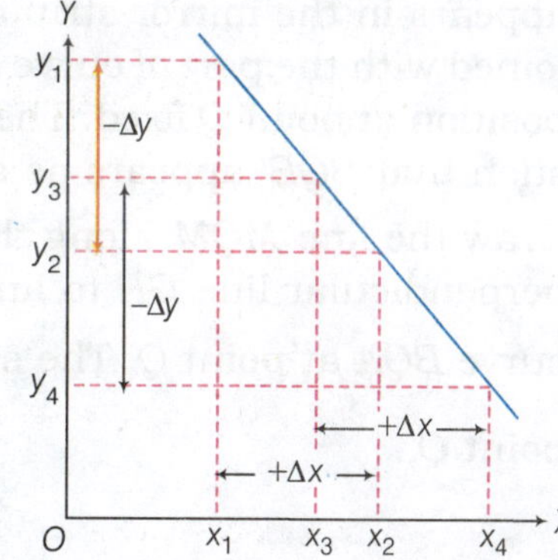

(c) Slope is fixed for a given straight line

Determination of the Slope of a Curve

The slope of the curve may have different values of slope at different points on the curve. Therefore, in case of curve, slope at a particular point is taken i.e. point Q.

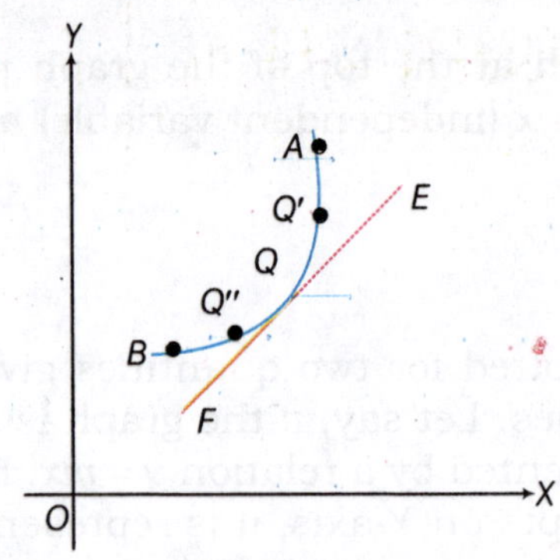

Tangent at point Q

To find the slope of a curve at a given point, one must draw a tangent to the curve at the desired point with the help of a plane mirror strip attached to a wooden block, so that it stands perpendicular to the paper on which the curve is to be drawn. This is shown in figures (a) and (b).

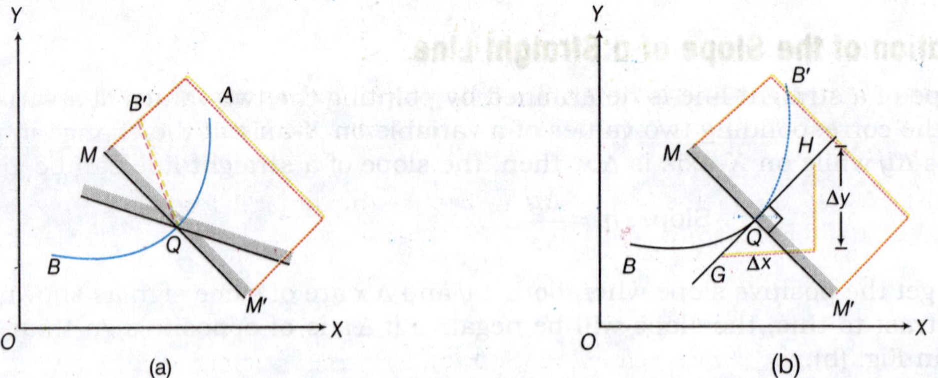

Determination of the slope of a curve

The plane mirror strips MM' is placed at desired point Q such that image $B'Q$ of part BQ of curve appears in the mirror strip as continuation of BQ. If image $B'Q$ will not appear to be smoothly joined with the part of curve BQ as shown in Fig. (a), then rotate the mirror strip MM', keeping its position at point Q fixed. The image $B'Q$ in the mirror will also rotate. Adjust the position of MM' such that BQB' appears as a continuous smooth curve as shown in Fig. (b).

Draw the line MQM' along the edge of the mirror for this setting and using a protractor, draw a perpendicular line GH to line MQM' at point Q. Therefore, GQH is the required tangent to the curve BQA at point Q. The slope of tangent GQH i.e. $\frac{\Delta y}{\Delta x}$, is the slope of curve AQB at point Q.

Section A

Experiment 1

AIM

To determine resistivity of two/three wires by plotting a graph for potential difference *versus* current.

Apparatus and Material Required

Two to three wires (of about 100 cm length) of unknown resistance, a battery eliminator or an accumulator (0 to 3 V), a rheostat, one-way plug key, a DC milliammeter (500 mA),DC voltmeter, thick connecting wires, a meter scale provided with terminals and a piece of sand paper.

Theory/Principle

Ohm's law states that

"The current flowing through a conductor is directly proportional to the potential difference between any two points of the conductor provided the physical conditions such as temperature, pressure, etc., remain constant".

If V is the potential difference across the ends of the conductor and I is the corresponding current, then according to Ohm's law,

$$V \propto I$$

$$\therefore \quad V = IR \qquad \ldots(i)$$

where, R = constant of proportionality called **resistance** of the conductor.

Determination of Resistance from the Graph

If we plot a graph between V and I by taking them along X and Y-axes respectively, we get a straight line passing through the origin.

From Eq. (i), $V = IR$

$$\frac{I}{V} = \frac{1}{R}$$

So, the slope of graph is $\frac{1}{R}$.

i.e. $$\text{Slope} = \frac{1}{R}$$

$$\Rightarrow \quad R = \frac{1}{\text{Slope}}$$

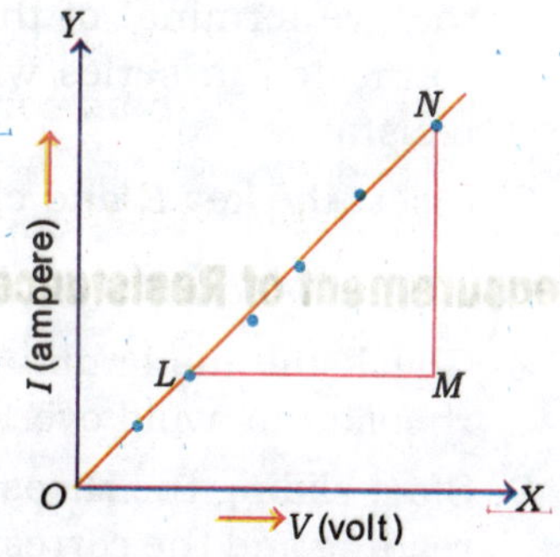

Graph showing linear relationship between V and I

If L is the length of the wire and r is the radius of the wire, then the resistivity of the wire is given as

$$\rho = \frac{RA}{L} = \frac{R \times \pi r^2}{L}$$

Procedure

Drawing the Circuit Diagram

1. First of all draw a neat circuit diagram as shown in figure below and arrange the apparatus in the same manner as shown in Fig. (1).

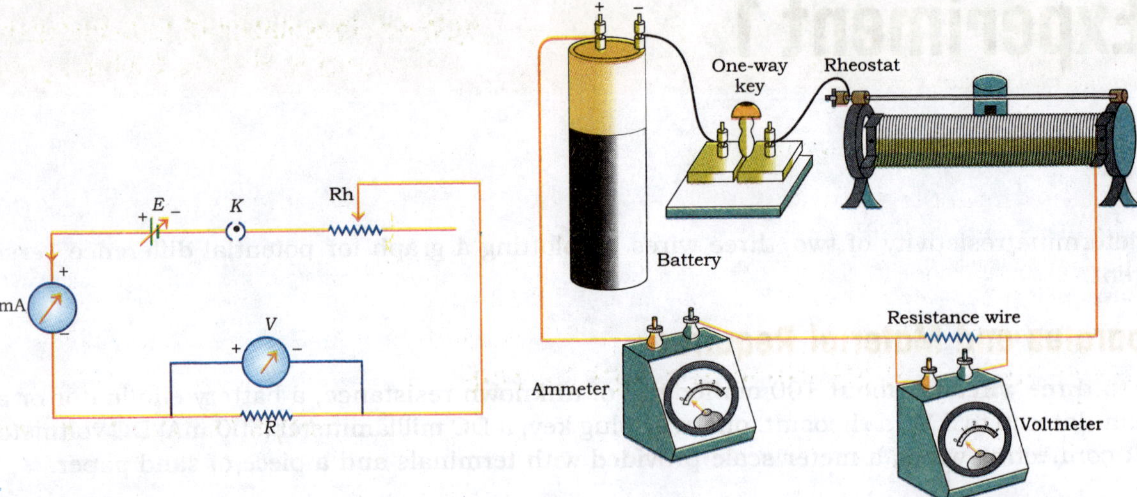

Fig. 1. Circuit diagram to verify the Ohm's law and to determine the resistance of a wire

Fig. 2. Experimental setup of Ohm's law

Setting up the Elements of Circuit

2. Remove the insulation coating from the ends of connecting wires by using sand paper.
3. Arrange all components from (resistor, rheostat, voltmeter, milliammeter, battery eliminator and key) as per the circuit diagram.
4. Check whether the pointers in milliammeter and voltmeter coincide with zero mark or not. If not, then adjust the screw provided near the base of pointer needle.
5. Note the range and least count of voltmeter as well as of milliammeter.
6. Now, by using copper wire make the tight connections according to the circuit diagram. It should be ensured that the +ve terminal of the voltmeter and ammeter are joined towards the +ve terminal of the battery as shown in Fig. (1). Also, ensure that the ammeter is connected in series with the resistance and voltmeter is connected in parallel with the resistance.
7. Insert the key K and check the milliammeter and voltmeter are working properly.

Measurement of Resistance of the Wire

8. Check the maximum and minimum readings on the ammeter and voltmeter using the rheostat to avoid overloading.
9. Start sliding the rheostat knob from the left to the right in steps. Note down the ammeter reading and the corresponding voltmeter reading every time. (Take care that the resistance does not get heated)
10. Pull out the key K and allow the wire to cool if it gets heated.
11. Insert the key K again and shift the rheostat contact slightly to increase the applied voltage.
12. Note again the milliammeter and voltmeter readings.

Note This time, we will get the increased value of current as the applied voltage has been increased.

13. Repeat steps (10) to (12) for few more times for different settings of rheostat and note the respective readings.
14. Plot the graph between V and I by taking them along X and Y-axes respectively and with the help of slope of the graph, determine the value of resistance by using the following relation.

$$\text{Resistance, } R = \frac{1}{\text{Slope}} = \ldots \Omega$$

15. Repeat the experiment for the second and third wire.

Determination of Resistivity of the Wire

16. Cut the wire at the points where it leaves the one terminal of the voltmeter and connected at the other.

Note It is to be ensured that the length of wire wound around the terminals of voltmeter should not be taken into account.

17. Now, remove the kinks in the wire (if any) and then stretch it against the meter scale.
18. Measure the resistivity of the wire $\rho = \dfrac{\pi r^2 R}{L}$.

Here, R is the value of resistance which is determined in step (14).

Observations and Calculations

1. Length of the wire, L = ... cm
2. Range of the ammeter = ... milliampere (mA)
3. Range of the voltmeter = ... volt (V)
4. Least count of ammeter = ... mA
5. Least count of voltmeter = ... V

Table for Milliammeter and Voltmeter Readings

S.N.	Voltmeter reading V (volt)	Milliammeter reading I (mA)	$R = V / I$ (ohm)
1.			
2.			
3.			
4.			
:			
8.			

6. Mean value of R = ... Ω
7. Least count of the screw gauge.
8. Pitch of the screw = ... mm
9. Total number of divisions on the circular scale, N = ...
10. Least count of the screw gauge $= \dfrac{\text{Pitch}}{N}$ = ... mm
11. Zero error of the screw gauge, e = ... mm
12. Zero correction for the screw gauge, $(-e)$ = ... mm

Table for the diameter (d) of the wire

S.N.	Linear Scale reading a (mm)	No. of circular scale division coinciding (n)	Circular scale reading $b = n \times LC$ (mm)	Observed diameter $d_0 = a + b$ (mm)
1.				
2.				
3.				

Mean corrected diameter, $d = d_0 + (-e) = \ldots\ldots$ cm.

Radius, $r = \frac{D}{2} = \ldots\ldots\ldots\ldots\ldots$ cm.

Plotting Graph

On plotting graph between V (along X-axis) and I (along Y-axis), we get a **straight line passing through the origin.** Hence, there is a linear relationship between the potential difference across the two ends of the conductor and current flowing through it.

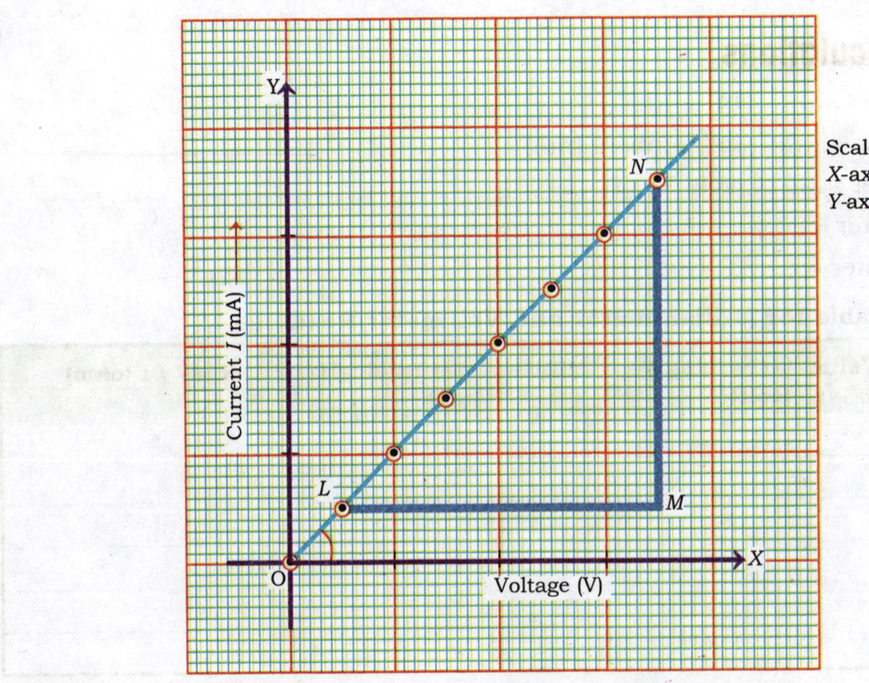

Graph showing relation between voltage and current

1. Find the slope of graph using formula, $\tan\theta = \text{Slope} = \frac{NM}{LM}$

$\therefore$ Resistance, $R = \frac{1}{\text{Slope}} = \ldots\ldots\Omega$

2. Determine resistivity of the wire $\rho = \frac{\pi r^2 R}{L} = \ldots\ldots\Omega$ cm.

Relative Error

As, $R = \frac{V}{I}$

∴ The relative error in the result can be estimated as, $\frac{\Delta R}{R} = \frac{\Delta V}{V} + \frac{\Delta I}{I} = ...$

Here, ΔR is the estimated error in the resistance value. ΔV and ΔI are the least counts of voltmeter and milliammeter respectively.

Result

(i) Resistivity of the first wire = ... Ω cm.

(ii) Resistivity of the second wire = ... Ω cm.

(iii) Resistivity of the third wire = ... Ω cm.

PRECAUTIONS

1. All the connections should be neat and clean and they should be tighten especially on the junctions.
2. To connect the elements or devices, a thick copper wire should be used after removing the insulations at its ends.
3. The wire used should be of uniform cross-section.
4. Take care that the voltmeter should be connected in parallel and the ammeter in series with the circuit. It must be remembered that current enters at the positive terminal and leaves at the negative terminal.
5. A low resistance rheostat must be used.
6. The plug in the key should be inserted only while taking observations otherwise the current would cause unnecessary heating in the circuit.
7. Measuring instruments of appropriate ranges should be used.

Sources of Error

1. The wire used may be of non-uniform cross-section.
2. The end resistance of wire may create some error in the result.
3. The instrument's screws may be loose.
4. The length of ends of the wire wound around the terminals of voltmeter may be included while measuring the total length of the wire.
5. The rheostat used may be of higher resistance value.
6. Due to the excessive heating, the resistance of the coil may be changed.

Viva-Voce

Q.1 State Ohm's law.

Ans. The current flowing between two points of a conductor is directly proportional to the potential difference between the same two points, provided that the temperature and other physical conditions of the conductor remain constant.

Q.2 On which factors does the resistance of a conductor depend?

Ans. Resistance of a conductor depends on

(i) nature of the material, i.e. resistivity (ρ),

(ii) length of the conductor (l) and

(iii) area of cross-section of conductor (A).

Q.3 Why should the resistance wire used in this experiment be of uniform cross-section and composition?

Ans. In order to get the resistance per unit length constant throughout the wire, the resistance wire should have uniform cross-section and composition.

Q.4 Why is it not advised to pass a large current through the conductor during the experiment?

Ans. If a large current is passed through a conductor, it will become hot which will increase the resistance of the conductor.

Q.5 How do the *V-I* graphs of non-ohmic resistors differ from those of ohmic resistors?

Ans. *V-I* graphs of ohmic resistors are always straight line, while *V-I* graphs of non-ohmic resistors are not straight line.

Q.6 Why a voltmeter is always connected in parallel with the circuit? [NCERT]

Ans A voltmeter is a high resistance device. If it is connected in series with the circuit then a very small current will flow through the circuit. So, a voltmeter is always connected in parallel with the circuit.

Q.7 Why an ammeter is always connected in series with the circuit?

Ans An ammeter is a low resistance device. If it is connected in parallel with the circuit then all the current will flow through the ammeter and it will cause a short circuit. So, an ammeter is always connected in series with the circuit.

Q.8 Why are copper wires normally used for connecting different components in an electric circuit? [NCERT]

Ans Because copper wire is a good conductor of electricity.

Q.9 What happens if the current is allowed to flow through the circuit continuously for long time? [NCERT]

Ans The circuit may get heated.

Experiment 2

AIM

To find the resistance of a given wire/standard resistor using a meter bridge.

Apparatus and Material Required

A meter bridge, a resistance box, a jockey, unknown resistance, a one-way key, a galvanometer, sand paper, connecting wires and a battery eliminator.

Meter Bridge

A meter bridge is also known as **slide wire bridge** used to measure an unknown resistance of a conductor by measuring its length. A circuit diagram showing a meter bridge is shown below.

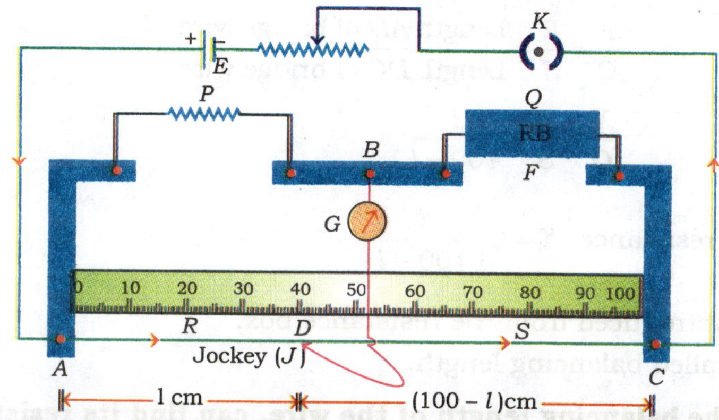

It is based on Wheatstone bridge. The resistance of the wire between the points A and D represents the resistance of arm R and the resistance between the points D and C represents the resistance of arm S. The resistance of the resistance box and unknown resistance represent the resistances of arm Q and P, respectively.

Theory/Principle

A meter bridge works on the principle of Wheatstone's bridge. A Wheatstone's bridge is an electrical network in which four resistors P, Q, R and S are connected to form the four arms of quadrilateral $ABCD$ as shown in the figure.

At the moment when the galvanometer shows zero deflection, then no current flows through the galvanometer and the **bridge is said to be balanced**. It happens when jockey is set at the point D called **null point** in the meter bridge.

Thus,

$$\frac{P}{Q} = \frac{R}{S} \qquad \text{...(i)}$$

Determination of Unknown Resistance

Since, the resistance (R) of a conductor is directly proportional to the length (l) of the conductor.

i.e.

$$R \propto l$$

Thus for bridge wire,

Resistance ratio = Length ratio

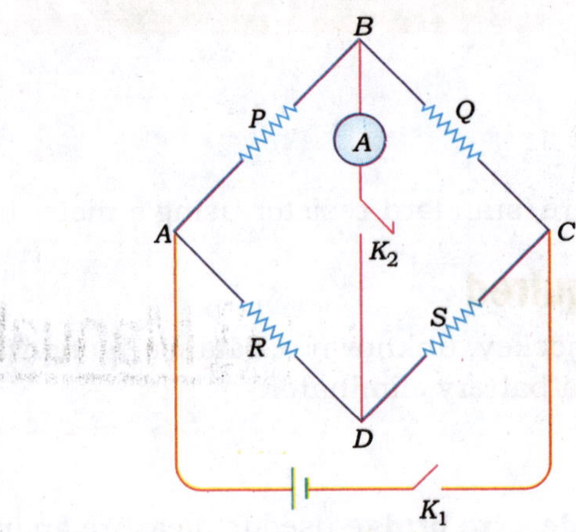

In the meter bridge, at null deflection in the galvanometer or when the bridge gets balanced,

$$\frac{P}{Q} = \frac{R}{S} = \frac{\text{Length } AD \text{ of bridge wire}}{\text{Length } DC \text{ of bridge wire}}$$

$$\therefore \quad \frac{X}{Q} = \frac{R}{S} = \frac{l}{100 - l}$$

$$\therefore \quad \text{Unknown resistance, } X = Q\left(\frac{l}{100 - l}\right)$$

where, Q = resistance introduced from the resistance box.

and l = length AD called balancing length.

Hence, by knowing the balancing length of the wire, can find its resistance.

Procedure

Set up the Meter Bridge

1. Take a piece of sandpaper and carefully remove the insulation from the ends of the connecting wires ensure proper electrical contact.
2. Arrange the components as per the circuit diagram of meter bridge and connect all the components with the help of connecting wire.

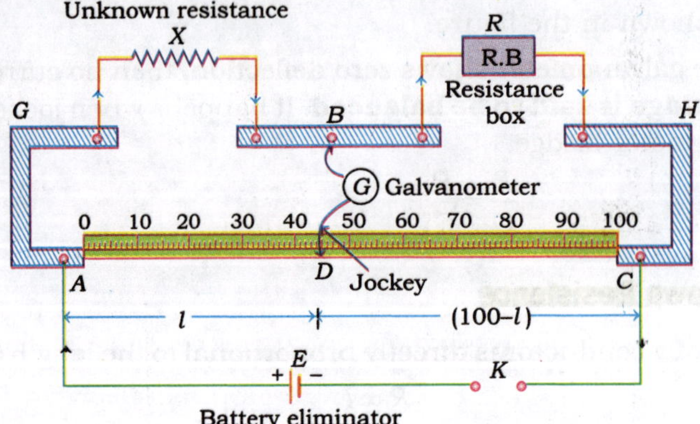

Circuit diagram of meter bridge

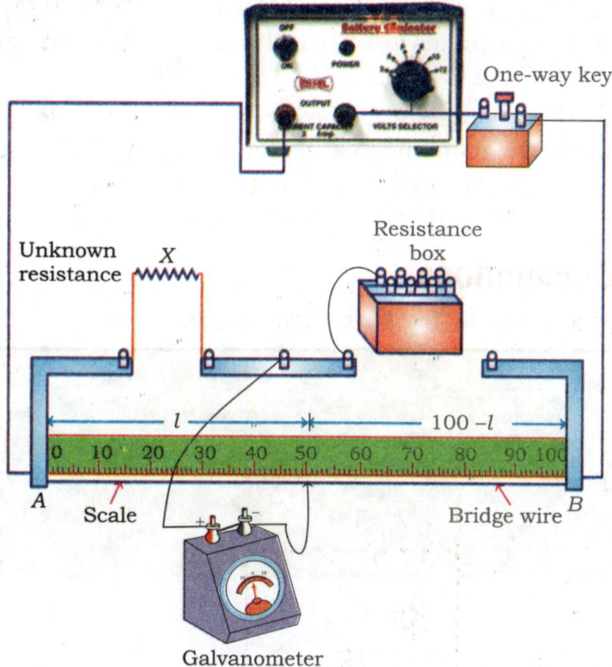

Experimental setup of meter bridge

3. Tighten all the plugs of the resistance box (RB) by pressing each plug downwards and then screwing them.
4. Connect the unknown resistance wire whose resistance is to be determined in the left gap between *G* and *B*. Take care that no part of the wire forms a loop.
5. Introduce a known resistance *R* from the resistance box in the circuit and insert the plug into the one-way key *K*, to complete the circuit.

Note Sometimes, a rheostat is provided to you instead of resistance box.

Testing the Correctness of the Connections

6. Touch the jockey gently to the left end *A* and right end *C* of the bridge wire and check the deflection in the galvanometer.
7. If the galvanometer shows deflections in the opposite directions at end *A* compared to deflection at end *C*, then the connections are made correct and null point will be somewhere in middle of the wire *AC*. If the galvanometer shows deflection in one side only, then adjust the resistance *R* so that the null point is somewhere in the middle of the wire *AC* (e.g. between 30 cm and 70 cm).
8. If the galvanometer still shows deflection to only one side, there may be a fault in the circuit. Check all connections, especially at functions and proper continuity.

Note When no current flows through the galvanometer, its pointer is expected to be at zero mark. Sometimes, it is observed that when no current flows through the galvanometer, the pointer may not exactly be at zero mark. In such cases, pointer can be adjusted to zero by gently moving the screw below the base of pointer using screw driver. Otherwise null point must be obtained by tapping the jockey on the wire.

Measurement of Balancing Length of the Wire

9. Now, slide the jockey along the wire nearly in the middle, so as to get a near null point in the galvanometer. The point where the galvanometer shows the zero deflection (say point *D*) on the wire is called **null** or **balanced point**.
10. When the null point is achieved on the wire, note down the balancing length *AD*.

11. By repeating the steps (7) to (10), take atleast four sets of observations in the similar way by introducing different resistances from the resistance box (in increasing order) into the one-way circuit.
12. Interchange the positions of resistance box R and wire of unknown resistance X and repeat the steps (7) to (10) for the same five values of R.

Note While interchanging the unknown resistance X and resistance box, it should be ensured that the length of wire of unknown resistance should be same in the right gap as it was in left gap.

Observations and Calculations

Table for Unknown Resistance

S.N.	X in the left gap				X in the right gap				
	Resistance from the resistance box, R (Ω)	Arms length		Unknown resistance,	Resistanc e from the resistance box R (Ω)	Arms length		Unknown resistance,	Mean resistance,
		Balancing length, AD = l (cm)	Length, DC = 100 − l (cm)	$X_1 = R \times \frac{l}{100-l}$ (Ω)		Balancing length AD′ = l′ (cm)	Length, D′C = 100 − l′ (cm)	$X_2 = R\frac{100-l'}{l'}$ (Ω)	$X = \frac{X_1 + X_2}{2}$ (Ω)
1									X_1 = ...Ω
2									X_2 = ...Ω
3									X_3 = ...Ω
4									X_4 = ...Ω
5									X_5 = ...Ω

Mean resistance, $X_{mean} = \frac{X_1 + X_2 + X_3 + X_4 + X_5}{5}$ = ...Ω

Result

The value of unknown resistance is found to be $X \pm \Delta X$ = (... ± ...) Ω.

PRECAUTIONS

1. *Plugs in the resistance box should be pressed and tighten by screwing them a little in the clockwise direction.*
2. *The bridge wire should not be pressed with the jockey too hard otherwise, cross-sections of the wire will change.*
3. *Try to obtain the null point near the middle of the wire (30 to 70 cm), so that the bridge can be used in most sensitive way.*
4. *Move the jockey gently on the wire and do not keep the jockey and the wire in contact for a long time.*
5. *Hold the jockey perpendicular to the wire of meter bridge.*
6. *The plug in key K should be inserted only when the observations are to be taken.*
7. *The wire should not make a loop.*

Sources of Error

1. The screws of meter bridge and of battery may be loosen.
2. The wire of meter bridge may be of non-uniform cross-section throughout its length.
3. The wire may get heated due to passage of current which increases its resistance.
4. The plugs may not be cleaned.
5. The keys of the resistance box may not be clean and tight.

Viva-Voce

Q. 1 Why are the appliances connected in parallel in domestic and industrial circuits?

Ans. (i) The potential across each appliance should be same.

(ii) Each appliance can be operated independently by using different switches.

(iii) If one appliance fuses, the other would continue functioning.

Q. 2 Why should we obtain the balance point in the middle of the bridge wire?

Ans. When the balance point is in the middle of the wire, very small error introduces in the value of unknown resistance. Thus, there is maximum probability of accuracy of the result.

Q. 3 What are end resistances?

Ans. The resistances of thick copper strips on either side of meter bridge wire are called end resistances.

Q. 4 What is the condition for maximum sensitivity of Wheatstone's bridge?

Ans. For maximum sensitivity of Wheatstone's bridge, all the four resistances P, Q, R and S should be of the same order.

Q. 5 Why we generally use constantan in the bridge wire?

Ans. The resistivity of constantan is very high and its temperature coefficient of resistance is very low, so it expands very less.

Q. 6 In what way the temperature affect the resistance of a conductor?

Ans. Resistance of a conductor increases with rise in temperature.

Q. 7 Why do we repeat the experiment by interchanging the position of unknown resistance and resistance box?

Ans. In order to eliminate the error due to contact resistances, we interchange the position of resistance box and unknown resistance wire.

Q. 8 Explain about sensitiveness of a Wheatstone bridge.

Ans. A Wheatstone bridge is said to be sensitive if it produces more deflection in the galvanometer for a small change of resistance in the resistance arm.

Q. 9 Why a meter bridge is also called as slide wire bridge?

Ans. While doing the meter bridge experiment, a jockey is made to slide over the bridge wire to get a null point. So, a meter bridge is also called as slide wire bridge.

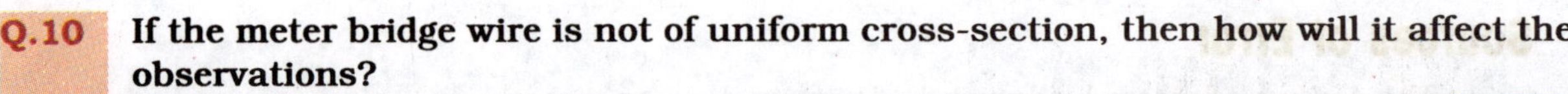

Q.10 If the meter bridge wire is not of uniform cross-section, then how will it affect the observations? [NCERT]

Ans. If the meter bridge wire is of non-uniform cross-section, then the resistance per unit length of bridge wire will be different over different lengths of meter bridge. Hence, we will not get the correct value of resistance.

Q.11 Is it necessary to keep the length of meter bridge wire 100 cm, i.e. 1 m ? What, if not? [NCERT]

Ans. No, the meter bridge works on the principle of Wheatstone's bridge. If the bridge is balanced the product of resistances in opposite arms is same, so we can use wire of any length in the meter bridge. Finally, we should find the resistance per unit length of wire and then the balancing length.

Q.12 Why is the meter bridge not suitable for measuring very high resistance? [NCERT]

Ans. The resistance forming bridge should be high and the current in the galvanometer reduces and the galvanometer will no longer be sensitive.

Q.13 If the meter bridge wire is not made of material of uniform density, how will it affect the observation? [NCERT]

Ans. For a wire, the density is given by

$$\sigma = \frac{m}{V} = \frac{m}{A \cdot l}$$

$$\therefore \quad \sigma \propto \frac{1}{A} \qquad \text{[where, } m \text{ and } l = \text{constants]}$$

Also, $\lambda \propto \dfrac{1}{A}$

$$\therefore \quad \lambda \propto \sigma \qquad \text{[where, } \lambda \text{ is the resistance per unit length]}$$

Thus, the resistance per unit length changes with density of the material. Hence, the resistance ratio will differ in our observation.

Q.14 The scale attached along the wire may not indicate the exact length as shown in figure. How would you minimise the error? [NCERT]

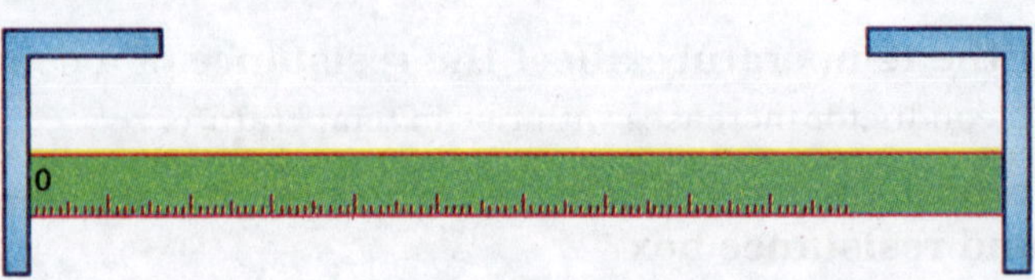

Ans. There are 102 divisions in the above scale, hence the correct formula to determine the unknown resistance will be

$$X = \left(\frac{102 - l}{l}\right) R$$

where, l = distance of null point from point A.

Experiment 3

AIM

To verify the laws of combination of resistances (series and parallel) using a meter bridge.

Apparatus and Material Required

A meter bridge, two unknown resistances, a resistance box, a sensitive galvanometer, a battery eliminator, a jockey, a one-way key, thick connecting wires and a piece of sand paper.

Theory/Principle

Resistances in Series

Resistances are said to be connected in series if they are connected end to end as shown in the figure (a). For n number of resistances connected in series, the equivalent resistance is given by

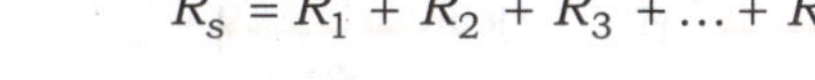

$$R_s = R_1 + R_2 + R_3 + \ldots + R_n$$

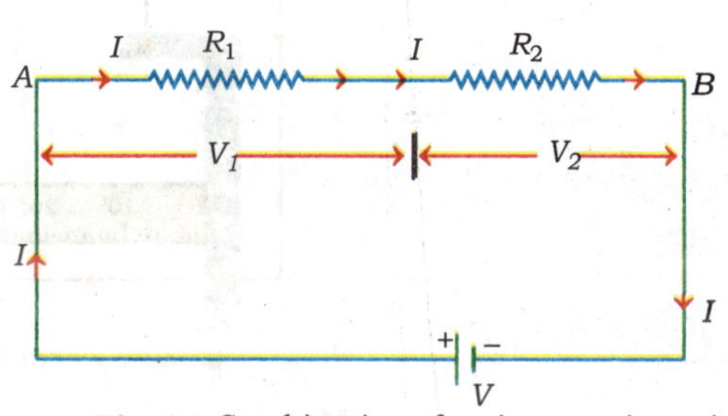

Fig. (a) Combination of resistances in series

Resistances in Parallel

Resistances are said to be connected in parallel when one end of each resistance is connected at one common point and their other ends are connected to other common point as shown in the figure (b).

For n number of resistances connected in parallel, the equivalent resistance is given by

$$\frac{1}{R_P} = \frac{1}{R_1} + \frac{1}{R_2} + \frac{1}{R_3} + \ldots + \frac{1}{R_n}$$

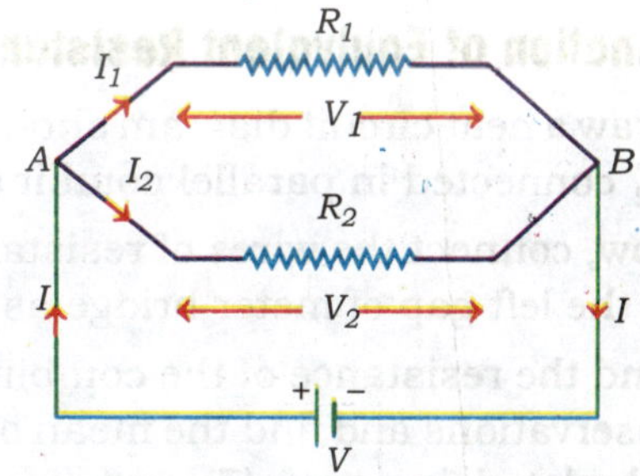

Fig. (b) Combination of resistances in parallel

The value of an unknown resistance X can be determined by using meter bridge as

$$X = \left(\frac{l}{100 - l}\right) R$$

where, l is the length of meter bridge wire from zero end to balance point and R is the resistance from resistance box.

Procedure

Determination of Two Resistances

1. Take two wires of resistances (say X_1 and X_2).
2. Follow the same steps as in Experiment 2 to determine the values of X_1 and X_2 one-by-one.

Determination of Equivalent Resistance of Series Combination

3. Take a sand paper and clean the insulation at the ends of the connecting wires.

4. Draw a neat circuit diagram showing the two resistances X_1 and X_2 connected in series combination and connect the resistances X_1 and X_2 in series in the left gap of meter bridge as shown in figure given below.
5. Check for deflection on both the sides by touching the jockey at both the ends of the meter bridge wire.
6. Find the equivalent resistance of series combination of resistors by following the same procedure as in Experiment 2.
7. Take five sets of observations for series combination.
8. Find the mean value of the five observations for series combination of resistances X_1 and X_2.

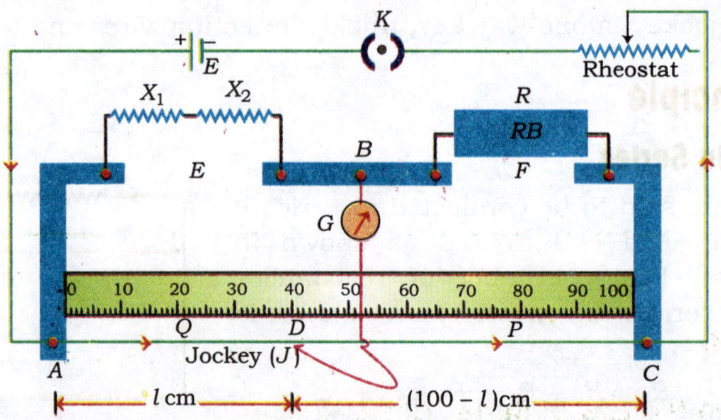

Meter bridge for verifying law of series combination of resistances

Determination of Equivalent Resistance of Parallel Combination

9. Draw a neat circuit diagram showing two resistances X_1 and X_2 connected in parallel combination.
10. Now, connect the wires of resistances X_1 and X_2 in parallel in the left gap of meter bridge as shown in the figure.
11. Find the resistance of the combination and take five sets of observations and find the mean of these five values same as calculated in steps (7) and (8) for series combination of resistances.

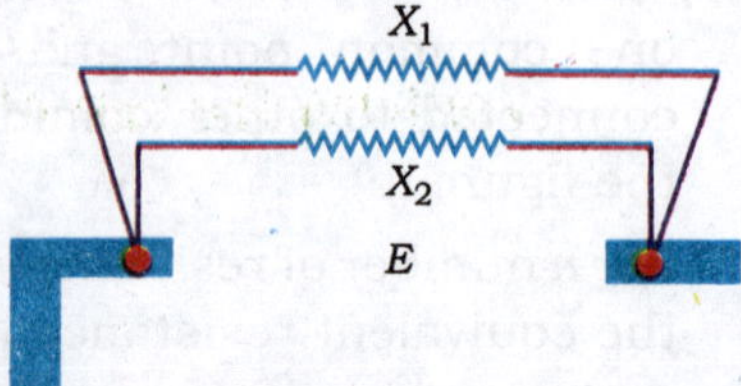

Meter bridge for verifying law of parallel combination of resistances

Observations

Table for Series and Parallel Combinations of Resistances

Resistance used in the left gap	No. of observation	Resistance from the resistance box, $R(\Omega)$	Balancing length, $AD = l$ (cm)	Length, $DC = 100 - l' = l'$ (cm)	Resistance, $X = \left(\frac{l}{l'}\right) \cdot R(\Omega)$	Mean resistance, $X(\Omega)$
	1					
	2					
X_1	3					$X_1 = \ldots$
	4					
	5					

X_2	1					$X_2 = \ldots$
	2					
	3					
	4					
	5					
X_1 and X_2 in series	1					$X_S = \ldots$
	2					
	3					
	4					
	5					
X_1 and X_2 in parallel	1					$X_P = \ldots$
	2					
	3					
	4					
	5					

Calculation

Verifying the Law of Series Combination

Experimental value of $X_s = \ldots \Omega$

Theoretical value of $X_s = X_s' = X_1 + X_2 = \ldots \Omega$

Difference $= X_s' - X_s = \Delta X_s = \ldots \Omega$

Verifying the Law of Parallel Combination

Experimental value of $X_p = \ldots \Omega$

Theoretical value of $X_p = X_p' = \dfrac{X_1 X_2}{X_1 + X_2} = \ldots \Omega$

Difference $= X_p' - X_p = \Delta X_p = \ldots \Omega$

Error

The error can be estimated in experimental value of X_s as

$$\therefore \quad \Delta X_s = X_s\left(\frac{\Delta l}{l} + \frac{\Delta l'}{l'}\right)$$

Similarly, for experimental value of X_P, $\Delta X_p = X_p\left(\frac{\Delta l}{l} + \frac{\Delta l'}{l'}\right)$

Result

Table for Verifying the Laws of Series and Parallel Combinations of Resistances

Combination of resistances	Theoretically expected value	Experimentally obtained value
Series	$R_1 + R_2 = \ldots\ldots\ldots\Omega$	$X_S \pm \Delta X_S = \ldots\ldots\ldots\Omega$
Parallel	$\dfrac{R_1 R_2}{R_1 + R_2} = \ldots\ldots\ldots\Omega$	$X_P \pm \Delta X_P = \ldots\ldots\ldots\Omega$

Within the limits of experimental error, the experimental and theoretical values of equivalent resistances are nearly equal. So, the **laws of combinations of resistances (series/parallel) are verified.**

PRECAUTIONS

Same as in Experiment 2.

Sources of Error

Same as in Experiment 2.

Viva-Voce

Q.1 If the balancing length is very close to one end of the wire, what can you infer about the unknown resistance compared to the known resistance?

Ans. The unknown resistance is either much smaller (if balancing point is near 0 cm) or much larger (if near 100 cm) than the known resistance.

Q.2 In a meter bridge experiment, even after proper connections the galvanometer shows no null point. What could be the possible reason?

Ans. The resistance in the left and right gaps may not be comparable, or there may be loose connections or broken wire.

Q.3 What do you mean by end resistance?

Ans. The resistances at the ends of bridge wire due to thick copper strips are called end resistances.

Q.4 How are the coils wound in a resistance box?

Ans. The coils are doubly wound in a resistance box to avoid electromagnetic induction.

Q.5 Give the definition of resistance.

Ans. The opposition offered by the material of wire to the flow of electric current through it is called the resistance of the wire (or conductor).

Q.6 How the temperature affects the resistance of a conductor?

Ans. The resistance of a conductor is directly proportional to the temperature.

Q.7 Why should we take null point near the middle of bridge wire?

Ans. In order to remove the end resistance, we prefer to take null point near the middle of bridge wire.

Q.8 Why is a meter bridge so called?

Ans. The bridge uses one metre (1 m) long wire, so it is called meter bridge.

Q.9 Why is it recommended to use resistance values close to each other in meter bridge arms?

Ans. To obtain a balancing point close to the center, which improves accuracy and reduces percentage error.

Q.10 Why should the jockey not be pressed too hard on the bridge wire?

Ans. If jockey is pressed hard, then it may change the thickness of the wire and hence, resistance changes.

Q.11 Why is meter bridge also called a slide wire bridge?

Ans. It is called so, because jockey slides over a one metre long wire provided in the meter bridge.

Q.12 When is Wheatstone bridge said to be balanced?

Ans. If no current flows through the galvanometer, then Wheatstone bridge is said to be balanced.

Q.13 Comment on the difference between theoretically expected and experimentally obtained values of the effective resistances. [NCERT]

Ans. For theoretically expected value of equivalent resistance first we should obtain the values of X_1 and X_2 from the colour code on the carbon resistor or from the given values in case of resistance made of wires of materials like nichrome, constantan, etc.

The equivalent resistance can be calculated using the formulae

$$X_s = X_1 + X_2 \quad \text{and} \quad X_p = \frac{X_1 \times X_2}{X_1 + X_2}.$$

On the other hand, for experimentally obtained value first the two wires should be connected in one of the gaps of bridge in series and parallel. Follow the same procedure for calculation of combinations of resistances. If any error is in the result, then find it. Finally, calculate the values as $(X_s \pm \Delta X_s)$ and $(X_p \pm \Delta X_p)$.

Q.14 Given *n* resistors of resistance *R* each, how will you combine them to get the maximum and minimum effective resistances? [NCERT]

Ans. In order to get the maximum effective resistance, all the resistors are combined in series and the effective resistance will be nR whereas for minimum effective resistance, all the resistors will be connected in parallel and the effective resistance will be $\frac{R}{n}$.

Q.15 How can we reduce the effect of end resistance at connections between the wire and copper strips? [NCERT]

Ans. The end resistance is caused due to improper soldering of wire. The end resistance can be reduced by interchanging the known and unknown resistances in the two gaps. The mean of the unknown resistances will give the result.

Q.16 A rheostat is connected in place of resistance box. How will the sensitivity of meter bridge change, if the rheostat head is moved from minimum resistance position to maximum resistance position?

Ans. If the rheostat head is at the minimum resistance position, then the order of known resistance may be less than that of other resistances. So, the bridge is less sensitive.

If the rheostat head is at the middle resistance position, then the order of known resistance may be same as that of other resistances. So, the bridge is more sensitive.

If the rheostat head is at the maximum resistance position, then the order of known resistance may be more than that of other resistances. So, the bridge is less sensitive.

Experiment 4

AIM

To determine the resistance of a galvanometer by half deflection method and to find its figure of merit.

Apparatus and Material Required

A moving coil galvanometer (weston type), a battery eliminator (0-6 V), two resistance boxes of range 0-10 kΩ and 0-200 Ω, two one-way keys, a rheostat, a voltmeter, connecting wires and sand paper.

Theory/Principle

Galvanometer

A galvanometer is a sensitive device used for detecting feeble electric current. It consists of rectangular coil pivoted between two poles (i.e. N and S) of a strong horse shoe permanent magnet. The coil in between the two poles is made up of a fine insulated copper wire. The resistance offered by this coil to the flow of current through it is called **resistance of galvanometer**.

Determination of Resistance of Galvanometer

The working principle of a galvanometer is that "*When an electric current passes through a coil placed in a uniform magnetic field, then the coil experiences a torque which rotates the coil.*" The deflection of the coil is determined by the movement of a pointer attached to the scale of galvanometer.

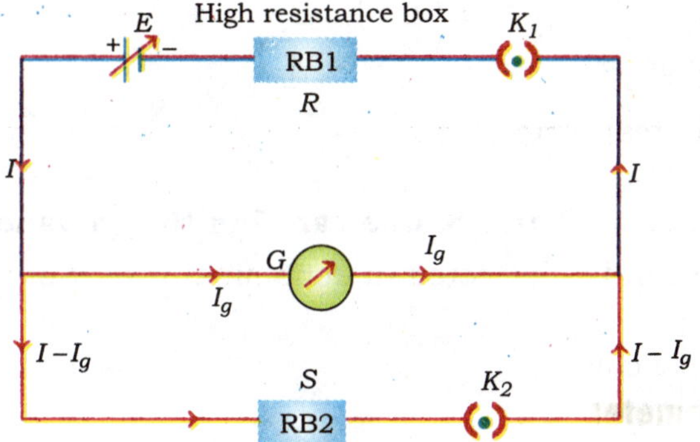

Circuit diagram for finding the resistance of galvanometer (G)

When a coil carrying current I is placed in a radial magnetic field, it experiences a deflection θ so that

$$I \propto \theta$$

$$\therefore \quad I = K\theta$$

where, K = constant of proportionality called **figure of merit**.

The given figure shows the circuit diagram required for finding the resistance of galvanometer by half deflection method.

When only key K_1 is closed the current I_g produces deflection θ in the galvanometer.

$$I_g = K\theta \Rightarrow \frac{E}{R+G} = K\theta$$

When the key K_2 is also closed, a small resistance is introduced from the resistance box RB2 as shunt resistance. The value of shunt resistance S is adjusted in such a way that the deflection in the galvanometer needle becomes half $\left(\text{i.e. } \frac{\theta}{2}\right)$.

As G and S are in parallel combination and R is in series with it, then the total resistance of the circuit,

$$R' = R + \frac{GS}{G+S}$$

Therefore, total current I due to the emf E of the cell in the circuit is given by

$$I = \frac{E}{R'} = \frac{E}{R + \frac{GS}{G+S}} \quad \text{...(ii)}$$

If I'_g is the current flowing through the galvanometer, then

$$\therefore \quad I'_g = \frac{IS}{G+S} \quad \text{...(iii)}$$

From Eqs. (i) and (iii), we get

$$I'_g = \frac{E}{R + \frac{GS}{G+S}}\left(\frac{S}{G+S}\right) = \frac{ES}{R(G+S)+GS} \quad \text{...(iv)}$$

For galvanometer current I'_g, if the deflection through the galvanometer is reduced to half of its initial value, then

$$I'_g = K\left(\frac{\theta}{2}\right) \quad \text{...(v)}$$

Using Eqs. (i), (iv) and (v), we get

$$\text{Galvanometer resistance, } G = \frac{RS}{R-S} \quad \text{...(vi)}$$

Hence, by knowing the values of R and S, one can find the galvanometer resistance G.

As S is very less than R, so S can be neglected in denominator part of Eq. (vi)

$$\therefore \quad G \approx S$$

Figure of Merit of a Galvanometer

By using Eq. (i), the figure of merit of galvanometer can be given as $K = \frac{1}{\theta}\left(\frac{E}{R+G}\right)$

Hence, by knowing the values of E, R, G and θ, one can find the figure of merit of a galvanometer.

Note Before measuring the figure of merit of galvanometer, the emf of the cell E is found by using a high resistance voltmeter.

Procedure

Setting up the Elements of Circuit

1. Make neat and tight connections as per the circuit diagram used for finding the resistance of the galvanometer. Open both the keys K_1 and K_2 by pulling out the plug from them.

Determination of Resistance R

2. From the high resistance box RB1, introduce a high resistance (say 5kΩ) and close the key K_1 while the key K_2 should be kept open.
3. Adjust the resistance R with the help of resistance box RB1 till the full scale deflection (or the maximum deflection) on the galvanometer dial is not achieved.
4. When the full scale deflection is achieved, note the corresponding reading of resistance R and deflection θ.

Determination of Resistance S

5. Now, keeping the value of R fixed, introduce some small resistance S (say 50 Ω) from the small resistance box RB2. Insert the plug into key K_2 to close it.
6. Now, adjust the value of S with the help of resistance box, till the deflection of galvanometer reduces exactly half the value you obtained in step (4).
7. When the deflection $\frac{\theta}{2}$ is observed, then note down the value of shunt resistance S. Take out the plug from key K_2 to close it after noting the value of shunt resistance, S.
8. Repeat the steps (5) to (7) and take at least five sets of observations, so that θ is even number of divisions and keep changing the value of R and corresponding adjustment of S for each set of observations.

Determination of Galvanometer Resistance G

9. Calculate the value of galvanometer resistance G by putting the observed values of R and S in the formula, $G = \frac{RS}{R-S}$

Determination of Figure of Merit K

10. With the help of high resistance voltmeter, measure the value of emf E of the cell.
11. For each set of observations, calculate the value of figure of merit K by putting the observed values of E, R, G and θ in the following formula.

$$K = \frac{1}{\theta}\left(\frac{E}{R+G}\right)$$

12. Take the mean of all values for G and K.

Observations and Calculations

1. The emf of the battery, E = ... V
2. Number of divisions on the galvanometer scale = ...

Table to Find the Resistance and Figure of Merit of Galvanometer

S. N.	High resistance from RB1, R (Ω)	Deflection in the galvanometer, θ (div)	Shunt resistance from RB2, S (Ω)	Half deflection in the galvanometer, $\frac{\theta}{2}$ (div)	$G = \frac{RS}{R-S}$ (Ω)	$K = \frac{1}{\theta}\left(\frac{E}{R+G}\right)$ (A/div)
1.					G_1 = ...Ω	K_1 = ...A/div
2.					G_2 = ...Ω	K_2 = ...A/div
3.					G_3 = ...Ω	K_3 = ...A/div
4.					G_4 = ...Ω	K_4 = ...A/div

3. Mean value of galvanometer resistance, $G = \frac{G_1 + G_2 + G_3 + G_4}{4}$ = ...Ω
4. Mean value of figure of merit, $K = \frac{K_1 + K_2 + K_3 + K_4}{4}$ = ... A/div

Result

1. Resistance of the given galvanometer by half deflection method, G = ... Ω
2. Figure of merit of given galvanometer, K = ... A/div

PRECAUTIONS

1. All the connections should be neat, clean and tight.
2. The key K_1 should be closed only after high value of R has been taken out from resistance box (RB_1), otherwise the galvanometer coil may burn.
3. To measure the value of emf, always use a high resistance voltmeter.
4. The emf E of cell or battery must be constant throughout the experiment.
5. Adjust the resistance R in such a way that deflection in the galvanometer should always be equal to even number of divisions.
6. Use high values of resistance R as practically as possible in order to get the correct value of galvanometer resistance G.

Sources of Error

1. The resistance of the coil in the Resistance Box (RB) used may not exactly be same as marked.
2. The emf of the battery may not be constant.
3. The divisions in the galvanometer may not be of equal size.
4. The plugs in the resistance box may be loosen or they may not be cleaned by sand paper.

Viva-Voce

Q. 1 What do you mean by full scale deflection current I_g?

Ans Maximum current which can be passed through the galvanometer for which the galvanometer needle shows maximum deflection is called full scale deflection current I_g.

i.e. $I_g = K\theta$

Q. 2 Why do we use galvanometer in electric circuit?

Ans The galvanometer is a sensitive device to detect current in the circuit. The galvanometer produces a deflection proportional to the current flowing through it.

Q. 3 Why do we use a high resistance in series with the galvanometer in half deflection method for finding resistance of a galvanometer?

Ans As we employ a high resistance in series with the galvanometer, then a low current passes through the galvanometer. Hence, the galvanometer is protected from damage due to excessive current.

Q. 4 Suppose no resistance is connected across the galvanometer, then what would be the reading in the galvanometer scale?

Ans Zero. Here in this case, the total current flows through the zero resistance shunt.

Q. 5 Under what condition, the galvanometer resistance is equal to the shunt resistance, i.e. $G = S$.

Ans $\because \quad G = \frac{RS}{R - S}$. If $R >> S$, then $G \approx S$

So, the galvanometer resistance is equal to the shunt resistance only when the series resistance R is more greater than shunt resistance.

Q. 6 How can we use galvanometer for measuring current? [NCERT]

Ans Actually, a galvanometer measures very small range of current. In order to measure current of higher order, a low resistance called shunt is connected in parallel to the galvanometer, so that maximum current passes through the shunt and galvanometer shows deflection for small current passing through it.

Q. 7 Out of galvanometer : ammeter and voltmeter, which has the highest resistance and which has the lowest? Explain. [NCERT]

Ans The voltmeter has very large resistance so that when put in parallel with the circuit, it should not divert much current from the parallel branch. The ammeter on the other hand has very less resistance, so that when put in series with the circuit, it should not reduce much the original current to be measured.

Q. 8 Which of the two meters has lower resistance a milliammeter or a microammeter? [NCERT]

Ans A milliammeter (mA) has current range more than that of microammeter (μA), so a milliammeter has lower resistance than a microammeter.

Q. 9 What are the factors on which sensitivity of a galvanometer depends? [NCERT]

Ans There are following factors on which sensitivity of galvanometer depends

(i) Number of turns (N) in the coil
(ii) Magnetic field (B)
(iii) Area (A) of coil
(iv) Torsional constant of springs

Q.10 Internal resistance of the cell is taken to be zero. This implies that we have to use a freshly charged accumulator in the experiment or use a good battery eliminator. If the internal resistance is finite, how will it affect the result? [NCERT]

Ans If the internal resistance of the cell is finite, it will cause a voltage drop and reduce the current flowing through the circuit, leading to measuring inaccuracies. It will also result in power dissipation within the cell, reducing the efficiency of power delivery.

Q.11 Is it possible to find the galvanometer resistance by taking $\frac{1}{3}$ deflection? If so, what changes would be required in the formula for calculation of value of G. [NCERT]

Ans Yes, it is possible to find the galvanometer resistance by taking $\frac{1}{3}$ deflection.

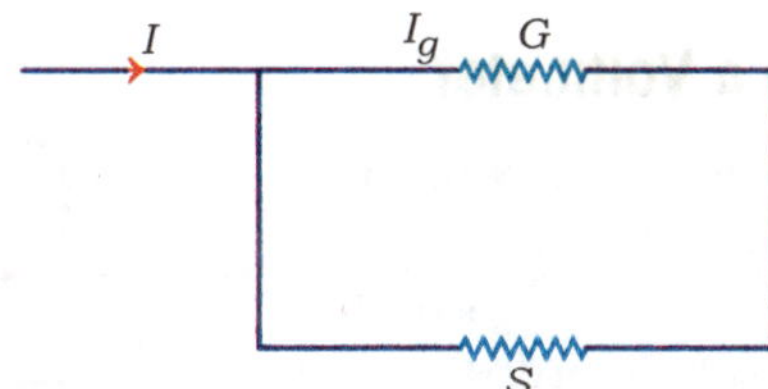

We can see that G and S are parallel to each other, therefore $(I - I_g)S = I_g G$

$$IS - I_g S = I_g G$$

$$\Rightarrow \quad IS = I_g G + I_g S$$

$$\Rightarrow \quad IS = (G + S)\, I_g$$

$$\Rightarrow \quad \frac{I}{I_g} = \frac{(G + S)}{S} \Rightarrow \frac{I_g}{I} = \frac{S}{G + S} \qquad \text{... (i)}$$

Now, by taking $\frac{1}{3}$ deflection, then the Eq. (i) becomes

$$\Rightarrow \quad \frac{1}{3} = \frac{S}{G + S}$$

$$\Rightarrow \quad G + S = 3S \Rightarrow G = 2S$$

Therefore, the $\frac{1}{3}$ deflection method can be used and in this case, the G equals twice the value of shunt resistance.

Q.12 We use a freshly charged accumulator whose internal resistance is zero for galvanometer experiment. If the internal resistance of the battery eliminator is finite, then how will it affect the result? [NCERT]

Ans For fresh charged accumulator ($r = 0$), the current sensitivity is ($r = 0$)

$$C = \frac{E}{R\theta} \qquad \text{...(i)}$$

When the internal resistance (r) is finite, then terminal potential difference is $V = E - Ir$.

Current sensitivity, $$C' = \frac{E - Ir}{R\theta} \qquad \text{...(ii)}$$

It is clear from Eqs. (i) and (ii) that, the current sensitivity decreases with r introduced in the cell, i.e. $C' < C$. Thus, the voltage sensitivity also decreases.

Experiment 5

AIM

To convert the given galvanometer (of known resistance and figure of merit) into a voltmeter of desired range and to verify the same.

Apparatus and Material Required

A galvanometer of known resistance and figure of merit, a rheostat of range 200Ω, a high resistance box of range 10 kΩ, a battery eliminator of range (0-5V), a one way key, a voltmeter of range (0-3V), connecting wires and a piece of sand paper.

Theory/Principle

Conversion of Galvanometer into a Voltmeter

By connecting a large resistance in series with the galvanometer, one can convert it into voltmeter, which is then connected in parallel to the conductor (or conductor across which potential difference is to be measured).

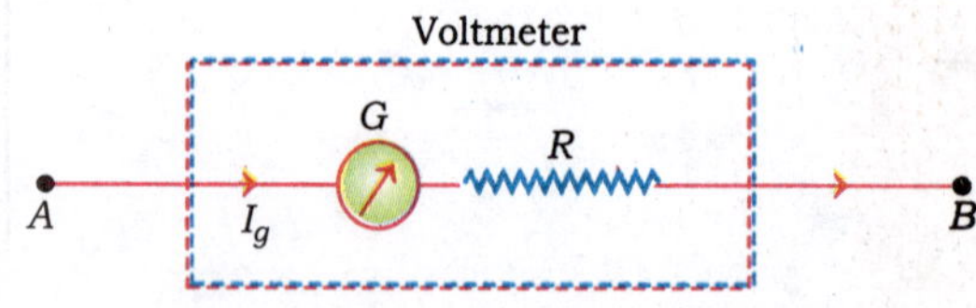

Galvanometer converted to voltmeter

Consider I_g is the current in the galvanometer and V is the required range of the voltmeter with a high series resistance R.

So, the total resistance in the circuit is $(R + G)$.

Here, G is the galvanometer resistance.

Using Ohm's law, we get

$$\text{Resistance, } R = \frac{V}{I_g} - G \quad \text{...(i)}$$

Procedure

Determination of Current for Full Scale Deflection

1. First of all note the given values of galvanometer resistance G and figure of merit K.
2. To find the value of current for full scale deflection, count the total number of divisions on either side of the zero mark of the scale of galvanometer. Let the number of those divisions be N.
3. Find the maximum current required for producing full scale deflection of N divisions by using the following relation.

$$I_g = NK$$

Determination of Value of High Series Resistance

4. Calculate the value of high series resistance R for given values of V, I_g and G by using the following relation.

$$R = \frac{V}{I_g} - G, \quad \text{where } V \text{ is the range of required voltmeter.}$$

Conversion of Galvanometer into Voltmeter

5. Connect that high resistance box in series with the galvanometer.
6. From the resistance box, take out a plug of resistance equal to the value of resistance you have calculated in step (4) and introduce it in series with the galvanometer. Now, the galvanometer is ready to use as a voltmeter of range 0 to 3 V.

Verification of Converted Galvanometer

7. Make the connections as per the circuit diagram shown in the figure. Connect a battery of emf E and a converted galvanometer and the voltmeter of nearly same range in parallel, with a high resistance rheostat.

Note If the voltmeter is not available of same range as that of galvanometer, then increase the range of voltmeter by connecting a suitable high resistance in series with it and we can also decrease the range of voltmeter by connecting a suitable resistance in parallel with it.

8. Close the key K and adjust the rheostat, so that the voltage shown in the voltmeter is equal to the desired range (say 3 V).
9. Keep on adjusting the position of the sliding contact of rheostat and also the resistance from the resistance box simultaneously till full scale deflection is observed on the galvanometer. When the full scale deflection is observed on the galvanometer, the voltmeter shows 3 V.
10. Note down the total resistance (say R') from the resistance box.
11. Observe the error by comparing the value of resistance R' with resistance R which has been calculated in step (4).

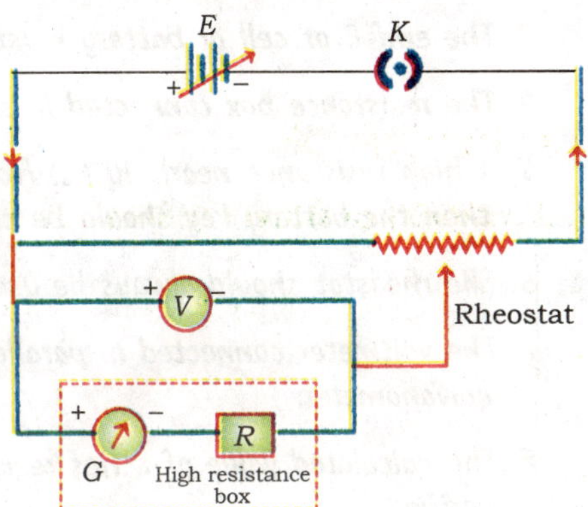

Circuit diagram to verify conversion of galvanometer into a voltmeter

Observations

Determination of Full Scale Deflection Current

1. Resistance of the given galvanometer, $G = \ldots \Omega$.
2. Figure of merit of the given galvanometer, $K = \ldots \frac{\text{A}}{\text{division}}$.
3. Total number of divisions on either side of zero of the galvanometer, $N = \ldots$ divisions.
4. Current through the galvanometer, $I_g = KN = \ldots$ A.

Determination of High Series Resistance

5. Required range of converted voltmeter, $V = \ldots$ V
6. Value of required series resistance, $R = \frac{V}{I_g} - G = \ldots \Omega$
7. Least count of the converted voltmeter $= \frac{V}{N} = \ldots\ldots$ volt
8. Least count of the standard voltmeter = ... volt.
9. The total resistance taken out from the resistance box, $R' = \ldots \Omega$.
10. Error in the value of high series resistance $= R - R' = \ldots \Omega$

Result

To convert the given galvanometer into voltmeter of range 0 to ...V

(a) The value of the calculated series resistance, $R = \ldots \Omega$.

(b) The value of observed series resistance, $R' = \ldots \Omega$.

(c) Current for full scale deflection, I_g = ... ampere.

PRECAUTIONS

1. *Before using the connecting wires, their ends should be cleaned with the help of sand paper, so that the insulation can be removed.*
2. *All the connections of wires and all the plugs in the resistance box should be tight.*
3. *The emf E of cell or battery must be constant throughout the experiment.*
4. *The resistance box connected in series with the galvanometer should be of high range.*
5. *A high resistance nearly 10 kΩ from the resistance box should be introduced in the circuit first and then the battery key should be closed. This is essential to avoid any damage to the galvanometer.*
6. *The rheostat should always be used as a potential divider.*
7. *The voltmeter connected in parallel with galvanometer should be of same range as that of galvanometer.*
8. *The calculated value of series resistance should be accurate otherwise the conversion would not be verified.*

Sources of Error

1. The wire may not be of uniform cross-section.
2. Calibration of resistance in the resistance box may not be correct.
3. The emf of the battery may be changed during the experiment.
4. The calculated value of resistance may have some error.
5. The resistant plugs in the resistance box may not be tight.
6. The galvanometer and voltmeter used may be of different ranges.

Viva-Voce

Q. 1 How do you convert a galvanometer into a voltmeter?

Ans. By connecting a high resistance in series with the galvanometer coil.

Q. 2 How can we use a rheostat, as a current divider or potential divider?

Ans. A rheostat can be used as a potential divider.

Q. 3 What should be the resistance of an ideal voltmeter?

Ans. Infinity (∞).

Q. 4 What do you mean by a resistance box?

Ans. A resistance box is a sequence of standard resistances connected in series. Resistance box helps us to connect any desired resistance in the circuit.

Q. 5 Can we increase/decrease the range of voltmeter?

Ans. Yes, the range of voltmeter can be increased or decreased.

Q. 6 A voltmeter and a millivoltmeter are converted from the same galvanometer. Out of these two, which one is having higher resistance?

Ans. A voltmeter, because it requires a large resistance to be put in series with the galvanometer.

Q. 7 What are the required properties of a voltmeter?

Ans A voltmeter must have a very large resistance and a very small current carrying capacity.

Q.8 Why is it necessary for a voltmeter to have a high resistance?

Ans A voltmeter needs to have high resistance because it is connected in parallel across two points in a circuit.

Hence, it has high resistance so that current flowing in the circuit would not disturbed and it can measure the correct value.

Q.9 Why is a high resistance connected in series with a galvanometer?

Ans A high resistance is connected in series with a galvanometer to increase the overall resistance of the voltmeter, thereby reducing its current carrying capacity.

Q.10 Why is a voltmeter always connected in parallel with the circuit? [NCERT]

Ans. A voltmeter when put in parallel in the circuit, it will not divert much current from parallel branch.

Q.11 In the experiment, if the galvanometer deflects fully but the standard voltmeter shows less voltage, what can be inferred?

Ans. The series resistance used is less than required; hence, voltage division is incorrect.

Q.12 Why is the coil wrapped on a conducting frame in a galvanometer?

Ans. When the coil is wrapped on a conducting frame the eddy current is set up in it which helps in bringing the coil to rest at once.

Experiment 6

AIM

To convert the given galvanometer (of known resistance and figure of merit) into an ammeter of desired range and to verify the same.

Apparatus and Material Required

A galvanometer of known resistance and figure of merit, a constantan or manganin wire of 26 or 30 SWG diameter, a battery eliminator, a rheostat of range 200Ω, an ammeter of 0-30 mA range, a one-way key, a screw gauge, a wire cutter, connecting wires and a piece of sand paper.

Theory/Principle

Conversion of Galvanometer into Ammeter

A galvanometer is a sensitive device which can detect the presence of very small current (~ 100mA) in a circuit but it cannot measure the current flowing through the circuit.

To measure the current of the order of an ampere, a low resistance called **shunt** is used in parallel to the galvanometer coil. This shunt resistance controls the current flowing through the galavanometer to prevent it from damage.

Determination of Shunt Resistance

If I is the total current in circuit for full scale deflection, then the current I_g only flows through the galvanometer and most of it $(I - I_g)$ passes through the shunt resistance S.

As the galvanometer and shunt are connected in parallel so the potential difference across both are same, i.e.

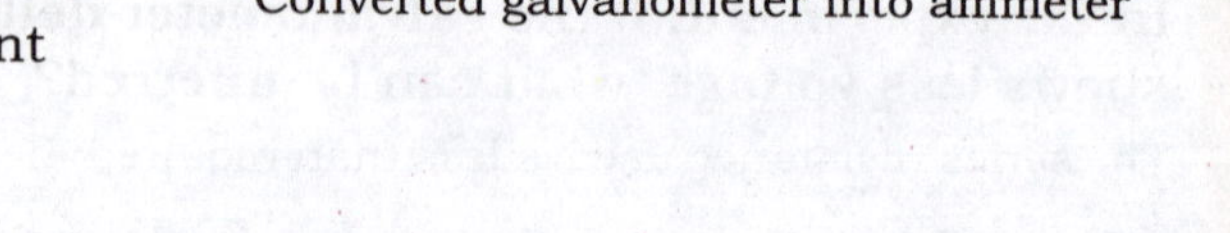

Converted galvanometer into ammeter

Potential difference across the galvanometer

= Potential difference across the shunt

$$\therefore \quad I_g G = (I - I_g)\, S$$

$$\therefore \quad \text{Shunt resistance,} \quad S = \frac{I_g G}{I - I_g} \qquad \ldots\text{(i)}$$

Note The instrument is calibrated into ampere to work as an ammeter.

Determination of Galvanometer Current

The figure of merit K represents the current corresponding to one scale division. If N is the total number of divisions on either side of the galvanometer scale, the value of galvanometer current I_g is given by

$$I_g = KN$$

Note If n represents the actual deflection in the converted galvanometer, then the total current will be $\frac{nI}{N}$.

Procedure

Determination of Shunt Resistance

1. Note the given values of galvanometer resistance (*G*) and figure of merit (*K*).
2. Count the total number of divisions *N* on both sides of the zero mark on the galvanometer scale.
3. Calculate the current I_g for full scale deflection of galvanometer by using the relation, $I_g = K N$.
4. Calculate the shunt resistance *S*, by putting the observed values of I_g, *G* and *I* in the following formula.

   Shunt resistance, $S = \frac{I_g G}{I - I_g}$

   Here, the current *I* is the range of the required ammeter.

Conversion of Galvanometer into Ammeter

5. Find the least count and zero error of screw gauge and measure the corrected average diameter of given resistance wire.
6. Determine the average corrected diameter of the wire using a screw gauge. Then, calculate the radius (*r*) using the formula

   Average corrected radius, $r = \frac{\text{Average corrected diameter } (d)}{2}$

7. Confirm the material of wire and find the specific resistance (ρ) of the wire from the standard table.
8. Calculate the length of the wire (*l*) needed for the resistance *S*, using the following formula

   Length of the wire, $l = \frac{\pi r^2 S}{\rho}$

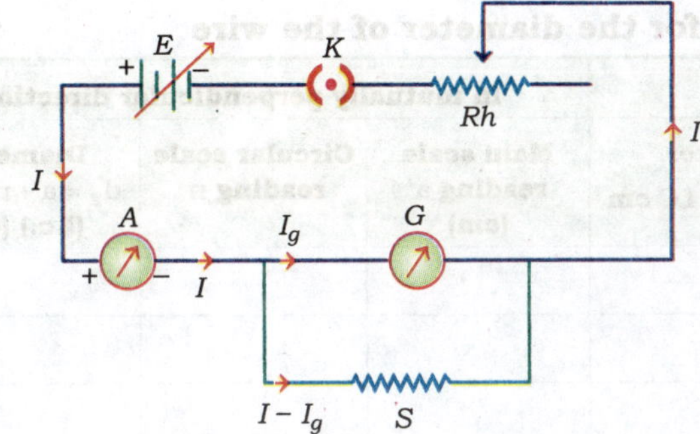

Circuit diagram to verify the conversion of galvanometer into an ammeter

9. Let the calculated length of wire be 10 cm, then cut 3-4 cm extra and put it in parallel to the galvanometer so that the length $l = 10$ cm remains exactly outside the terminals of the galvanometer as shown in the figure. The resistance of this wire will be nearly equal to the value of shunt resistance.
10. Connect all the components as shown in the figure after cleaning the ends of the connecting wires with the help of sand paper to remove the insulation.
11. Adjust the length of wire till the full scale deflection in the galvanometer is shown.
12. When the full scale deflection is shown on the galvanometer scale, measure the length of the wire. Now, the galvanometer is converted to an ammeter whose range is 30 mA.

Verification of Converted Galvanometer

13. To verify the converted galvanometer, measure the exact length of the shunt wire (say l') and calculate its resistance by the same formula, you have used in step (8).

$$l' = \frac{\pi r^2 S}{\rho} \Rightarrow S = \frac{l' \rho}{\pi r^2}$$

Note The specific resistivity (ρ) of the material of the wire and the radius (r) of wire will remain same.

14. Now, compare the new calculated value of shunt resistance S with the value of S you have calculated in step (4) to verify the converted galvanometer.

Observations and Calculations

Resistance of the given galvanometer, $G =$ ....Ω

Determination of Galvanometer Current

Figure of merit of the given galvanometer, $K =$ ....A/div.

Total number of divisions on either side of zero of the galvanometer scale, $N =$ ......divisions.

Current required for producing full scale deflection of N divisions (galvanometer current), $I_g = KN =$ ....A.

Determination of Shunt Resistance

Range of required ammeter, $I =$ ....A

Shunt resistance, $S = \frac{I_g G}{I - I_g} =$ ....Ω

Measurement of Radius of the Wire

Least count of the screw gauge, LC = ... mm = ... cm

Zero error of the screw gauge, $e =$ .... mm = ... cm

Table for the diameter of the wire

S. N.	In any direction			In mutually perpendicular direction			Mean observed diameter
	Main scale reading a (cm)	Circular scale reading n	Diameter $d_1 = a + n \times LC$ cm	Main scale reading a' (cm)	Circular scale reading n'	Diameter $d_2 = a' + n' \times LC$ (l.c.) (cm)	$d' = \frac{d_1 + d_2}{2}$ (cm)
1.							$d_1' =$...... cm
2.							$d_2' =$...... cm
3.							$d_3' =$...... cm
4.							$d_4' =$...... cm

Mean diameter of the wire, $d_0 = \frac{d_1' + d_2' + d_3' + d_4'}{4} =$ .... cm

Mean corrected diameter of the wire, $d = d_0 - e =$ .... cm

Mean corrected radius of the wire, $r = \frac{d}{2} =$ .... cm

Determination of Length for Shunt Resistance

Resistivity of material of wire shunted for the galvanometer (or value from the standard table), ρ = ...Ω-m = ...Ω-cm

Required length of the wire, $l = \dfrac{\pi r^2 S}{\rho}$ = ... cm

where, $\pi = 3.14$

Verification of Converted Galvanometer

The observed length of the shunt wire of converted galvanometer, l' = ... cm

Shunt resistance of the converted galvanometer, $S' = \dfrac{l' \times \rho}{\pi r^2}$ = ... Ω

Calculated value of the shunt resistance, S = ... Ω

Difference (error), $S - S'$ = ... Ω

Observe the difference to verify the converted galvanometer.

Result

To convert the given galvanometer into an ammeter of range 0 to .... A,

(a) The calculated resistance of the shunt wire is S = ... Ω

(b) The observed resistance of the shunt wire is S' = ... Ω

PRECAUTIONS

1. Before using the connecting wires, their ends should be cleaned with the help of sand paper to remove the insulation.

2. The diameter of the wire should be calculated accurately.

3. Ensure all wire and component connections are tight and secure.

4. Use a freshly charged battery, so that its emf may remains constant throughout the experiment.

5. The ammeter needed for the verification should be of the same range as the range of conversion.

6. After adjusting the length of the wire, measure the length of the wire between the two plugs carefully.

7. The value of new shunt resistance should be measured accurately.

8. Use wire with a uniform cross-section for consistent resistance.

9. Always cut some extra length of the wire, i.e. 3 to 4 cm more than required.

Sources of Error

1. The wire may not be of uniform cross-section.
2. The calculated value of shunt resistance may have some error.
3. The emf of the battery may change during the experiment.
4. The ammeter used for verification may be of different ranges.

Viva-Voce

Q. 1 Which information would you wish to know about the galvanometer before converting it into an ammeter?

Ans. We should know the following parameters before conversion

(i) Resistance of galvanometer (G)

(ii) Current required (I_g) to produce full scale deflection

Q. 2 What is the resistance of an ideal ammeter?

Ans. Zero (0)

Q. 3 What is meant by the range of an ammeter?

Ans. It is the maximum value of current that an ammeter can measure.

Q. 4 When a galvanometer said to be sensitive?

Ans. A galvanometer is said to be sensitive, if it shows large scale deflection for a small current passed through it.

Q. 5 Can we increase/decrease the range of an ammeter or not?

Ans. We can increase the range of an ammeter but we cannot decrease the range of an ammeter.

Q. 6 Write the formula for shunt resistance (*S*).

Ans.

$$S = \frac{I_g}{I - I_g} G$$

where, G = Galvanometer resistance,

I_g = Current through the galvanometer

and $I - I_g$ = Current passes through the shunt.

Q. 7 What should be the characteristics for a good ammeter?

Ans Large current tolerance and low resistance.

Q. 8 Why is an ammeter always connected in series with the circuit? [NCERT]

Ans An ammeter is connected in series with the circuit because it measures the whole current passed through it.

Q. 9 How can you increase the range of the converted galvanometer to 0-60 mA? [NCERT]

Ans The range of converted galvanometer can be increased by connecting a resistance in series with it.

Q.10 How can you decrease the range of the converted galvanometer to 0-20 mA? [NCERT]

Ans We cannot decrease the range of converted galvanometer (ammeter) because for $I < I_g$, the value of shunt resistance becomes negative which cannot be made possible.

Experiment 7

AIM

To find the frequency of AC mains with a sonometer.

Apparatus and Material Required

A sonometer with a soft iron wire stretched over it, an electromagnet with a step-down transformer, a 500 g hanger, seven 500 g slotted weights, a physical balance, two sharp edge wedges, a weight box, a meter scale and a clamp stand.

Theory/Principle

Determination of Frequency of AC Mains by using Sonometer

If an electromagnet having AC current in its coil is held close to the middle of stretched sonometer wire, the wire will be attracted twice during each cycle towards the electromagnet.

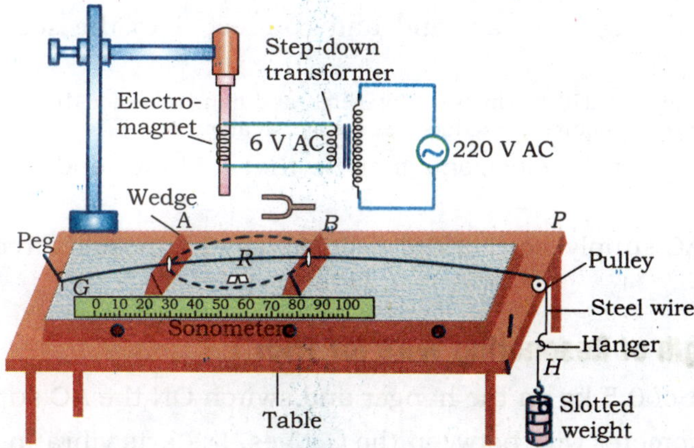

Set up for finding the frequency of AC mains using an electromagnet and sonometer

It is because, the attractive force experienced by the stretched wire will be proportional to the magnetisation produced in the core of the electromagnet and the current magnetises and demagnetises the cylindrical core of electromagnet twice for each cycle.

The given figure shows the experimental set up for finding frequency of AC mains using an electromagnet and a sonometer. Since in each cycle, the stretched wire will be pulled twice and hence at resonance, the wire will vibrate with a frequency which is twice the frequency of alternating current.

Let frequency of alternating current = f

$$\therefore \quad f = \frac{n}{2} = \frac{1}{2 \times 2l}\sqrt{\frac{T}{m}} \quad \text{or} \quad l^2 = \frac{1}{4n^2 m} \times T \qquad \text{...(i)}$$

where, n = frequency with which the sonometer wire vibrates,

l = length of vibrating string,

T = tension in the wire = Mg,

M = mass suspended from the string

and m = linear mass density of the wire

Eq. (i) is in the form of $y = mx$, which is the equation of straight line. So, on plotting a graph with T on X-axis and l^2 on Y-axis, we get a straight line. The slope of this line gives the relation between frequency of the AC mains and that of stretched vibrating wire. So, the frequency of alternating current f can be determined by using the formula.

$$f = \frac{n}{2} = \frac{1}{4\sqrt{m \times \text{slope}}} \quad \ldots\text{(ii)}$$

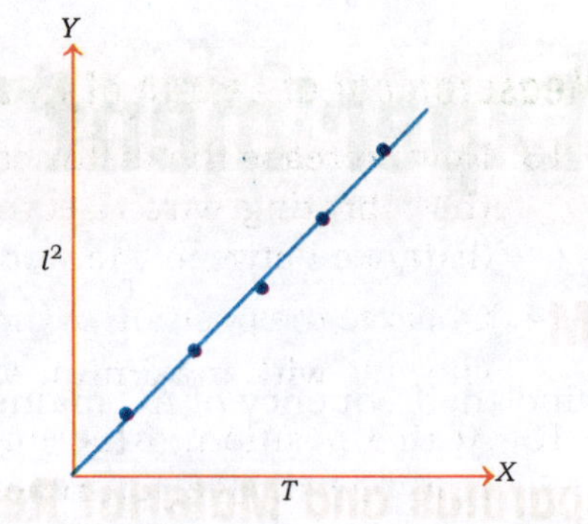

Graph showing relation between l^2 and T

Procedure

Setting up the Apparatus

1. First of all, fix the sonometer on the table in such a manner that its one end carrying pulley sets on the edge of the table, so that the hanger can be suspended without touching the table to stretch the wire. Make the groove clean in order to confirm that it has minimum friction.
2. Now, place the two wooden blocks or bridges having wedges A and B to remove the kink in the wire.
3. Clamp the electromagnet in a stand and connect it to the secondary of a step down transformer.

Note The voltage of AC mains is 220 V which is quite high and dangerous for the winding of electromagnet, so a step-down transformer is required to reduce the voltage to about 6 V.

4. Adjust the position of the electromagnet, so that its lower end lies close to the middle of stretched wire AB.
5. Switch ON the AC supply, so that the electromagnet impose its frequency on the soft iron wire.

Measurement of Length of Resonating Wire for Trial 1

6. Place the weight of 0.5 kg on the hanger and switch ON the AC supply.
7. Observe the sonometer wire between the wedges. It starts vibrating.

Note The current flowing in the electromagnet core is of alternating nature, so the force which acts on the sonometer wire is also oscillatory in nature. Thus, the wire vibrates.

8. Adjust the length of vibrating wire by slowly increasing the distance between the wedges A and B.
9. Keep on increasing the length of the vibrating wire till it vibrates with maximum amplitude.
10. In order to attain the final adjustment, take a small piece of paper and then fold it to give it the V-shape looking like a paper rider. Now put this paper rider R at the middle of the wire between wedges A and B.
11. Observe the position of the paper rider. It starts moving and finally falls down when the wire vibrates with maximum amplitude.
12. At this position, with the help of meter scale, measure the length of the resonating wire between the wedges and also note down the corresponding load suspended from the hanger. This reading will give you the **resonant length for trial 1**.

Measurement of Length of Resonating Wire for Trial 2

13. Now increase the distance between the wedges by 2-4 cm and put the paper rider back on the vibrating wire. Decrease the length of the vibrating wire by slowly decreasing the distance between the wedges.
14. Observe the position of the paper rider, it starts moving and finally falls down when the wire vibrates with maximum amplitude.
15. At this position, measure the value of resonating wire with the help of meter scale. This reading will give you **resonating length for trial 2**.
16. Find the mean of the values measured in steps (12) and (15).
17. Now, increase the load in steps of 0.5 kg and by repeat the steps (8) to (18) each time, find the mean resonating length.

Determination of Linear Mass Density of the Wire

18. Switch OFF the AC supply. Remove the load and untie the sonometer wire from its peg.
19. Using physical balance, find the mass of 100 cm sonometer wire. Hence, find the mass per unit length or linear mass density m of the wire by dividing mass of wire by the length (100 cm).
20. Note your observations in the tabular form.

Observations

1. Length of the sonometer wire, L = ... cm = ... m
2. Mass of the sonometer wire = ... g(gram) = ... kg
3. Linear mass density, m = ... g/cm = ... kg/m
4. Acceleration due to gravity, g = ... ms^{-2} [$9.8 \ m/s^2$]

Table to Determine the Frequency of Alternating Current

S. N.	Load, M (kg)	Tension in the wire, $T=Mg$	Resonating length, l (cm), when distance between wedges		Mean, $l = \frac{l_1 + l_2}{2}$ (m)	Fundamental frequency of wire, $n = \frac{1}{2l}\sqrt{\frac{T}{m}}$ (Hz)
		T (N)	Trial 1 (Increased) l_1	Trial 2 (Decreased) l_2		
1.	0.5				l_1 = ... m	n_1 = ... Hz
2.	1.0				l_2 = ... m	n_2 = ... Hz
3.	1.5				l_3 = ... m	n_3 = ... Hz
4.	2.0				l_4 = ... m	n_4 = ... Hz

Calculations

1. For each set, calculate the value of fundamental frequency of stretched iron wire using the formula

$$n = \frac{1}{2l}\sqrt{\frac{T}{m}}$$

Find the mean of four values of n, $n_{mean} = \frac{n_1 + n_2 + n_3 + n_4}{4}$ = ... Hz

2. Plot a graph of l^2 against T with l^2 on Y-axis and T on X-axis. Determine the slope of the graph.
3. Using the value of slope, determine the frequency f of alternating current as

$$f = \frac{n}{2} = \frac{1}{4\sqrt{m \times \text{slope}}}$$

Result

1. The graph between l^2 and T is a straight line.
2. Slope of the graph $= \frac{1}{4\,mn^2} =$ ....
3. Frequency of alternating current, $f = \frac{n}{2}$ is

   (i) .... Hz (from calculation) (ii) .... Hz (from graph)
4. Difference in experimental value and standard value = ...
5. Percentage of error $= \frac{\text{Difference}}{\text{Standard value}} \times 100 =$ ... %

PRECAUTIONS

1. The sonometer wire should be of soft iron or any other magnetic material and of uniform cross-section.

2. The pulley used in the experimental set up should be frictionless.

3. The paper rider should always be placed exactly on the middle of wire between the wedges.

4. Loading of wire should be done within their elastic limits to avoid breaking of wire.

5. The tip of electromagnet should be very close to the sonometer wire in its middle.

6. The edges of the wedge should be sharp so that exact length of the vibrating wire can be measured.

7. The length of vibrating wire should be noted when the amplitude of vibration is maximum.

8. After each set of observation, the circuit should be switched OFF for few minutes.

9. Never touch the wire carrying either AC or DC. It is very dangerous to touch the wire or metallic surface carrying current.

Sources of Error

1. The wire may not be of uniform cross-section, also its composition may not be of the same material.
2. The two wedges may not be sharpened.
3. The values marked on slotted weights and hanger may not be true.
4. The resonant length of the string may not be noted accurately. Due to parallax error, this wrong observation may be taken.
5. The main AC frequency may not be stable.

Viva-Voce

Q.1 What are the positions of nodes and antinode in the vibrating wire?

Ans. The nodes are situated at the sharp edges of two wedge and antinode at the middle of stretched wire.

Q.2 Why do we use a step-down transformer with the electromagnet?

Ans. The voltage of AC mains is 220 V which is quite high and dangerous for the winding of electromagnet, so a transformer is required to reduce the voltage to about 6 V which is step-down transformer.

Q.3 What is an electromagnet?

Ans. An electromagnet is a temporary magnet, so it behaves like a magnet till the current passes through its coil.

Q.4 When does the sonometer wire resonate?

Ans. The resonance occurs when the natural frequency of vibrating wire is equal to the frequency of alternating current.

Q. 5 Write the voltage and frequency of AC in India.

Ans. 220 V, 50 Hz.

Q. 6 Define the term resonance.

Ans. Resonance is said to occur when the frequency of oscillation coincides with the frequency of external agency maintaining the oscillation.

Q. 7 Define rms value of alternating current.

Ans. It is that value of direct current which produces the same heating effect in a given resistor as is produced by the given AC current when passed for the same time.

Q. 8 What is the unit of frequency?

Ans. Hertz (Hz).

Q. 9 How can we generate AC?

Ans. An AC can be generated by a dynamo or AC generator.

Q.10 Which value of current do we read with an AC ammeter?

Ans. The rms value of current, i.e. I_{rms}.

Q.11 For what purpose, we use sonometer?

Ans. Sonometer is used to measure the frequency of sound.

Q.12 What is meant by unidirectional current?

Ans. A unidirectional current is a type of current that flows in the same direction while its magnitude varies between a maximum value and zero.

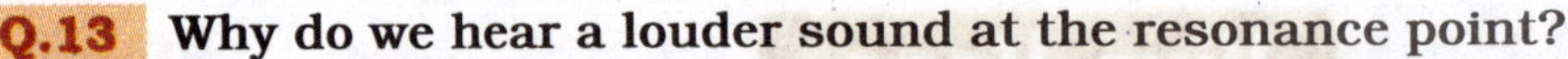

Q.13 Why do we hear a louder sound at the resonance point?

Ans. Because constructive Interference occurs, amplifying the vibrations.

Q.14 Is there any fixed north or south pole of the electromagnet, when AC is passed through it?

Ans. No, there is no fixed north or south pole in an electromagnet when alternating current is passed through it because the AC continuously changes in magnitude and reverses direction after each half-cycle.

Q.15 Draw the curve showing the variation of X_L and X_C with frequency.

Ans. The graph below shows these variations.

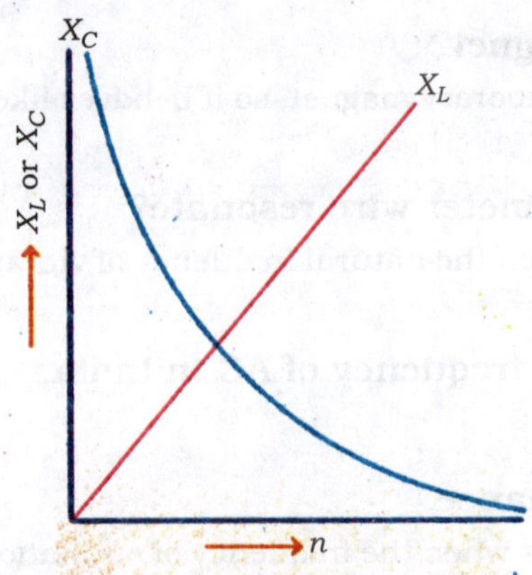

Q.16 How is AC different from DC? **[NCERT]**

Ans. A type of electric current whose magnitude and direction changes periodically is called an AC, whereas DC is the type of electric current having same magnitude and direction. So, DC repels while AC attracts.

Q.17 Define frequency of AC. **[NCERT]**

Ans. The number of cycles made by Alternating Current (AC) in one second is called frequency of AC (f).

Q.18 What should be the property of the iron for making it a good electromagnet? **[NCERT]**

Ans. The core of electromagnet should be made up of soft iron.

Q.19 How does the sonometer wire vibrate? **[NCERT]**

Ans. The current flowing in the electromagnet core is of alternating nature, so the force which acts on the sonometer wire is also oscillatory in nature. Thus, the wire vibrates.

Q.20 Identify the rule which helps us to find the direction of force acting on the stretched wire. **[NCERT]**

Ans. Fleming's left hand rule.

Q.21 Explain Fleming's left hand rule. **[NCERT]**

Ans. Stretch the fore finger, the middle finger and thumb of your left hand, so that they are perpendicular to each other. If the fore finger points towards the direction of magnetic field and the middle finger indicates the direction of current, then the thumb will indicate the direction of force acting on the conductor.

Activity 1

AIM

To measure the resistance and impedance of an inductor with or without iron core.

Apparatus and Material Required

Inductor coil (diameter ≈ 2 cm and 2000 turns), soft iron core (diameter ≈ 1.75 cm) of length equal to that of inductor, resistance box (0 to 10 kΩ), battery eliminator (0 to 6 V), a step-down transformer with tappings (0-2-4-6 V, 50 Hz), DC milliammeter (0 to 500 mA), AC milliammeter (0-500 mA), DC voltmeter (0-5 V), AC voltmeter (0-5 V), one-way key, connecting wires and a piece of sand paper.

Theory/Principle

Inductor

An inductor is a cylindrical coil of very large number of turns of copper wire wound on a hollow cylinder.

Resistance and Impedance of an Inductor

The hindrance to the flow of current (AC or DC) in a circuit is known as **resistance** R. The resistance of this coil is given by,

$$R = \frac{V}{I}$$

where, V = potential difference across the coil, I = DC current through the coil.

On introducing a soft iron core inside the coil, new values of potential difference across the coil V' and current I' through it change the value of resistance as

$$R' = \frac{V'}{I'}$$

The hindrance to the flow of Alternating Current (AC) due to generation of back emf in the coil is known as **impedance** Z. If V_{AC} is an alternating voltage through the coil without iron core and I_{AC} is the corresponding current flowing through the coil.

Then, the impedance of the coil is

$$Z = \frac{V_{AC}}{I_{AC}}$$

On introducing the iron core inside the coil, the value of alternating voltage becomes V'_{AC} and the corresponding alternating current flowing through the core becomes I'_{AC} through the coil. So, the new value of impedance is given by

$$Z' = \frac{V'_{AC}}{I'_{AC}}$$

Procedure

Measurement of Resistance of an Inductor without Iron Core

1. Arrange the apparatus and elements as per the circuit diagram as shown in figure and keep the key K, open.

2. Connect the DC source and DC milliammeter in series with inductor. Also, connect the voltmeter in parallel with inductor coil.
3. Close the key K by inserting the plug into it. Adjust the battery eliminator to the lowest reading and switch ON the battery.
4. Adjust the resistance R with the help of resistance box, so that the readings are within the scale of milliammeter and voltmeter.
5. Note the DC current and DC voltage across the inductor from milliammeter and voltmeter.

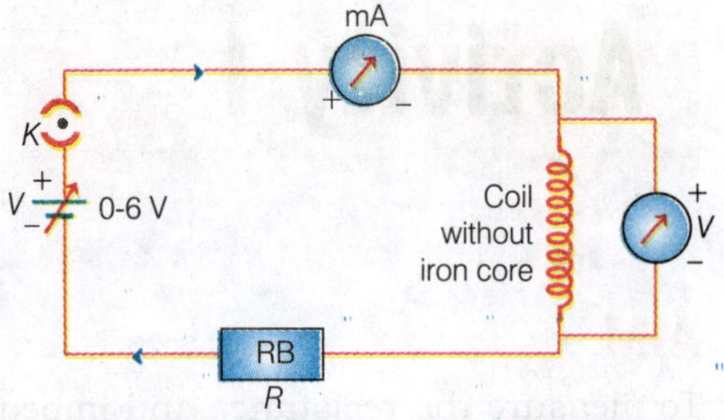

Circuit diagram to measure the resistance of an inductor without iron core

6. Set the knob of battery eliminator to higher voltages in regular steps and note the readings of DC current and DC voltage across the inductor.
7. After taking three to four observations of V and I, find the resistance of the coil without iron core for each set of observation by using the following relation and then find the mean of all different values of resistance.

$$R = \frac{V}{I}$$

Measurement of Resistance of an Inductor with Soft Iron Core Inside It

8. Introduce the soft iron core such that it is completely inside the coil and parallel to the length of inductor as per the circuit diagram as shown in figure.
9. Repeat the steps (5) to (10) and record the current and voltage across the inductor to find the new resistance R'.

Note Since, there is no inductive effect in the DC circuit, so within the experimental errors, you will find that the value of resistance remains same.

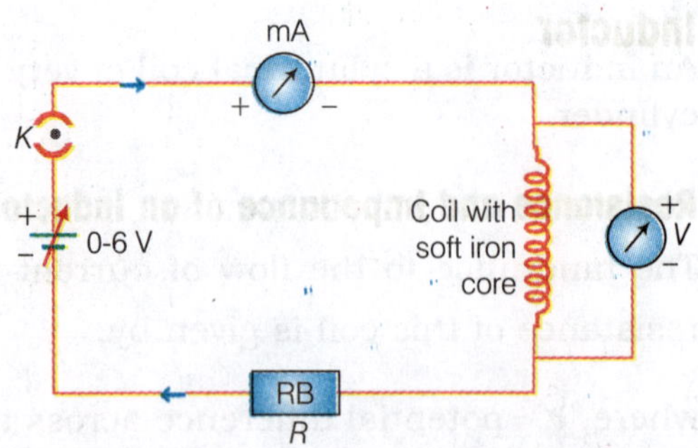

Circuit diagram to measure the resistance of an inductor with soft iron core inside it

Measurement of Impedance of an Inductor Without Iron Core

10. Make the electrical connections as per the circuit diagram as shown in figure by keeping the key K open and using step-down transformer with various tappings (0 V, 2 V, 4 V, 6 V), AC voltmeter (0-5 V) and AC ammeter (0-0.3 A).
11. Close the key K by inserting the plug into it and adjust the voltage of transformer to minimum value by tapping it to 0 V. Note the readings of AC ammeter and AC voltmeter.

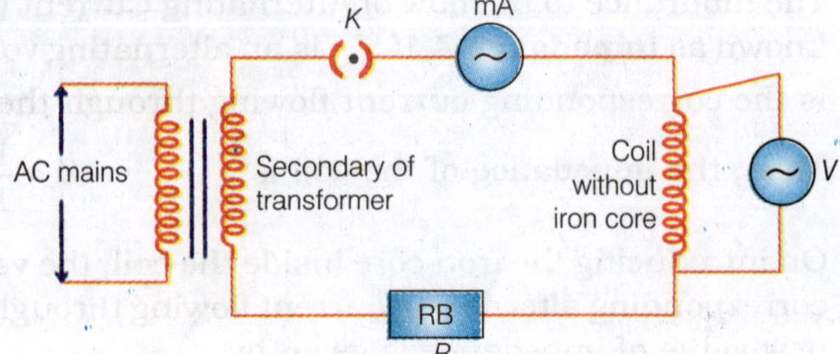

Circuit diagram to measure the impedance of an inductor without iron core

12. Repeat the steps (13) and (14) by changing the tappings of transformer 2, 4, 6 V.
13. Find the value of impedance of inductor without iron core for each set of observations by using the following relation and then take the mean of different values of impedance.

$$Z = \frac{V}{I}$$

Measurement of Impedance of an Inductor with Soft Iron Core Inside it

14. Introduce the core of soft iron such that it is fully inside the coil and parallel to the length of inductor as per the circuit diagram as shown in figure below.
15. Repeat the steps (13) to (15) for measuring alternating currents and voltages. Record the currents and voltages across the inductor and find the new value of impedance for each set of observations.

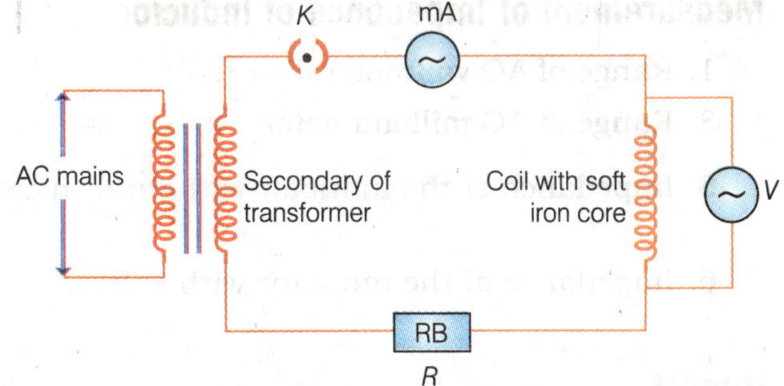

Circuit diagram to measure the impedance of an inductor with soft iron core inside it

Note Since, the inductive effect in the AC circuit affects the value of impedance. Hence, you will find that the new impedance will be larger than the old one.

Observations and calculations

Measurement of Resistance of Inductor

1. Range of DC voltmeter = 0 to ... V
2. Least count of DC voltmeter = ... V
3. Range of DC milliammeter = 0 to ... mA
4. Least count of DC milliammeter = ... mA
5. Resistance of the inductor without iron core, $R_{mean} = \frac{R_1 + R_2 + R_3}{3} = \ldots\Omega$

Table for Resistance of Inductor Coil With and Without Iron Core

S. No.	Applied voltage or battery eliminator setting, E(V)	Without iron core			With soft iron core		
		DC voltmeter reading, V_{DC}(V)	DC milliammeter reading, I (mA)	$R = \frac{V}{I}$ (Ω)	DC voltmeter reading, V′ (V)	DC milliammeter reading, I′ (mA)	$R' = \frac{V'}{I'}$ (Ω)
1				R_1 = ... Ω			R_1' = ... Ω
2				R_2 = ... Ω			R_2' = ... Ω
3				R_3 = ... Ω			R_3' = ... Ω

6. Resistance of the inductor with iron core, $R'_{mean} = \frac{R_1' + R_2' + R_3'}{3} = \ldots\Omega$

Table for Impedance of Inductor Coil with and Without Iron Core

S. No.	AC voltage source setting (V)	Without iron core			With soft iron core		
		AC voltmeter reading, V_{AC}(V)	AC milliammeter reading, I_{AC} (mA)	$Z = \frac{V_{AC}}{I_{AC}}$ (Ω)	AC voltmeter reading, V'_{AC}(V)	AC milliammeter reading, V'_{AC} (mA)	$Z' = \frac{V'_{AC}}{I'_{AC}}$ (Ω)
1				Z_1 = ... Ω			Z_1' = ... Ω
2				Z_2 = ... Ω			Z_2' = ... Ω
3				Z_3 = ... Ω			Z_3' = ... Ω

Measurement of Impedance of Inductor

1. Range of AC voltmeter = 0 to ... V
2. Least count of AC voltmeter =... V
3. Range of AC milliammeter = 0 to ... mA
4. Least count of AC milliammeter =...mA
5. Impedance of the inductor without iron core, $Z_{mean} = \frac{Z_1 + Z_2 + Z_3}{3} = ...\Omega$
6. Impedance of the inductor with soft iron core, $Z'_{mean} = \frac{Z'_1 + Z'_2 + Z'_3}{3} = ...\Omega$

Result

1. Resistance of inductor coil without iron core, R_{mean} =... Ω
2. Resistance of inductor coil with iron core, R'_{mean} =... Ω
3. Impedance of inductor coil without iron core, Z_{mean} =... Ω
4. Impedance of inductor coil with iron core, Z'_{mean} =... Ω

PRECAUTIONS

1. The ammeter should be connected in series with the inductor coil and the voltmeter should be connected in parallel with it.

2. The ammeter and voltmeter used in experiment should be of suitable ranges.

3. Open the key after each observation to avoid excessive heating.

4. The iron core should be inserted completely within the induction coil.

5. Zero error of ammeter and voltmeter should be multified to zero by adjusting the pointer at zero when no current is flowing.

Source of Error

The least count of the AC milliammeter and AC voltmeter may not be small enough to accurately record the difference in impedance on inserting the iron core.

Viva-Voce

Q 1 Name the category of circuit for which we need to calculate the impedance.

Ans. L-R circuit. Here, impedance, $Z = \sqrt{R^2 + X_L^2}$ L-C circuit. Here, impedance, $Z = \sqrt{X_L^2 + X_C^2}$

R-C circuit. Here, impedance, $Z = \sqrt{R^2 + X_C^2}$ L-C-R circuit.

Here, impedance, $Z = \sqrt{R^2 + (X_L - X_C)^2}$

Q 2 With the passage of direct current through the coil, is there any inductance in the coil?

Ans. No, as no change of magnetic flux takes place with the direct current.

Q 3 Define the term reactance.

Ans. The effective resistance offered by an inductor or a capacitor to the flow of AC current is known as reactance.

Q 4 What do you mean by capacitive reactance?

Ans. The resistance offered by a capacitor to the flow of AC current is called capacitive reactance.

Q 5 **What do you mean by inductive reactance?**

Ans. It is the resistance offered by an inductor to flow of AC current through it.

Q 6 **What is the self inductance of a coil?**

Ans. The self inductance (L) of a coil is defined as the induced emf set up in the coil to unit rate of change of current through it .

Q 7 **Define an ideal inductor.**

Ans. An inductor having self inductance only and not having any ohmic resistance/capacitive reactance is called an ideal inductor.

Q 8 **Why can't we use DC ammeter and voltmeter to measure AC?**

Ans. In AC, the direction of current changes periodically. So, the pointers of DC ammeter and voltmeter cannot follow the direction change and will remain at rest. Thus, we cannot use DC ammeter and voltmeter to measure AC.

Q 9 **Is it possible to have a resistor without inductance?**

Ans. Yes, for a wire wound resistor having non-inductive winding.

Q 10 **What will be the effect of frequency of AC voltage on the reactance of an inductor?**

Ans. The reactance offered by an inductor increases with increase in frequency of AC voltage.

Q 11 **Define admittance of an AC circuit.**

Ans. It is the reciprocal of impedance of an AC circuit.

Q 12 **If frequency of AC is increased, what happens to impedance of the inductor?**

Ans. Impedance increases because inductive reactance X_L is directly proportional to frequency.

Q 13 **How does the presence of an iron core affect the inductive reactance?**

Ans. It increases the inductance L, thus increasing $X_L = 2\pi fL$.

Q 14 **Define the term impedance of a circuit.** [NCERT]

Ans. The total effective resistance offered by resistance of coil and capacitor/inductor or both to the passage of AC current is called impedance of a circuit.

Q 15 **What differences do you observe in DC and AC ammeters and voltmeters?** [NCERT]

Ans. The DC voltmeter and ammeter measure actual value of voltage and current respectively whereas, the AC voltmeter and ammeter measure rms value of voltage and current respectively.

Activity 2

AIM

To measure resistance, voltage (AC/DC), current (DC) and check the continuity of a given circuit using a multimeter.

Apparatus and Material Required

A multimeter with its test leads, a resistance box, a step-down transformer ($V_{out} \approx 6V$), a rheostat, a cell, a key, connecting wires and a piece of sand paper.

Theory/Principle

To Measure the Resistance

When a resistor of resistance *R* is connected in a circuit, the potential difference across the two ends of the resistor can be measured by connecting the multimeter (with proper voltage setting) in parallel with the resistor.

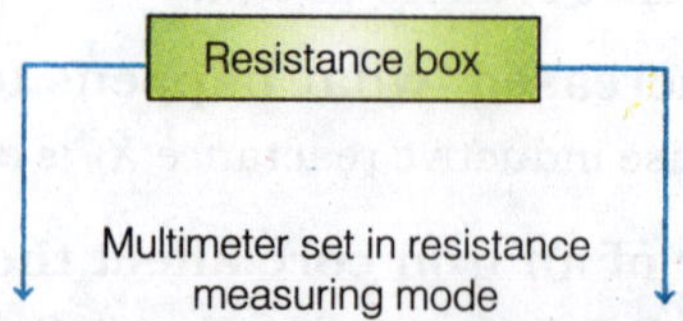

Fig. 1 Use of multimeter as ohmmeter

To Measure the Direct Current and Voltage

When a Direct Current (DC) is passed through the coil of multimeter, the multimeter shows a deflection proportional to DC. For measuring DC current, the multimeter is connected in series with the circuit and to measure DC voltage, it is connected in parallel with the two ends across which the DC voltage is to be measured.

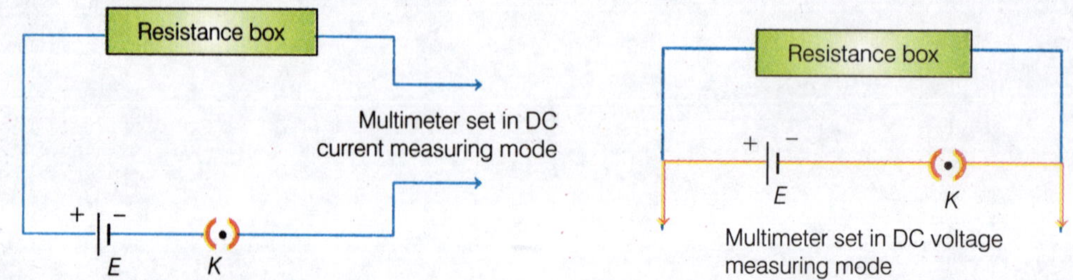

Fig. 2 Use of multimeter as DC ammeter

Fig. 3 Use of multimeter as DC voltmeter

To Measure the AC Voltage

In order to measure the AC voltage, the root mean square (rms) values of current and voltage are measured with proper setting of voltage and current. To measure the AC voltage, first the AC voltage is step down upto 6 V by using step-down transformer and the multimeter is connected to the two ends of the secondary coil of step down transformer.

By adjusting the rheostat, the multimeter reading for AC voltage drop across the resistor is noted.

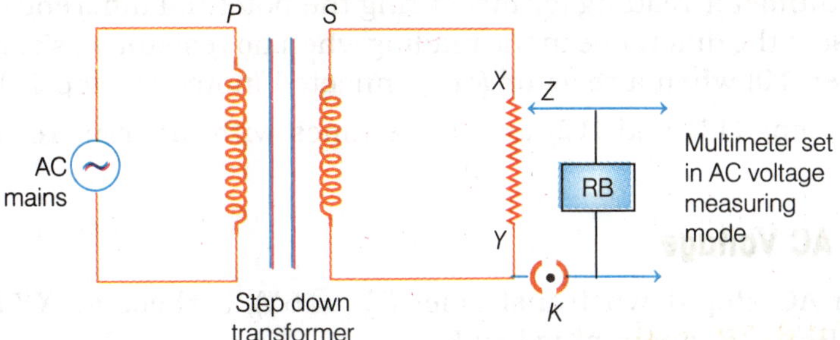

Fig. 4 Use of multimeter as an AC voltmeter

To Check the Continuity of an Electrical Component

To check the continuity of any electrical component, resistance of the component is measured. A very low resistance ($\leq 0.1\Omega$) between the two ends of a component indicates that the component under test has a short circuit. If the component under test shows infinite resistance, it indicates the discontinuity.

Procedure

Setting up the Analog Multimeter

1. Set the multimeter in resistance measuring mode. Connect the red and black probes to the multimeter. Take care that the end of test leads should not have any insulating layer on them.
2. Touch free ends of both the leads and adjust the zero adjustment knob till the multimeter reads zero ohm on resistance scale.

Measurement of Resistance

3. Separate the two metallic ends of the test probes (leads) and connect the resistance box with the multimeter.
4. Now insert a known resistance R in the circuit by taking out a resistance key from the resistance box and note the multimeter reading R_M indicating the value of resistance of the resistor used in the circuit. Repeat this step four more times by taking out different resistors.
5. Carefully observe the reading .

Note That its zero lies at the extreme right of the scale. Use the multiplication factor appropriately to the range selected. e.g. 4 divisions of deflection in $R \times 100$ scale means resistance measured is $4 \times 100\Omega = 400\Omega$.

Measurement of DC Voltage

6. Take a source of DC like battery eliminator.
7. Set the multimeter pointer to DC voltage range.
8. Set the test probes in the multimeter socket with proper polarity. It is a convention to use red lead as positive and black lead as negative.
9. Touch the free end of black lead with negative terminal of the battery and that of red lead to the positive terminal of the battery.
10. Insert the plug key K in the circuit and switch ON the battery to read the multimeter reading. Do not insert any resistance from the resistance box in the circuit. Record the observations and then open the key K.

11. Next insert a resistance R by taking out a resistance plug key or $R (\approx 10\Omega)$ from the resistance box. Close the key K by the inserting the plug into it.
12. Read the multimeter reading for measuring the potential difference across two ends of the resistor R. Note the difference in the reading when no resistor was connected with the circuit (noted in step 10) when a resistor R is connected (noted in step 11).
13. Repeat the steps (11) and (12) four more times with different resistors connected to the battery.

Measurement of AC Voltage

14. Connect an AC step-down transformer ($V_{out} = 6V$), a rheostat XY as potential divider, a Resistance Box (RB) and a plug key K.
15. Set the multimeter in (AC) voltage measuring mode of the range 0 of 10 V.
16. Connect the free ends of two leads of multimeter to the ends of secondary coil of the transformer, a potential divider (rheostat) XY, key K and Resistance Box (RB) setting as shown in the figure 4.
17. Bring the variable connector Z of the rheostat close to point X, so that the resistance of the rheostat coil would become minimum.
18. Close the key K and record the multimeter reading for AC voltage drop across the resistance R.
19. Repeat the step (17) for atleast four positions of Z of rheostat coil XY.

Measurement of DC Current

20. Select the function switch and the range switch/sockets suitable for proper DC current measurement.
21. Connect the multimeter in series with the ends of the secondry coil of the transformer.
22. Note the multimeter reading for multimeter set in DC current measuring mode.
23. Bring a resistance R in the circuit from the resistance box and close the key K, then note the multimeter reading for measuring DC current flowing in the circuit.
24. Repeat step (24) for four more values of resistance R.

Digital Multimeter

25. For digital multimeter, the procedure for measuring voltage, current and resistance is similar to that of analog measurement. The digital multimeters can accept voltage even with reversed polarities and display the number when the magnitude of the measured quantity crosses the upper limit of the range used so that the digital multimeter is not damaged as easily as the analog multimeter.

Observations

1. Range of resistance scale on multimeter panel = 0 to... Ω
2. Least count of resistance scale =... Ω

Table for Measuring Resistance

S. No.	Resistance from the resistance box, R (Ω)	Multimeter reading for resistance, R_M (Ω)	Difference, $R - R_M$ (Ω)
1			
2			
3			
4			

3. Range of DC voltage scale on multimeter = 0 to ... V
4. Least count of voltage scale = ... V

Table for Measuring DC Voltage

S. No.	Resistance from the resistance box, R (Ω)	Multimeter reading for DC voltage (V)
1		
2		
3		
4		

5. Range of AC voltage scale selected on multimeter = 0 to ... V
6. Least count of voltage scale = ... V

Table for Measurement of AC Voltage Drop Across Resistor R

S. No.	Position of variable connection (Z) on rheostat coil, XY	Multimeter reading for AC voltage (V)
1	Close to point X	
2		
3		
4		

7. Range of DC current selected scale on multimeter = 0 to ... mA
8. Least count of current scale = ... mA

Table for Measurement of DC Current

S. No.	Resistance from resistance box, R (Ω)	Multimeter reading for DC current (mA)
1.		
2.		
3.		
4.		

Result

1. The DC/AC voltage, DC current and resistance have been measured by using a multimeter.
2. AC/DC voltage measured by multimeter is same as that of voltage marked on AC/DC source.
3. The values of resistance measured by multimeter is same as that measured by colour coding.

PRECAUTIONS

1. *Allow the AC current for minimum possible time for safety consideration.*
2. *Appropriate selection of function switch and range switch for a given measurement of voltage or current and resistance should be made.*
3. *Before using the multimeter, its zero ohm should be achieved by connecting its probes together and by adjusting its knob.*
4. *While dealing with high voltages, the probes of the multimeter should be held from their insulating cover.*
5. *While measuring the voltage or current, the range of the multimeter should be selected high then it is reduced to low as per the requirement.*
6. *If the two leads of the multimeter are not identical, then the measurement will be affected.*

Viva-Voce

Q 1 What is a multimeter?

Ans. It is an electronic device used for measuring AC/DC voltage, DC current and resistance.

Q 2 Which type of resistors we use in electrical/electronic circuits?

Ans. Carbon composition resistors.

Q 3 Distinguish between AC voltage and DC voltage.

Ans. The magnitude of DC voltage is always constant. On the other hand, the magnitude of AC voltage changes periodically.

Q 4 Can the measurement of DC voltage/current be done using AC voltage/current function switch? [NCERT]

Ans. No.

Q 5 Why a multimeter also called as AVO meter?

Ans. A multimeter measures current in ampere (A), voltage in volt (V) and resistance in ohm (Ω). So, it is also called as AVO meter.

Activity 3

AIM

To assemble a household circuit comprising three bulbs, three (ON/OFF) switches, a fuse and a power source.

Apparatus and Material Required

Three bulbs (40 W, 220 V each), three bulb holders, three ON/OFF switches, a fuse of 1 A, a fuse holder, three pin plug, flexible two coloured insulating copper wire, main switch.

Theory/Principle

The electricity of 220 V and 50 Hz is supplied to us for domestic purposes. In household circuit, all appliances are connected in parallel with the mains. Consider P_1, P_2, P_3, P_4, P_5.... be the power consumed by different domestic electrical appliances in a circuit. Then the total power consumed P at any instant is given by

$$P = P_1 + P_2 + P_3 + P_4 + P_5 + \dots$$

At a potential V, the current I drawn from the mains is given by

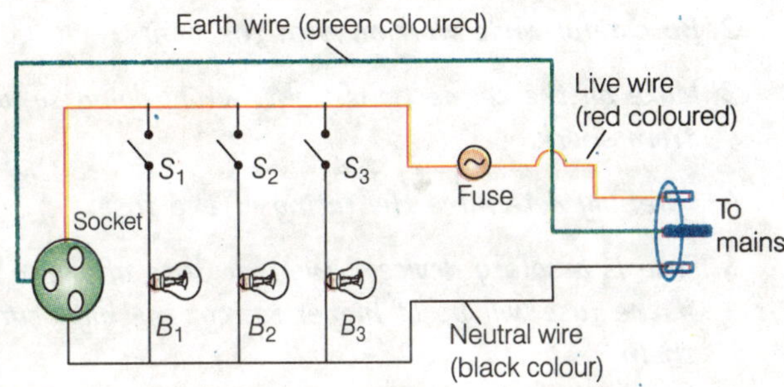

Circuit diagram for wiring of three bulbs

$$I = \frac{P}{V} \qquad [\because P = VI]$$

where, P is in watt, I is in ampere and V is in volt.

Sometimes the terminals of electric appliances get accidentally connected so a high current is drawn from the circuit which may burn the appliances, hence, they may get damaged. A fuse of rating little higher than the current drawn is connected in series with the appliances.

Whenever high current flows in the circuit the fuse gets burnt which saves the appliances from damage. A fuse is a short piece of wire made up of material of high resistivity and low melting point so that it gets easily melt due to overheating when excessive current passes through the circuit and hence, the current flowing in the circuit is stopped.

Procedure

1. Take three bulbs B_1, B_2 and B_3 and connect them in series with switches S_1, S_2 and S_3 respectively.
2. $B_1 - S_1$, $B_2 - S_2$ and $B_3 - S_3$ connections should be parallel with each other as shown in the circuit diagram. Hence, each bulb can be OFF and ON individually by using its switch connected in series with it.
3. Connect a fuse in series with the set up and connect a plug and socket at the end of two leads. Also connect a wire from the earth pin of the plug.
4. Insert the plug in socket provided in the main electric board.

5. Put the switches S_1, S_2 and S_3 ON one by one and observe the bulb glowing independently of the other bulb.
6. Press all the switches ON simultaneously and observe the bulbs glowing together.
7. Put the switches S_1, S_2 and S_3 OFF one by one and observe the bulbs not glowing.

Observation

The bulb glows when the switch is made ON. It stops glowing when the switch is made OFF.

Result

The circuit for the connection of three bulbs is completely installed with safety.

PRECAUTIONS

1. *Always make the connections of the switches and fuse with the live wire.*
2. *Be careful while working with the mains.*
3. *Make all the connections tight. While doing so, use an insulating cover on your hand to keep away from shock.*
4. *Carefully determine the rating of the fuse.*
5. *Fuse is a safety device. Never use fuse of much higher rating than the recommended value. Because if the fuse will be of higher rating, the high current flows to the electrical appliances and damage them.*
6. *Always use that supply which is connected to the distribution board which divides the power into different circuits.*

Viva-Voce

Q 1 Why is the fuse always connected in the live wire and not the neutral?

Ans. To cut off the current from the source immediately in case of overload or short circuit.

Q 2 What do you mean by fuse wire?

Ans. A fuse is a type of low resistance resistor that acts as a sacrificial device to provide overcurrent protection for either of load or short circuit.

Q 3 Why three pin sockets and plugs are preferred over two pin ones?

Ans. The two pin connection have live wire and neutral wire, whereas the three pin sockets and plugs have earth connections for safety purpose.

Q 4 Which is better the ring main system or the parallel circuit system?

Ans. The ring main system.

Q 5 The electric cable have wires of three different colours. Why?

Ans. The green coloured wire is used for earth connection, the red coloured wire is for live line and the black coloured wire is for neutral line.

Q 6 Write the formula for electric power.

Ans. $P = \frac{W}{t} = VI = I^2R = \frac{V^2}{R}$, where, W = work done or electric energy,

t = time taken , V = voltage, I = current and R = resistance.

Q 7 **How much is the resistance of a closed plug key?**

Ans. Negligibly small.

Q 8 **How much is the resistance of air gap?**

Ans. Infinity (∞).

Q 9 **Give two advantages of ring main system.**

Ans.
(i) A new power point can be installed without putting long leads all the way to the distribution box.
(ii) A separate fuse can be connected with each plug. In case if one fuse is not working, the other appliances can work without any affect.

Q 10 **Calculate the maximum current drawn for three bulbs used in the circuit?** [NCERT]

Ans. From the experiment, the rating of each of the bulbs is 40 W, 220 V.

$$P = VI$$

Current in each bulb,

$$I = \frac{P}{V} = \frac{40}{220} = \frac{2}{11}$$

Total current, $I = I_1 + I_2 + I_3$

$$= \frac{2}{11} + \frac{2}{11} + \frac{2}{11} = \frac{6}{11}$$

Q 11 **Why do we connect household appliances in parallel combination?** [NCERT]

Ans. This arrangement allows appliances to function properly without affecting each other and if one appliance fails, it doesn't impact the operation of others. Aditionally, parallel connections allow for consistent voltage across all devices, ensuring they operate efficiently.

Activity 4

AIM

To assemble the components of a given electrical circuit.

Apparatus and material required

A voltmeter (0-5 V), an ammeter (0-1.5 A), a resistor, a rheostat, a battery, a one-way key, connecting wires and sand paper.

Procedure

1. First of all, current various components as shown in figure.
2. Open the key K by taking out the plug from it.
3. To measure the current in the circuit, connect the ammeter in series with the circuit and to measure the potential difference across the resistance, connect a voltmeter in parallel to the resistance. It should be ensured that the positive terminals of voltmeter and ammeter must be connected with the positive terminal of the battery E.

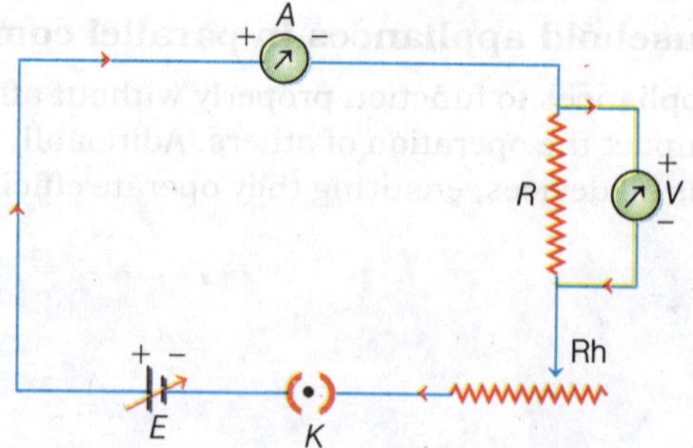

Assembling of electrical components for Ohm's law

4. Close the key K by inserting the plug into it and check whether the voltmeter and ammeter show deflections on the right hand side or not.
5. The circuit has been assembled completely. Check the continuity of assembled circuit by using a multimeter.

Note With the help of this assembled circuit, one can measure the unknown resistance by knowing the values of current and potential difference.

Result

The components of the electrical circuit have been assembled correctly.

PRECAUTIONS

1. Take care that the ammeter should be connected in series with the resistor and the voltmeter should be connected in parallel with the resistor.

2. Clean the connecting ends with a piece of sand paper. However, do not rub the plugs and keys with sand paper to clean them. Excessive use of sand paper will make the plug unfit to be used with the socket or key.

3. Before connecting the element, the key should be opened.

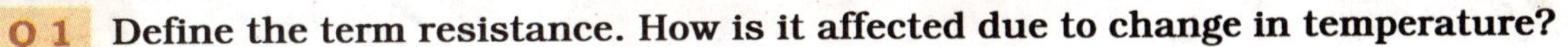

Viva-Voce

Q 1 Define the term resistance. How is it affected due to change in temperature?

Ans. The opposition to the flow of electric current through any cross-section of a conductor is called the resistance. The resistance of a conductor increases with rise in temperature of conductor.

Q 2 Define Ohm's law.

Ans. When the physical condition of a conductor like temperature, pressure, etc remains same then current passing through the conductor is directly proportional to the potential difference applied across its ends.

i.e. $I \propto V \Rightarrow V = IR$

Q 3 Why do we use voltmeter in electrical circuitry?

Ans. In order to measure potential difference between two points in an electrical circuit, we use a voltmeter.

Q 4 What do you mean by a battery?

Ans. The combinations of primary cells in series is termed as a battery.

Q 5 What do you mean by emf of a cell? [NCERT]

Ans. The electromotive force (emf) of a cell is the potential difference across the terminals of the cell when no current is drawn from the cell.

Q 6 Does the current drawn from the cell remain constant? If not, why? [NCERT]

Ans. No, due to internal resistance of a cell there is a potential drop in the cell and the terminal potential difference decreases. Thus, the current will decrease slowly.

Q 7 Why is an ammeter always connected in series with the circuit? [NCERT]

Ans. An ammeter has very low resistance. So, by connecting an ammeter in series with the circuit, it measures the current through a circuit without changing the magnitude of current.

Q 8 Why is a voltmeter always connected in parallel with the component across which voltage is to be measured? [NCERT]

Ans. A voltmeter measures potential drop across two points without changing its magnitude when it is connected in parallel. So, the voltmeter is always connected in parallel with the component across which voltage is to be measured.

Activity 5

AIM

To study the variation in potential drop with length of a wire for a steady current.

Apparatus and Material Required

A battery eliminator of constant voltage, potentiometer, a DC power supply (or lead accumulator), a rheostat, a voltmeter and an ammeter of suitable range, one-way key, jockey, connecting wires and a piece of sand paper.

Theory/Principle

If a steady current is flowing through a wire of uniform area of cross-section, then the potential drop V across any two points of the wire is directly proportional to the length l between these two points.

i.e. $$V \propto l \quad \ldots \text{(i)}$$

Here, resistance per unit length of the wire is constant due to flow of constant current through the same cross-section.

As, $$V \propto l$$

$$V = kl \quad \Rightarrow \quad k = \frac{V}{l}$$ where, k is a constant called **potential gradient**.

From Eq. (i), it is clear that if we plot a graph between V and l by taking them along Y- and X-axes respectively, we get a straight line passing through the origin. Thus, **there is linear relationship between length of the wire and potential drop across it.**

Procedure

Setting up the Elements of Circuit

1. Arrange the electrical components as per the circuit diagram.
2. Open the key by pulling out the plug from it.
3. Connect the positive terminals of the battery to zero length of potentiometer wire, i.e. at point A.
4. Connect the negative terminal of the battery to the maximum length of potentiometer wire, i.e. at point B through an ammeter, plug key and rheostat. Take care that the negative terminal of ammeter should be connected with negative terminal of the battery.

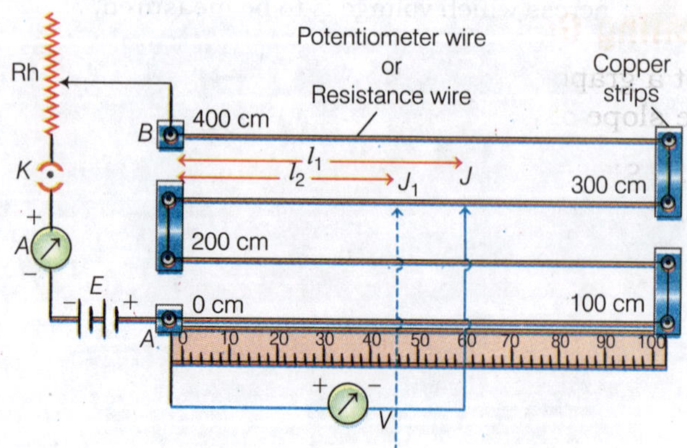

Circuit diagram of potentiometer for the variation of potential drop with length of wire

5. Connect positive end of voltmeter to point A and negative end of voltmeter to the jockey J which can slide over the wire.

Studying the Variation in Potential Drop with Length of Wire

6. Now close the key K by inserting the plug into it and place the jockey at point A. Adjust the rheostat to get full scale deflection in the voltmeter.
7. Again place the jockey at point B you will get zero deflection in the voltmeter.

Note If the zero deflection is not shown then by adjusting the sliding contact of the rheostat, the current flowing in the circuit is also adjusted hence, one can get the full scale deflection in the voltmeter.

8. Now, place the jockey at different points in between 40 cm to 60 cm of the wire and note the corresponding voltmeter readings.
9. Repeat the observations by placing the jockey at the lengths 80 cm, 120 cm or upto 400 cm of wire.

Note During the experiment, it should be ensured that the ammeter gives the constant reading.

10. Plot a graph between V and l by taking them along Y- and X-axes, respectively. The graph will be a straight line passing through the origin.

Observations and Calculations

Range of voltmeter = 0 to ...V   Least count of voltmeter = ...V   Zero error of voltmeter = ... V

Table for Variation in Potential Drop Across the Length of Wire

S.No.	Length of potentiometer wire over which potential drop is measured, l (cm)	Voltmeter reading, V (V)	Potential gradient, $k = \frac{V}{l}$ (V/cm)
1			k_1 = ...
2			k_2 = ...
3			k_3 = ...
4			k_4 = ...

Calculate the potential gradient $k = (V/l)$ at different lengths of the wire. The value of (V/l) is almost same for each observation.

Mean value of potential gradient, $k = \frac{k_1 + k_2 + k_3 + k_4}{4}$ = ... V/cm

Plotting Graph

Plot a graph of V *versus* l, with V on Y-axis and l on X-axis. The slope of graph gives potential gradient k.

Slope of graph, $k = \frac{BC}{AB} = \frac{V}{l}$ = ... V/cm

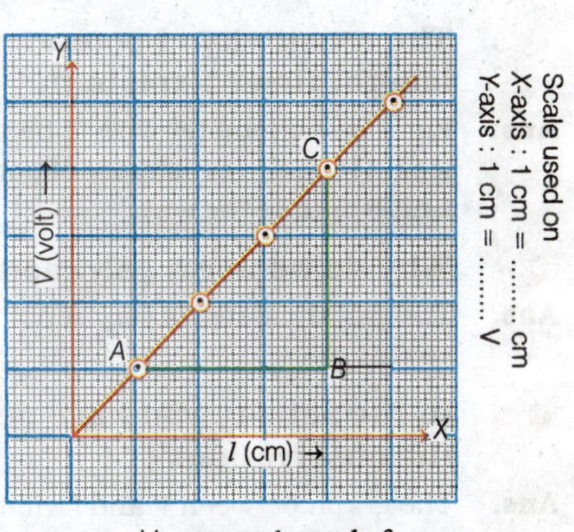

V *versus* l graph for potentiometer wire

Result

1. The potential gradient $\frac{V}{l}$ for given potentiometer wire is found to be constant within the limit of experimental error.
2. The V *versus* l graph is a straight line showing a **linear relationship between** V **and** l.
3. Mean value of potential gradient, k =... V/cm.
4. From graph, the value of k =... V/cm

PRECAUTIONS

1. The electrical connections should be neat, clean and tight.
2. Check the uniformity of potentiometer wire at its various points. If the potentiometer wire has non-uniform cross-section, replace it with the wire of uniform cross-section.
3. The readings of ammeter should remain constant throughout the experiment.
4. The positive terminals of the battery and voltmeter should be connected at the same point A of the potentiometer wire.
5. Do not press the jockey too hard on the potentiometer wire. It may destroy the uniformity of the wire.
6. Plug should be inserted into the key, only at the time of taking observations otherwise excessive heating of wire may affect the observations.
7. Always use a rheostat to control the current in the circuit and allow the steady current in the wire.
8. The placement of jockey should vary from 40 cm to 400 cm of potentiometer wire to take different observations.

Viva-Voce

Q 1 What is the principle of a potentiometer?

Ans. The principle of a potentiometer is that the potential drop across any length of wire of uniform cross-section and composition is directly proportional to the length.

Q 2 Define the term potential gradient.

Ans. The potential drop per unit length of potentiometer wire is called potential gradient.

Potential gradient, $k = \frac{V}{l}$

Q 3 The sensitivity of potentiometer wire depends upon the potential drop per unit length. How? Explain it.

Ans. For a potentiometer wire to be more sensitive, the potential drop per cm of wire should be very less. Thus, the sensitivity of potentiometer wire is inversely proportional to the potential drop per unit length of the wire.

Q 4 Why do we use a galvanometer in an electric circuit?

Ans. The galvanometer is very sensitive device and it is used to measure the current flow in an electric circuit.

Q 5 In the activity you have performed, how does the non-uniformity of wire affect the observations?

Ans. The graph between V and l will be non-linear, if the potential drop is not proportional to the length. It is caused due to non-uniformity of wire and improper adjustment of rheostat slider.

Activity 6

AIM

To draw the diagram of given open circuit comprising at least a battery, resistor/rheostat, key, ammeter and voltmeter. Mark the components that are not connected in proper order and correct the circuit and also the circuit diagram.

Apparatus and Material Required

A battery eliminator or a battery, rheostat, resistor, ammeter, voltmeter, plug key, connecting wires and a piece of sand paper.

Theory/Principle

An electrical circuit is functional only if all the components of circuit are connected in proper order and the components and devices are in working condition when the key is closed.

An open circuit means a break in some part of a circuit due to open key or broken wire or burnt out components or loose connections. The examples of open circuit are shown in the figures.

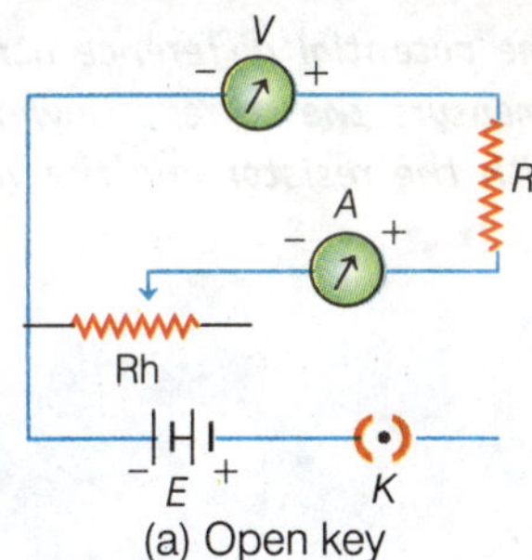

(a) Open key

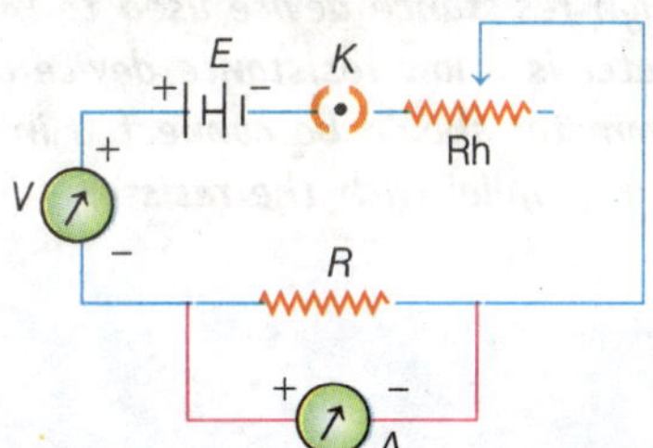

(b) Incorrect connection as ammeter in parallel and voltmeter in series with the resistor

Procedure

Making Correction in the Circuit Diagram

1. Draw the circuit diagram in your notebook as given by your teacher or from any of the above figures.
2. In the observation table, mark the various components which are not connected in proper order by (X) and by (T) which are in correct order.
3. Next, do the correction in the circuit diagram.

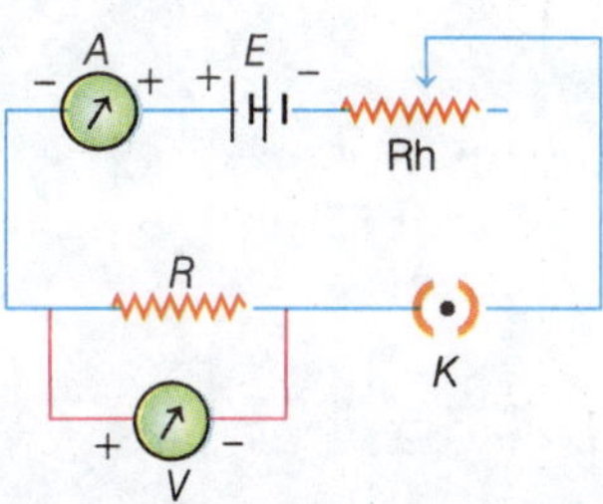

A proper arrangement of components in a circuit

Verification of Corrected Circuit Diagram

(or How the Components Should be Connected in a Circuit)

4. Connect all the electrical components according to the corrected circuit diagram.
5. Finally close the key and check whether the corrected circuit is functioning or not.

Observations

Table for Mark a (✔) or (✗) in Appropriate Column

S. No.	Circuit component	Correct connection	Incorrect connection
1	Battery/cell		
2	Resistor		
3	Rheostat		
4	Ammeter		
5	Voltmeter		
6	Key		

Result

The electrical components assembled as per the corrected circuit diagram is functional.

PRECAUTIONS

1. *Ends of connecting wires should be cleaned with sand paper before making connections.*
2. *The positive terminal of the battery should be connected to the positive terminals of the voltmeter and ammeter. Also, the negative terminal of the battery should be connected with rheostat.*
3. *As a voltmeter is a high resistance device used to measure the potential difference across the resistor and an ammeter is a low resistance device used to measure the current flowing through the circuit. Hence, the ammeter should be connected in series with the resistor and the voltmeter should be connected in parallel with the resistor.*

Viva-Voce

Q 1 What do you mean by open circuit?

Ans. Combination of primary components of electrical circuit in such a way that no current is drawn from the cell is called open circuit.

Q 2 What do you mean by closed circuit?

Ans. If all the primary components of electrical circuit are connected in a proper way, so as the current is drawn from the cell then the circuit is termed as closed circuit.

Q 3 What do you mean by an electric circuit?

Ans. The conducting path consisting of electric components between two terminals of a cell is called the electric circuit.

Q 4 What will happen, if an ammeter is directly connected across a battery?

Ans. If an ammeter with very low resistance is connected directly across a battery, a large current will flow through it, potentially causing the coil to burn out.

Q 5 What do you expect, if a voltmeter is connected in series and ammeter in parallel with the resistance *R* by mistake?

Ans. If a voltmeter is mistakenly connected in series and an ammeter in parallel with the resistance R, the combined resistance of R and the ammeter will be low. However, since the voltmeter is in series, the overall resistance of the circuit will be high, resulting in only a small current flowing through the circuit. The small current will pass entirely through the ammeter, so neither the voltmeter nor the ammeter will be damaged.

Q 6 What is the function of sand paper in setting up the electric circuit? [NCERT]

Ans. The ends of connecting wires are rubbed with the sand paper in order to remove the insulation from their surfaces.

Q 7 What do you mean by ampere-hour capacity of a battery?

Ans. The ampere-hour (Ah) capacity of a battery indicates the total amount of charge, it can store. For example, a battery with a capacity of 5 Ah can supply a current of 1 A for 5 h or 0.5 A for 10 h.

Q 8 A rheostat and a resistance box can change the resistance in a circuit, yet their functions are different. Explain it. [NCERT]

Ans. Resistance box will provide resistance of discrete values such as 1, 2, 3 ohm. So, interim values are not possible. On the other hand, rheostat gives a chance to vary the resistance continuously. It may be 5Ω or 5.769Ω. So just to fix current for specified value such as 1.5 A, resistance box is not suitable but rheostat is most suitable.

Section B

Experiment 1

AIM

To find the value of v for different values of u in case of a concave mirror and to find the focal length.

Apparatus and Materials Required

An optical bench along with three uprights, concave mirror, mirror holder, two optical needles, index needle and meter scale.

Terms Related To Experiment

Index Correction

It is defined as the difference of the actual distance and the observed distance between two uprights. It is also known as **bench-correction**. The readings of two uprights do not give the actual distance between the tip of the pin O and pole P of the mirror. Hence, a correction must, be applied. It is called the index correction.

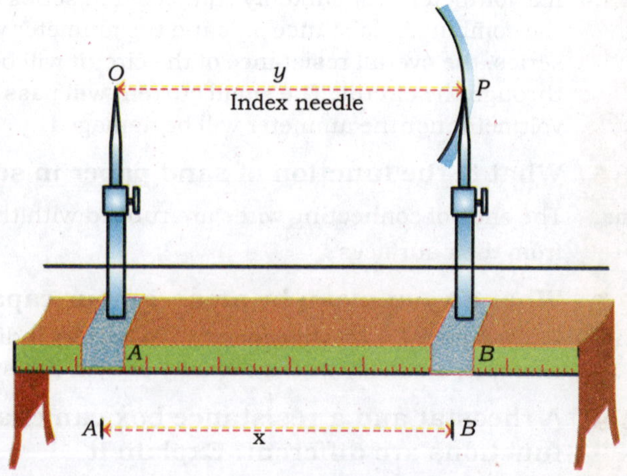

In order to determine the index correction, an index needle is used to measure the distance between two uprights by using a meter scale. But before measuring the distance between two uprights, the height of the needle O is adjusted so that its tip and the pole of the mirror lie in the same horizontal line. Then, the index needle is held in such a way that its one end touches the tip of the needle O and the other end touches the pole P or centre of the mirror. If the distance x is measured by considering the uprights positions on the optical bench and y is the distance between tip of the needle and centre of mirror measured by using index needle, then difference x-y gives the **index correction** and y-x gives the **index error**.

Removal of Parallax

The method of locating the position of an image on the optical bench by a pin is called **parallax method**. As we know, the position of an object is always known to us but its image is to be projected. The parallax is to be removed between the tip of real inverted image of object needle and the tip of erect image needle.

Firstly, the heights of image needle and object needle are so adjusted that their tips lie on a horizontal straight line passing through the pole of mirror and then keep one eye closed and the other eye open which is moved to left and right. If the image needle moves in the opposite direction of eye, then one needs to take away the image needle from the mirror but if the image needle sets closer to the eye, then one needs to take the needle towards the mirror. The position of the image needle is adjusted till the tips of the erected image needle and image of the object needle coincide with each other. When they both coincide, the parallax gets removed.

Theory/Principle

Object and Image Distances for Concave Mirror

In a spherical mirror, the distance of the object from its pole is called the **object distance** (u). The distance of the image from pole of the mirror is called the **image distance** (v).

Focal Length

The distance of the principal focus from the pole is called **focal length** (f). The relation between quantities (u, v and f) is called **mirror formula**.

It is expressed as $$\frac{1}{f}=\frac{1}{u}+\frac{1}{v} \text{ or } f=\frac{uv}{u+v}$$

where u, v and f are used with their signs.

This formula is valid in all situations for all spherical mirrors and for all positions of the object.

Determination of Focal Length of a Concave Mirror

Consider an object like an iron needle is placed in front of the reflecting surface of the concave mirror in such a way that the position of an object lies in between principal focus of the mirror F and the centre of curvature C. Then a real, inverted and magnified image is formed in between the centre of curvature of mirror and infinity (∞) as shown in the figure.

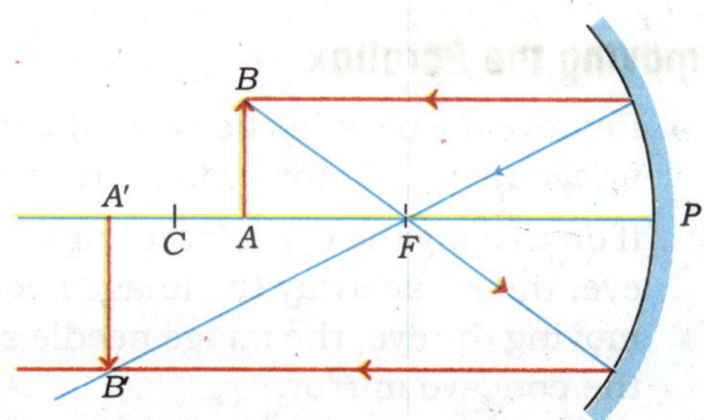

Formation of image of an object in C and F of the concave mirror

The image formed in this case will be clear and easier to be seen. Thus, the focal length of the concave mirror can be found by placing the object in between the point C and focus F.

Procedure

Determination of Approximate Focal Length

1. Find the approximate focal length of the given concave mirror by focusing the image of a distant object. This can be done by obtaining a bright and clear image of a distant building or tree on a sheet of paper.
2. Measure the distance between the mirror and the image which gives approximate focal length f of the concave mirror.

Setting up the Apparatus

3. Place the optical bench on a horizontal adjusted rigid table. If the table is not horizontal, then set it with the help of levelling screws and spirit level.
4. Place the three uprights on the optical bench.
5. Clamp the concave mirror with the mirror holder to the upright nearest to the one end of the optical bench.

Note It is to be ensured that the mirror should be vertical and perpendicular to the length of the optical bench.

6. Fix the two optical needles P_1 and P_2 to the uprights in front of the reflecting surface of the mirror.
7. Now adjust the heights of both the needles, so that their tips and pole (or centre) of the mirror lie in the same horizontal line.

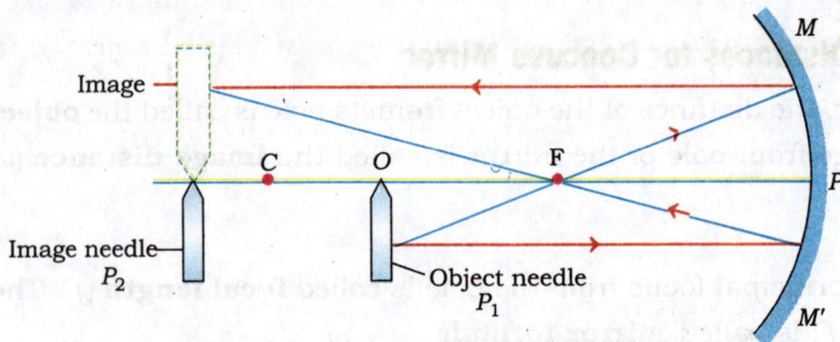

Experimental setup for determination of focal length of a concave mirror

8. Adjust the position of the upright holding object needle P_1, so that it lies in between the centre of curvature C and focus F of the concave mirror.
9. Move an object needle P_1 on the optical bench back and forth so that its image touches to the tip of the image needle P_2 and ensure that this meeting of the two tips is seen at the pole of the concave mirror.

Removing the Parallax

10. Remove the parallax between the image of the object needle and image needle by moving the image needle P_2 towards or away from the mirror.
11. If on moving the eye left and right, the image needle moves in a direction opposite to that of eye, then take away the image needle from the concave mirror. In the contrast to this, if on moving the eye, the image needle sets closer to the eye, then take the image needle towards the concave mirror.

Determination of Image and Object Distances

12. When the parallax gets removed, note the position of the uprights holding the concave mirror, object needle and image needle on the optical bench. The distance between the pole of the mirror and image needle P_2 will give you the **observed image distance** (v) of the object whereas, the distance between the pole of the mirror and object needle P_1 will give you the **observed object distance** (u).

Applying the Index Correction

13. To find the index correction, place a thin straight index needle in such a way that its one end touches the tip of the needle P_1 and the other end touches the pole P of the mirror.
14. Now, by using meter scale determine the actual distance by measuring the length of the index needle touching the tip of the needle P_1 and centre of pole P of the mirror. This will give you the actual length between the object needle P_1 and pole of the mirror. The difference between observed distance (measured in step 12) and actual distance will give you the correction to be applied to the observed object distance.
15. Find the index correction for the image needle P_2 by following the same steps (13) to (14) and apply the correction to the observed image distance.

Determination of Focal Length

16. Find the focal length f by using the following relation, $\frac{1}{f}=\frac{1}{u}+\frac{1}{v}$

    Here, u and v represent the corrected object and image distances respectively.
17. Repeat the experiment for at least five different positions of object u and determine the corresponding values of v.
18. Find the focal length for each set of observations and then take the mean of all values of focal length.
19. Note your observations in the tabular form.

Observations and Calculations

For Approximate Focal Length

1. Rough or approximate focal length of the given concave mirror = ... cm

For Index Correction

2. Actual distance of the object from the pole of the mirror using index needle, i.e. l_0 =...... cm
3. Observed distance of the object from the mirror = Position of mirror upright – Position of object needle upright on the scale, l_0' ...... cm
4. Index correction for object distance, i.e. e_0 =Actual distance –Observed distance = $l_0 - l_0'$=... cm
5. Similarly, for image needle, $e_i = l_i - l_i'$ = ... cm

Table for Determination of Focal Length of Given Concave Mirror

S. N.	Position of			Observed distances		Corrected distances		Focal length $f=\frac{uv}{u+v}$ (cm)	Δf (cm)
	Mirror (cm)	Object needle, P_1 (cm)	Image needle, P_2 (cm)	u' (cm)	v' (cm)	$u = u' + e_0$(cm)	$v = v' + e_i$ (cm)		
1								f_1 = ... cm	
2								f_2 = ... cm	
3								f_3 = ... cm	
4								f_4 = ... cm	
5								f_5 = ... cm	
6								f_6 = ... cm	

6. Calculate the corrected values of u and v by using

$$u = u' + e_0 \text{ and } v = v' + e_i$$

For Focal Length

7. Compute the value of f by using mirror formula, $\frac{1}{f}=\frac{1}{u}+\frac{1}{v}$ or $f=\frac{uv}{u+v}$

   Find the value of focal length for each set of observations.
8. Find the mean value of focal length, $f=\frac{f_1+f_2+f_3+f_4+f_5+f_6}{6}$ =... cm

Error

The error in focal length, $\frac{\Delta f}{f^2} = \frac{\Delta u}{u^2} + \frac{\Delta v}{v^2}$

$$\Delta f = f^2\left(\frac{\Delta u}{u^2} + \frac{\Delta v}{v^2}\right)$$

where, Δu and Δv are the least counts of optical bench scale, with the help of which, they are measured, u and v are the corrected object and image distances respectively and f is the mean value of focal length of concave mirror.

Result

1. The values of v (image distance) for different values of u (object distances) are recorded in the observation table.
2. The focal length of the given concave mirror is $f \pm \Delta f = \ldots \pm \ldots$ cm.

PRECAUTIONS

1. *The optical bench should be levelled properly.*
2. *The uprights supporting the optical elements should be rigid and mounted vertically on the optical bench.*
3. *The object needle should be kept in between the centre of curvature and the focus of the mirror.*
4. *The aperture of mirror should be small else the image formed will not be distinct.*
5. *To locate the position of the image, the eye should be atleast 30 cm away from the needle.*
6. *Do not place the object needle closer to the rough focal length of the mirror. This will produce a virtual image.*
7. *The tip of the inverted image of the object needle must touch the tip of the image needle and must not overlap.*
8. *Index correction for u and v should be properly determined and must be applied.*
9. *The image and object needles should not be interchanged throughout the experiment.*
10. *A white screen or plane background may be used for seeing the clear image of the pin.*

Sources of Error

1. If the top of the optical bench is not horizontal then error arises.
2. If the tips of needle and pole of the mirror are not in the same horizontal level, then error may occur.
3. The concave mirror may not be front-coated so that multiple reflections may occur from the reflecting surface of the mirror.
4. The parallax and index correction may not have been considered.
5. The uprights may not be set vertically on the optical bench.

Viva-Voce

Q.1 Why is it advised to use a small aperture of mirrors for doing the experiments?

Ans. It is advised to use a small aperture of mirrors for doing the experiments because it allows a very narrow beam of rays through the mirror. As a result of it, a clear and distinct image free from aberrations is formed by the mirrors.

Q.2 Which mirror is used by a surgeon and why?

Ans. A concave mirror of small aperture is used by a surgeon to throw a narrow and sharp beam of light into the ear, eye, nose and throat for medical check-up.

Q.3 Does the focal length of a mirror change due to (i) change in medium and (ii) colour of light?

Ans. No, the focal length of a mirror does not change. Since, focal length of a mirror does not depend upon the external medium and wavelength of light.

Q.4 What are paraxial and marginal rays?

Ans. The rays which are very close to the principal axis or subtend a very small angle are called paraxial rays. The rays which are away or subtend large angle with principal axis are called marginal rays.

Q.5 Why do we not use a concave mirror for search light?

Ans. We do not use a concave mirror for search light as large aperture of concave mirror will cause spherical aberration. Rays from sources of light coming at the focus, will not be parallel after reflection from mirror.

Q.6 If the optical bench is not levelled properly, what difficulty will it pose in locating the position of the image?

Ans. The line joining the tips of the image needle, object needle and the centre of the mirror will not remain horizontal. As a result, it becomes difficult to locate the image.

Q.7 Is silvering done by depositing silver coating or some other material?

Ans. Silvering is done by depositing silver nitrate only in good quality mirrors. But in commercial mirrors, silvering is done by depositing mercuric oxide.

Q.8 Suggest a very simple method for determining the focal length of a concave mirror in the laboratory.

Ans. One pin-method is a very simple method for determining the focal length of a concave mirror in the laboratory.

Q.9 Write the nature of the image formed by a concave mirror when the object is placed between its pole and the focus?

Ans. The nature of the image formed is virtual, erect and magnified.

Q.10 If the plotted graph between $\frac{1}{u}$ and $\frac{1}{v}$ is a straight line, what does the intercept give?

Ans. The intercept on the $1/v$ axis gives the reciprocal of focal length $\left(\frac{1}{f}\right)$.

Q.11 Why should the object pin and the screen be at the same horizontal level?

Ans. To avoid parallax error and obtain accurate image distance v.

Q.12 Name the type of mirror which is used in a solar furnace. How is high temperature achieved by this device?

Ans. Concave mirror is used in a solar furnace. The sun rays are focused at a point by the concave mirror. The concentrated beam of sun light at a point increases the temperature at that point.

Q.13 A man standing in front of a mirror finds his image having a very large head and legs of normal size. What type of mirrors are used in designing such a mirror?

Ans. The upper part of such a mirror is concave mirror and the lower part is a plane mirror.

Q.14 The image formed is observed to be virtual, erect and larger than the object. Identify the mirror and the position of the object.

Ans. The mirror used is concave mirror. The position of the object is in between the pole of the mirror and its principal focus.

Q.15 What is the principal focus of a concave mirror?

Ans. Principal focus of a concave mirror is the point on the principal axis at which the light rays incident on the mirror parallel to the principal axis meet after reflection from the mirror.

Q.16 What is the relation between focal length and radius of curvature of a spherical mirror?

Ans. The focal length of a spherical mirror is half of its radius of curvature. So, mathematically, it is given by

$$f = \frac{R}{2}$$

where, f = focal length,
R = radius of curvature.

Q.17 What do you mean by focal length of a spherical mirror?

Ans. The distance between pole and principal focus of a spherical mirror is called the focal length of spherical mirror.

Q.18 Why are the mirrors silvered at the back surface?

Ans. The mirrors are silvered at back surface to avoid damaging of mirror due to rough handling.

Q.19 Define index correction.

Ans. The difference between the corrected distance and observed distance of the tip of the needle from the pole of a mirror is called the index correction.

Q.20 A dentist uses concave mirror to see the tooth. In what way, does it help the dentist? [NCERT]

Ans Dentists use concave mirror to see the large image of the teeth to examine the teeth of a person. He/She holds a small concave mirror in such a way that the tooth lies within its focus and a magnified image of the tooth is seen by the dentist.

Q.21 Can you determine the focal length of a concave mirror, if $u < f$? [NCERT]

Ans If the object distance (u) is less than the focal length (f) of a concave mirror, the image formed is virtual and located behind the mirror.

In this case, it is not possible to find the position of this virtual image using a needle. However, a plane mirror can be used to determine the position of the image.

Experiment 2

AIM

To find the focal length of a convex mirror, using a convex lens.

Apparatus and Material Required

Optical bench with uprights, convex mirror, convex lens, two needles, knitting or index needle, mirror holder, lens holder, meter scale and spirit level.

Theory/Principle

Determination of Focal Length of Convex Mirror

When an object *AB* is placed at point *P′* in front of a thin convex lens then its real, inverted and magnified image *A′ B′* is formed at position *C* on the otherside of the lens as shown in Fig. (b). If a convex mirror is introduced in between point *C* and the convex lens, then the real and inverted image *A′ B′* coincides with the object *AB* at point *P′* as shown in Fig.(a).

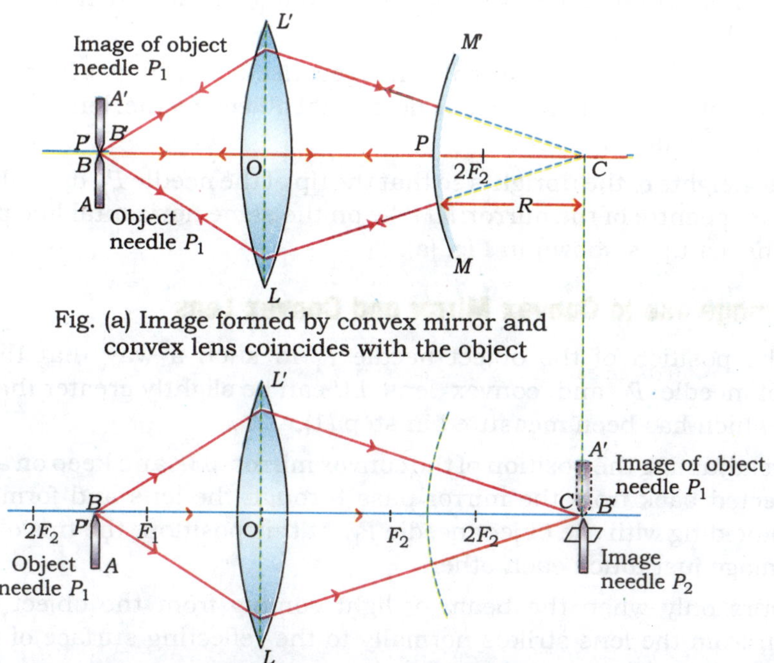

Fig. (a) Image formed by convex mirror and convex lens coincides with the object

Fig. (b) Image formed by a convex lens is inverted and magnified

This happens when rays of light coming from the object get refracted from the lens and then fall normally to the reflecting surface of the mirror and hence, retrace their path after reflection from the mirror. Any normal ray to a spherical surface has to be along the radius of that imaginary sphere of which mirror is a part, so that *C* must be the centre of curvature of the convex mirror.

Thus, the light rays are directed towards the centre of curvature C of the mirror which is formed behind the reflecting surface of the mirror. Hence, the image of the object pin AB is formed at itself, i.e. $A'B'$.

In the figure, PC is the radius of curvature R and half of radius of curvature is the focal length of the convex mirror. It is expressed as

$$f = \frac{PC}{2} = \frac{R}{2}$$

By locating the position of point C, the distance PC (or distance between pole and centre of curvature of the mirror) can be measured.

Therefore, by measuring the radius of curvature of the mirror, one can measure the focal length of that mirror.

Procedure

Determination of Rough Focal Length

1. Find the rough or approximate focal length of the convex lens by following the steps (1) and (2) of Experiment 1. Ensure that the focal length of convex lens is more than that of convex mirror.

Setting up the Apparatus

2. Place the optical bench on a horizontally adjusted rigid table. It should be confirmed that the table is horizontal or not by using spirit level. If it is not, then set it horizontally with the help of levelling screws.
3. Now place three uprights mounted with object needle P_1, convex lens LL' and convex mirror MM' on the optical bench. It must be noted that object needle, lens and mirror should be set vertically on the table.
4. Adjust the heights of the uprights so that the tip of the needle P_1, optical centre of the lens LL' and pole P or centre of the mirror MM' lie on the same horizontal line parallel to the optical bench. The set up is shown in Fig. (a).

Formation of Image due to Convex Mirror and Convex Lens

5. Adjust the position of the object needle P_1 in such a way that the distance between the object needle P_1 and convex lens LL' can be slightly greater than the focal length of the lens which has been measured in step (1).
6. Now start adjusting the position of the convex mirror MM' and keep on adjusting till the light rays reflected back from the mirror pass through the lens and form a real and inverted image coinciding with the object needle P_1. At this position, the tips of the object needle P_1 and its image just touch each other.

   This occurs only when the beam of light coming from the object needle after getting refraction from the lens strikes normally to the reflecting surface of the mirror and then reflected back along its path to retrace it.
7. Remove the parallax between the image of the object needle and object needle by following the steps (10) and (11) given in Experiment 1.

Note It should be ensured that the exact meeting of the tips of the object needle P_1 and its image must also be seen at the centre of the convex mirror.

8. Now, read the position of the uprights holding object needle P_1, lens LL' and convex mirror MM' and note the observations in the tabular form.

Formation of Image due to Convex Lens

9. Place the fourth upright holding an another optical needle, i.e. an image needle P_2 on the right side of the convex mirror on the optical bench.
10. Remove the convex mirror from its upright without disturbing the position of object needle and convex lens. The set-up is shown in Fig. 2 (b).
11. Adjust the height of the image needle P_2 in such a way that its tip, optical centre of the lens LL' and the tip of the object needle P_1 lie on the same horizontal line parallel to the optical bench. At this position, the tip of the needle P_2 also lies on the principal axis of the lens.

Note To differentiate the image needle P_2 from the object needle P_1, one can put a piece of paper on the image needle P_2.

12. A real, inverted and magnified image of object needle on the other side of the lens is formed. Now remove the parallax between the image needle P_2 and the real and inverted image of object needle P_1 by adjusting the position of image needle P_2 and without changing the position of lens LL' and object needle P_1.
13. Keep on adjusting the position of image needle P_2 till it coincides with real and inverted image of object needle P_1 formed by the convex lens. Follow the same steps (10) and (11) given in Experiment (1) to remove the parallax.
14. When the parallax gets removed, the image needle P_2 lies at the centre of curvature C of the convex mirror MM'. Note the position of the image needle P_2 on the optical bench.

Measurement of Radius of Curvature of Convex Mirror

15. Find the distance between the centre of curvature C and pole of the convex mirror by measuring the distance between the image needle P_2 and the position of the convex mirror MM'. This distance gives you the **radius of curvature** R **of the convex mirror** MM'.

Note The convex mirror is removed, so that the upright which was holding the mirror will be taken into account.

16. Now, repeat the experiment by changing the separation between object needle P_1 and lens LL' by 1-2 cm each time. Take at least five sets of observations in this manner.
17. Note your observations in the tabular form.

Applying the Index Correction

18. Here the radius of curvature R of the convex mirror MM' has been found, so that the index correction will be applied for R. Follow the steps (13) to (15) given in Experiment 1 to find the index correction to be applied in the distance measured between the image needle P_2 and convex mirror.

Determination of Focal Length of Convex Mirror

19. Find the corrected radius of curvature of the convex mirror for each set of observations.
20. Take mean of all values of corrected radius of curvature and find the focal length of the convex mirror by using the following relation.

$$f = \frac{R_{\text{mean}}}{2}$$

where, R_{mean} = mean of all corrected radius of curvature of the convex mirror.

Observations and Calculations

For Approximate Focal Length

1. Rough or approximate focal length of the convex lens = ... cm.

For Index Correction

2. Least count of the optical bench/meter scale = ... cm.
3. Actual length of the index needle, l = ... cm.
4. Observed length of the index needle, l' = Position of mirror upright – Position of upright holding the image needle P_2 = ... cm
5. Index correction, e = Actual length – Observed length = $l - l'$ =...... cm

Table for Determination of Radius of Curvature of Convex Mirror, (*R*)

S. N.	Upright position of				Observed distance, $R' = c - d$ (cm)	Corrected distance, $R = R' + e$ (cm)	Focal length, f (cm)	Δf (cm)
	Object needle P_1, a (cm)	Convex lens LL, b (cm)	Convex mirror MM', c (cm)	Image needle, P_2, d (cm)				
1						R_1 = ... cm		
2						R_2 = ... cm		
3						R_3 = ... cm		
4						R_4 = ... cm		
5						R_5 = ... cm		

For Focal Length

6. Calculate the mean value of radius of curvature of convex mirror.

$$R_{mean} = \frac{R_1 + R_2 + R_3 + R_4 + R_5}{5} = \text{......} \text{ cm}$$

7. Focal length of the convex mirror, $f = \frac{R_{mean}}{2}$ = ... cm.

Error

Here the error will be estimated in the focal length, you have calculated above.

$$\Delta f = f\left[\frac{\Delta c}{c} + \frac{\Delta d}{d} + \frac{\Delta l}{l} + \frac{\Delta l'}{l'}\right]$$

where, Δc, Δd, Δl and $\Delta l'$ are the least counts of the measuring instruments and f is the focal length calculated by using R_{mean}.

Maximum of the five values of Δf is to be reported with the result as the experimental error.

Result

The focal length of the given convex mirror is given by

$$f \pm \Delta f = \ldots \pm \ldots \text{ cm}$$

PRECAUTIONS

1. All the uprights supporting the needles, lens and mirror must be rigid and mounted vertically on the optical bench.
2. The apertures of the given convex lens and convex mirror should be small, otherwise the image formed will be distinct.
3. The tip of the needle, centre of the mirror and centre of lens should be at the same height.
4. While removing the parallax, the eye should be kept at a minimum distance of 25 cm.
5. Index correction should be applied between the image needle and back surface of the convex mirror.
6. The convex lens should be held close to the convex mirror.
7. While removing the convex mirror, the object needle, image needle and lens should not be disturbed.
8. To avoid multiple reflections, the convex mirror should be front-coated.
9. The focal length of convex lens used should be larger than that of convex mirror given in the experiment.

Sources of Error

1. If the top of the optical bench is not horizontal, then error arises.
2. If the tips of needles, pole of the mirror and lens are not in the same horizontal level, then error may occur.
3. The concave mirror may not be front-coated, so that multiple reflections may occur from the reflecting surface of the mirror.
4. The parallax and index correction may not have been considered.
5. The uprights may not be set vertically on the optical bench.
6. Personal error such as eye defects can be tedious to remove parallax.

Viva-Voce

Q.1 Is it possible to obtain the focal length of a convex mirror on the screen? Explain.

Ans. No, it is not possible to find the focal length of a convex mirror because the image formed by a convex mirror is always virtual and cannot be obtained on the screen.

Q.2 What is the focal length of a lens?

Ans. The focal length of a lens is the distance of principal focus of the lens from the optical centre of the lens.

Q.3 Write the relation between the radius of curvature and the focal length of spherical mirror.

Ans. The relation between the radius of curvature and the focal length is given by $R = 2f$.

Q.4 How do you calculate index correction?

Ans. Index correction is the difference between the actual distance and observed distance. It may be positive or negative.

Q.5 Which has larger field of view, a convex or a concave mirror?

Ans. A convex mirror has a larger field of view as compared to a concave mirror.

Q.6 Which mirror is used as a driving mirror in vehicles and why?

Ans. Convex mirror is used as a driving mirror in vehicles because it forms virtual, erect and diminished image for all positions of an object.

Q.7 Identify the point from where all distances are measured along the principal axis.

Ans. The point from where all distances are measured along the principal axis is the pole in case of mirror and optical centre in case of lens.

Q.8 Can we photograph a virtual image?

Ans. Yes, we can photograph a virtual image because the rays diverging from the virtual image are real and can be focused.

Q.9 State a property of optical centre of a lens.

Ans. A ray of light passing through optical centre of a lens suffers no refraction.

Q.10 Where should an object be placed in front of a convex lens to get a real image of the size of object?

Ans. To get a real image of the size of the object, it should be placed at twice the focal length of a convex lens.

Q.11 If the convex mirror is removed after adjusting the image, what change is observed?

Ans. The image position will change significantly, confirming the mirror's contribution in image formation.

Q.12 If focal length of the concave mirror is determined, by using convex lenses of different focal lengths, do you expect any change in the result? If yes, what type of change is there? [NCERT]

Ans Yes, the focal length of the concave mirror changes as we are using different convex lenses of different focal length.

Q.13 How will the result change, if a convex lens of different refractive indices were used? [NCERT]

Ans If a convex lens of different refractive indices were used, then the focal length of convex lens is changed and it is positive. The relation used is $\frac{1}{f} = \left(\frac{\mu_2 - \mu_1}{\mu_1}\right)\left(\frac{1}{R_1} - \frac{1}{R_2}\right)$

Q.14 If the convex lens selected for the experiment has focal length less than that of the convex mirror, how would this selection limit the experiment? [NCERT]

Ans If the convex lens selected for the experiment has focal length less than that of convex mirror, this selection limit the experiment as the convex mirror forms virtual and erect image. The focal length of convex mirror cannot be determined.

Experiment 3

AIM

To find the focal length of a convex lens by plotting graphs between u and v or between $\frac{1}{u}$ and $\frac{1}{v}$.

Apparatus and Materials Required

An optical bench, two sharp edged needles (pins), convex lens, a lens holder, three uprights (with clamps), knitting needle (or index needle), a meter scale and spirit level.

Theory/Principle

Determination of Focal Length of Convex Lens

Consider an object placed at a distance u from the optical centre of a thin convex lens whose focal length is f, then a real and inverted image is formed on the other side of the lens at a distance v from the optical centre O.

The relation between u, v and f is given by

$$\frac{1}{f} = \frac{1}{v} - \frac{1}{u} \qquad \text{...(i)}$$

This is called **lens equation** or **Gaussian form of lens equation**. This lens formula is valid in all situations for any spherical lens.

To Show Linear Relationship between Object and Image Distances

The focal length of a lens can also be determined by plotting graphs between u and v or between $1/u$ and $1/v$.

From Eq. (i), it is understood that **the graph between $\frac{1}{u}$ and $\frac{1}{v}$ will be a straight line with negative slope.**

If $\frac{1}{v} = 0$, then $\frac{1}{u} = \frac{1}{f}$ and if $\frac{1}{u} = 0$, then $\frac{1}{v} = \frac{1}{f}$. ...(ii)

Hence, the intercepts of the graph on both the axes are $\frac{1}{f}$.

Therefore, the graph between u and v will be a hyperbola.

Eq. (ii) shows that the values of u and v are interchangeable. This means that when an object is placed at a distance $2f$ from the optical centre, then a real and inverted image is formed at distance $2f$ from the optical centre on the other side of the lens.

If an object is placed between distance $2f$ and distance f, then its real and inverted image is formed beyond the $2f$ from the optical centre on the other side. **This proves the linear relationship between u and v.**

Procedure

Determination of Rough Focal Length of Convex Lens

1. First, determine the rough focal length of the given convex lens by focussing the image of a distant object.
2. To determine the rough focal length, obtain a sharp image of the distant object such as tree, building, etc., on a screen, say a plane wall or a sheet of paper placed on the other side of the lens.
3. By using a meter scale, measure the distance between the optical centre of the lens and wall on which image of the object appears. This distance will give you the **rough focal length of convex lens**.

Setting up the Apparatus

4. Now, place the three uprights holding the convex lens LL', the object needle AB and the image needle CD in such a way that the two needles lie on both the sides of the optical bench and upright holding the lens lies in the middle of the other two uprights holding the optical needles (i.e. image needle and object needle).

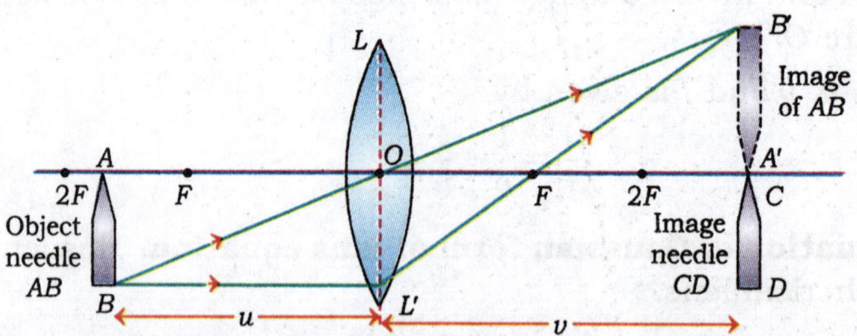

Set up to determine the focal length of convex lens

5. Ensure that the object needle, lens and image needle should be set vertically on the optical bench, so that principal axis is parallel to the optical bench.
6. Adjust the height of the uprights holding the object needle and image needle so that the optical centre of the lens and the tips of these two needles lie on the same horizontal line.

Note One can also put a piece of white paper on image needle to differentiate it from the object needle.

Determination of Object and Image Distances

7. Next adjust the position of the object needle AB until it lies in between F and $2F$ of the lens. At this position of the object needle AB, a real, inverted and magnified image is formed at a point beyond $2F$ from the optical centre unit other side of the lens.
8. Now, adjust the image needle CD until its tip coincides with the tip of the image $A'B'$ of the object needle AB. Also, ensure that the meeting of these two tips can also be seen at the centre of lens.
9. Now move your eye left and right and observe the meeting of the tips of the image needle CD and image $A'B'$ of the object needle. If on moving the eyes, these two are seen separate from each other, then one needs to remove the parallax.
10. Remove the parallax between the tip of the image needle CD and image $A'B'$ of the object needle by following the steps (10) and (11) given in Experiment 1.

11. Once the parallax gets removed, note the position of the object needle *AB*, convex lens *LL'* and the image needle *CD* on the optical bench. The distance between the object needle *AB* and convex lens *LL'* will give you the **object distance** (*u*) and the distance between the image needle *CD* and the convex lens *LL'* gives the image distance (*v*).
12. Repeat the experiment for five more different observations by slightly changing the position of the object needle *AB* (say 2-3 cm) from the optical centre of the lens.

Applying the Index Correction

13. In step (11), you noted the image and object distances. Now apply the index correction in these two readings.
14. To determine the actual length, of the lens use an index needle. Adjust it horizontally such that its one end touches one of the curved surfaces of the lens and the other end touches the tip of the needle. Determine the length of the index needle in between these two points to find the actual length between the lens and the respective needle.

Note The actual length (or the distance between the tip of the needle and optical centre of the lens) is determined by measuring the length of index needle plus half of the thickness of the lens because optical centre of a double convex lens with surfaces of equal curvature is at its geometrical centre. But if one is using a thin convex lens, then the thickness of the lens can be ignored.

15. Find the difference between the observed distance (or distance noted in step 11) and actual distance (or distance noted in step 14). This difference will give you the **index correction for the distance between lens and respective needle.**

Note Index correction for both the distances i.e. image and object distances is to be found.

16. After applying the index correction, find the corrected distances *u* and *v* for each set of observations.

Determination of Focal Length

17. Find the focal length of the given convex lens by using the following relation.

$$f = \frac{uv}{u+v}$$

Note Here *u* and *v* represent the corrected object and image distances respectively.

18. For each set of observations, find the focal length and calculate the mean of all the focal length values.
19. Plot a graph between *u* and *v* and $\frac{1}{u}$ and $\frac{1}{v}$ by taking them along negative *X*-axis and positive *Y*-axis respectively and find the focal length from the slope of the graph also.

Observations and Calculations

1. Least count of the meter scale = ... cm.

Determination of Rough Focal Length

2. Approximate rough focal length of convex lens = ... cm.

Determination of Index Correction

3. Length of the index/knitting needle measured by the meter scale, L_0 = ... cm.
4. Thickness of the thin convex lens (given), t = ... cm.
5. Actual length between optical centre *O* of the lens and tip of object needle,
$l_0 = L_0 + \frac{t}{2}$ = ... cm.

6. Observed length of object needle, l_0' = Distance between the centre of convex lens and tip of the object needle

= Position of lens upright on the scale – Position of object needle upright on the scale

= ...... – ...... = ... cm.

7. Index correction for object distance, $e_0 = l_0 - l_0'$ = ... cm

8. Similarly, one can find the index correction for image distance, $e_i = l_i - l_i'$ = ... cm

Table to Determine the Focal Length of Convex Lens

S. N.	Lens upright, a (cm)	Object needle upright, b (cm)	Image needle upright, c (cm)	Observed distance of object, $u' = a - b$ (cm)	Observed distance of image, $v' = a - c$ (cm)	Corrected object distance, $u = u' + e_0$ (cm)	Corrected image distance, $v = v' + e_i$ (cm)	$\frac{1}{u}$ (cm^{-1})	$\frac{1}{v}$ (cm^{-1})	$f = \frac{uv}{u+v}$ (cm)	Δf (cm)
1										f_1 = ... cm	
2										f_2 = ... cm	
3										f_3 = ... cm	
4										f_4 = ... cm	

Determination of Focal Length of Lens

9. Focal length, $f = \dfrac{uv}{u+v}$

10. Mean of the different values of focal length, $f = \dfrac{f_1 + f_2 + f_3 + f_4}{4}$

Error

Same as given in Experiment 1.

Determination of Focal Length by Plotting Graphs

1. Graph between u and v

Take, u along negative X-axis and v along positive Y-axis. The scales of X and Y-axes should be same. For different values of u and v, draw a graph to obtain hyperbola. Label the points u_1, u_2, u_3 ...... along negative X-axis and v_1, v_2, v_3 ...... points on positive Y-axis.

Thus, focal length of the lens is given by

Distance OA (= $2f$) on Y-axis = ... cm

Distance OB (= $2f$) on negative X-axis = ... cm

Mean focal length of convex lens,

$$f = \frac{OA + OB}{4} = \text{......} \text{ cm}$$

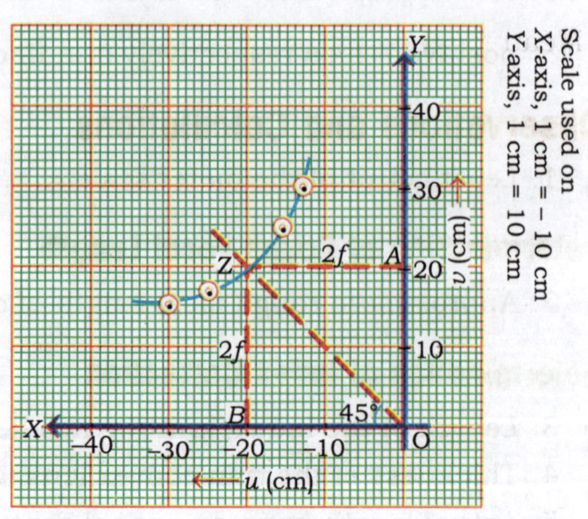

Graph showing relation between u and v of convex lens

2. Graph between $\frac{1}{u}$ and $\frac{1}{v}$

Now, consider $\frac{1}{u}$ along negative X-axis and $\frac{1}{v}$ along positive Y-axis and draw a graph to obtain a straight line.

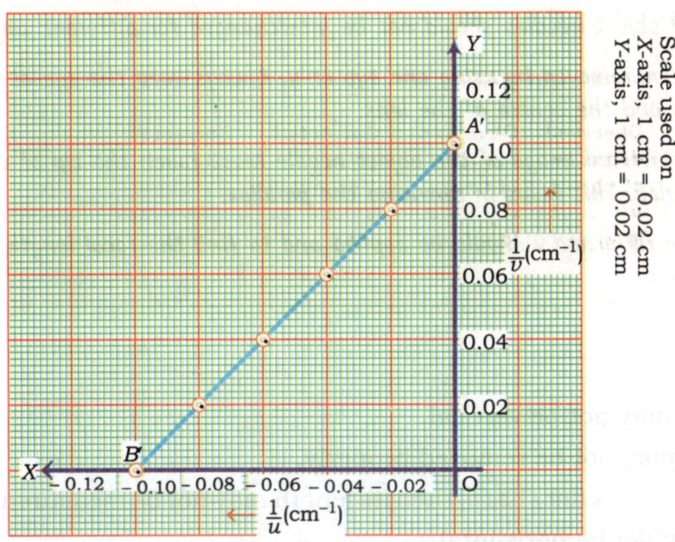

Graph showing relation between $\frac{1}{u}$ and $\frac{1}{v}$ of convex lens

Both the intercepts OA' on Y-axis and OB' on negative X-axis will be equal to distance $\frac{1}{f}$. Thus, the focal length is given by

$$\frac{1}{f} = \text{Intercept on } X\text{-axis, } OB = \ldots\ldots \text{ cm}^{-1}$$

and $$\frac{1}{f} = \text{Intercept on } Y\text{-axis, } OA' = \ldots\ldots \text{ cm}^{-1}$$

$$\therefore \text{ Mean focal length } (f) \text{ of the convex lens, } = \frac{\frac{1}{OA'} + \frac{1}{OB'}}{2} = \ldots\ldots \text{ cm}$$

Result

The focal length of the given convex lens

(i) From calculations, $f \pm \Delta f = \ldots\ldots$ cm

where, f is the mean value of the different values of focal length and Δf is maximum of six values determined for error.

(ii) From u *versus* v graph, $f = \ldots\ldots$ cm

(iii) From $\frac{1}{u}$ *versus* $\frac{1}{v}$ graph, $f = \ldots\ldots$ cm

PRECAUTIONS

1. The aperture of the lens should be small otherwise the image formed will not be distinct.
2. Eye should be kept at a distance more than the least distance of distinct vision, i.e. 25 cm from the image needle.
3. The image and object needles should not be interchanged for different sets of observations.
4. Parallax should be removed by using one eye only. Always keep the eye at the same height as the tips of needles and the centre of the lens.
5. The tip of the inverted image of the object needle must touch the tip of the image needle and should not overlap. This helps in removing the parallax.
6. Index correction for u and v should be applied and to find the focal length, corrected values of u and v should be used.

Sources of Error

1. The uprights may not be vertical.
2. The parallax may not be removed properly.
3. If the index needle is not sharp, then its length may not be measured accurately on scale.
4. The table may not be horizontal.
5. In plotting $1/v$ *versus* $1/u$ graph, if scales for both the two axes are not same, then the straight line graph may (rather will) not be at 45° to negative X-axis. This may result in confusions and error in drawing the graph.

Viva-Voce

Q.1 Focal length of a given lens is f_v for violet colour and f_r for red colour. Which one is larger?

Ans. The refractive index of the lens material is greater for violet than for red colour. Hence, the lens is more refracting for violet than red, so $f_r > f_v$.

Q.2 Write three practical uses of lenses.

Ans. Practical uses of lenses are

(i) Spectacles (ii) Optical instruments (iii) Photographic camera

Q.3 Draw the ray diagram for image formation in case of a convex lens for an object placed at the infinity.

Ans.

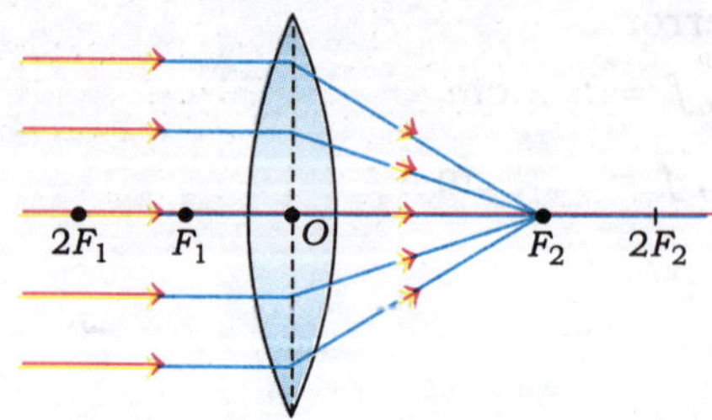

Q.4 What are the differences between the image formed by convex lens and a concave lens?

Ans. The image formed by the concave lens is virtual, erect and diminished.
The image formed by the convex lens is real, inverted and the size of the image increases as the object moves near the lens.

Q.5 Where does the centre of curvature of the plane surface of a plano-convex lens lie?

Ans. The plane surface of a plano-convex lens is flat. So it has no centre of curvature (its radius of curvature is infinite). Only the curved surface has a centre of curvature which lies on the curved side, along the principal axis.

Q.6 Define the principal axis of a plano-convex lens.

Ans. The principal axis of a plano-convex lens is defined as that straight line that is perpendicular to the plane surface and passes through the centre of curvature of the curved surface.

Q.7 What is the relation between focal length and radius of curvature of a plano-convex lens?

Ans. The relation between the focal length and radius of curvature is given by

$$\frac{1}{f} = (\mu - 1)\left(\frac{1}{R_1} - \frac{1}{R_2}\right)$$

where, μ = refractive index,
R_1 and R_2 = radii of curvatures

Q.8 How does the focal length of a thick convex lens differ from that of a thin lens? [NCERT]

Ans. A thin lens is one whose thickness is negligible as compared to the image and object distances, so a thin lens has a larger focal length than the thick lens.

Q.9 How can you recognise a convex lens, a circular glass slab and a concave lens, without touching them? [NCERT]

Ans. When the glass piece is put on a printed page and the virtual image of the printed page is seen. Then, the magnification of the image is judged.

(i) The glass piece is a glass slab, if the image has same size as that of object.
(ii) The glass piece is a convex if the image is magnified.
(iii) The glass piece is a concave if the image is diminished.

Q.10 How does the focal length of a convex lens change, if it is dipped in water? [NCERT]

Ans. The focal length of lens changes when immersed in water, as the lens works according to the refraction of light. The change in focal length can be found by using lens maker's formula.

$$\frac{1}{f} = \left(\frac{\mu_g}{\mu_w} - 1\right)\left(\frac{1}{r_1} - \frac{1}{r_2}\right)$$

where, μ_g and μ_w are refractive indices of glass and water. As we know that, μ_w is 1.33. If the refractive index of lens is greater than that of water, then the focal length is reduced.

Q.11 Can a virtual image produced by a lens be inverted? [NCERT]

Ans. No, a virtual image produced by a lens cannot be inverted.

Experiment 4

AIM

To find the focal length of a concave lens, using a convex lens.

Apparatus and Material Required

Optical bench with four uprights, a thin concave lens, a convex lens of focal length smaller than that of concave lens, two lens holders, index needle, a meter scale and a spirit level.

Theory/Principle

Formation of Image due to Concave Lens

As concave lens diverges the rays, the image formed by a concave lens alone will not be real and cannot be taken on a screen. To converge these diverging rays and hence to form a real image, convex lens is used.

Therefore, in order to determine the focal length of a concave lens, a convex lens is placed in between object and concave lens. This results in producing a real and inverted image of the object.

Determination of Focal Length of Concave Lens

In the given figure the light rays coming from the object needle are being converged through the convex lens L_1 so that the real and inverted image $A'B$ is formed at position I_1q.

When a concave lens L_2 is inserted in between convex lens L_1 and the image I_1, then for concave lens L_2, image $A'B$ behaves as a virtual object as shown in figure and this diverging lens L_2 forms a real and inverted image $A''B''$ at point I_2. Thus, OI_1 and OI_2 be the distances u and v respectively for concave lens L_2.

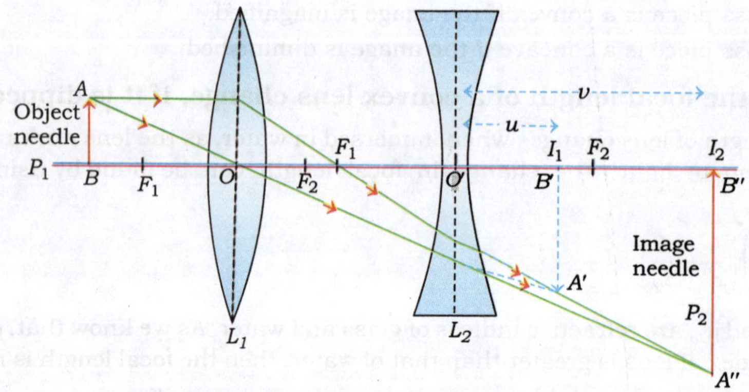

Ray diagram for determination of Concave lens

Note The focal length of convex lens L_1 is smaller than the focal length of the concave lens L_2. Also, the second image $A'B'$ is formed only when the distance between the lens L_2 and first image $A'B'$ is less than the focal length of L_2.

Using lens formula, we can calculate the focal length of concave lens L_2 as

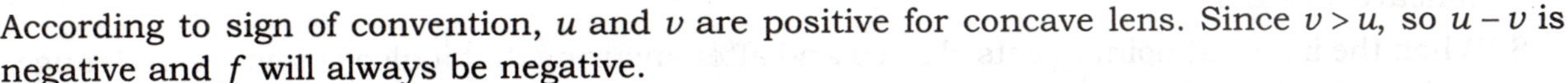

$$\frac{1}{f} = \frac{1}{v} - \frac{1}{u} \quad \Rightarrow \quad f = \frac{uv}{u - v}$$

According to sign of convention, u and v are positive for concave lens. Since $v > u$, so $u - v$ is negative and f will always be negative.

Thus, by using convex lens, one can find the focal length of concave lens.

Procedure

Determination of Rough Focal Length of Convex Lens

1. Estimate the rough focal length of convex lens (if it is not known) by following the steps (1) to (3) given in Experiment (3).
2. Confirm that the focal length of convex lens is less than that of concave lens.

Setting up the Apparatus

3. Set up the apparatus by following the steps (4) to (6) given in Experiment (3).

Determination of Object and Image Distances for a Convex Lens

4. Find the distance of object u and image distance v for a convex lens after removing the parallax and applying the index correction. Follow the same steps (7) to (18) given in Experiment (3).

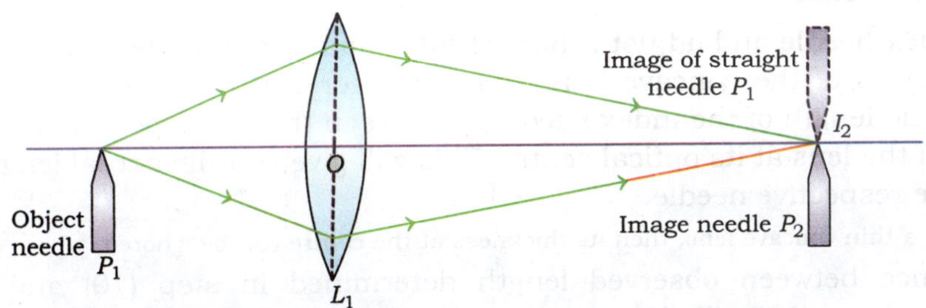

Determination of object and image distances for a convex lens

Introducing the Concave Lens

5. Now, place a fourth upright holding a concave lens L_2 in between convex lens L_1 and image needle P_2. Now, the light rays coming from an object needle P_1 which were being converged at point I_1 by the convex lens will be refracted further by the concave lens L_2 and then finally will be converged at point I_2.
6. Adjust the position of the concave lens so that the point I_2 is sufficient away from the point I_1. Here, at point I_2 the real image of a virtual object at point I_1 will be formed.

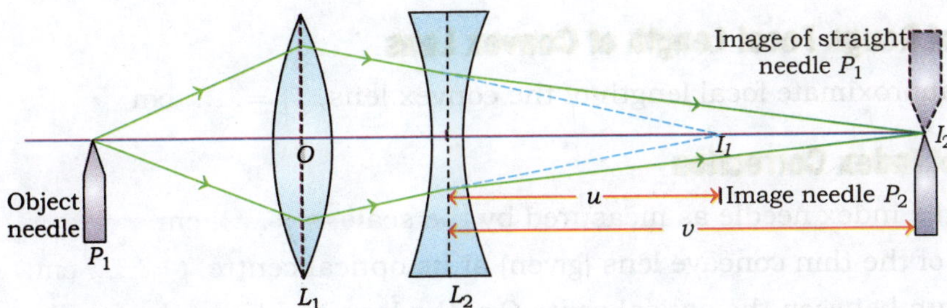

Determination of focal length of concave lens with the help of convex lens

7. If the image formed at point I_2 is not distinctly visible, then try to adjust the concave lens slightly nearer to the point I_1. One can locate the image by using a pencil held in hand and keeping the image needle P_2 at point I_1, so as to guide to decide which way to shift the concave lens L_2.
8. When the image at point I_2 gets cleared and after ensuring that it also lies within the range of the optical bench, start removing the parallax between the image formed at point I_2 and the image needle P_2. To remove the parallax, follow the steps (10) and (11) given in Experiment (1).

Determination of Object and Image Distances for Convex Lens

9. When the parallax gets removed note the position of upright holding concave lens and position of image I_1 of the image needle. The difference between these two readings will give you the **observed distance of the object**.
10. Note the position of upright holding image needle P_2 at point I_2. The difference between the readings of position of upright holding the concave lens and upright holding the image needle P_2 will give you the **observed distance of the image**.
11. Now, repeat the steps (4) to (10) and take at least five more sets of observations by slightly changing the position of the upright holding the object needle P_1 by 1-2 cm for each set of observations.
12. Note your observations in tabular form.

Apply the Index Correction

13. Take an index needle and adjust it horizontally such that its one end touches one of the curved surfaces of the concave lens and the other end touches the tip of the needle. Determine the length of the index needle in between these two points and add half of the thickness of the lens at its optical centre. This will give you the actual length between the lens and the respective needle.

Note If one is using a thin concave lens, then its thickness at the centre can be ignored.

14. The difference between observed length determined in step (10) and actual length determined in step (13) will give you the index correction for image distance.

Determination of Focal Length

15. Find the focal length of the given convex lens by using the following relation

$$f = \frac{uv}{u-v}$$

Note Here, u and v denote the corrected object and image distances respectively from the concave lens.

16. For each set of observations, find the focal length and take the mean of all different values.

Observations and Calculations

Determination of Rough Focal Length of Convex Lens

1. Rough or approximate focal length of the convex lens, f_L = ... cm.

Determination of Index Correction

2. Length of the index needle as measured by the scale, s = ... cm.
3. Thickness of the thin concave lens (given) at its optical centre, t = ... cm.
4. Actual length between the optical cente O of the lens and tip of the needle,

$$l = s + \frac{t}{2} = \text{......}\ \text{cm.}$$

5. Observed length of the index needle,

l' = Distance between the pole (or centre) of the lens and tip of the needle

l' = Position of lens upright on the scale – Position of needle upright on the scale

l' = ... cm.

6. Index correction, $e = l - l'$ =...... cm.

Determination of Focal Length of Concave Lens

Table for Determination of Focal Length of Concave Lens

S.N.	Position of					Observed object distance, $u' = c - d$ (cm)	Observed image distance, $v' = g - d$ (cm)	Corrected object distance, $u = u' + e$ (cm)	Corrected image distance, $v = v' + e$ (cm)	$f = \frac{uv}{u-v}$ (cm)	Δf (cm)
	Object needle upright P_1, a (cm)	Convex lens L_1 upright, b (cm)	Image formed by L_1 at point I_1, c (cm)	Concave lens L_2 upright, d (cm)	Image formed by L_1 and L_2 at point I_2, g (cm)						
1										f_1 = ... cm	
2										f_2 = ... cm	
3										f_3 = ... cm	
4										f_4 = ... cm	
5										f_5 = ... cm	
6										f_6 = ... cm	

7. Find the focal length of concave lens by using, $f = \frac{uv}{u - v}$ = ... cm

Note Here, u and v denote the corrected object and image distances respectively.

8. Find the focal length for each set of observations and then, calculate the mean value of given concave lens,

$$f = \frac{f_1 + f_2 + f_3 + f_4 + f_5 + f_6}{6} = \ldots \text{ cm}$$

Error

The error will be estimated in the calculated value of focal length as

$$\therefore \quad \frac{\Delta f}{f^2} = \frac{\Delta v}{v^2} + \frac{\Delta u}{u^2} \Rightarrow \Delta f = f^2\left[\frac{\Delta u}{u^2} + \frac{\Delta v}{v^2}\right]$$

Result

The focal length of the given concave lens is $f \pm \Delta f$ = ...± ...cm.

PRECAUTIONS

In addition to precautions of Experiment (3), some are discussed below:

1. *The focal length of the convex lens should be less than the focal length of concave lens.*
2. *All the four uprights must be vertical.*
3. *The concave lens must be placed near the convex lens. In fact, the second image I_2 is formed only when the distance between concave lens L_2 and first image I_1 (which acts as virtual object for concave lens) is less than the focal length of the concave lens.*
4. *The image formed at I_2 is quite enlarged, it may be blurred. So, it should be preferred to use a thin and sharp object pin and shine it with light.*
5. *The convex lens and the object needle P_1 must not be disturbed during the second part (or when the concave lens is inserted) of the experiment.*
6. *Do not get confused with bold and bright image formed by the combination of convex and concave lens.*
7. *Index correction/bench correction for u and v should be taken into account.*
8. *Use sharply pointed object needle for greater accuracy.*

Sources of Error

Same as Experiment (3).

Viva-Voce

Q.1 Under what condition, the nature of lens changes?

Ans. The refractive index of surrounding medium is greater than that of material of lens. The convex lens acts as concave lens and *vice-versa.*

Q.2 What type of lens is an air bubble inside water?

Ans. Concave lens

Q.3 Is virtual image ever inverted?

Ans. No, when the object is erect, a virtual image is always erect and a real image is always inverted.

Q.4 What are the signs for the power of a convex lens and concave lens?

Ans. The power of a convex lens is positive, since its focal length is positive while the power of a concave lens is negative, since its focal length is negative.

Q.5 Under what condition, a lens does not show refraction?

Ans. When refractive index of surrounding medium is equal to refractive index of material of lens, then

$$P = \frac{1}{f} = \left(\frac{n_2}{n_1} - 1\right)\left(\frac{1}{R_1} - \frac{1}{R_2}\right)$$

$\because \quad n_1 = n_2$

$\therefore \quad P = 0$

Q.6 Which of the convex lens (thick or thin) has a larger focal length?

Ans. A thin convex lens has a larger focal length.

Q.7 State the practical uses of lenses.

Ans. Lenses are used in optical instruments like microscope, telescope, photographic camera and for correcting defects of vision.

Q.8 Can you name the factors on which focal length of a lens depend?

Ans. Focal length of a lens depends upon

(i) Radii of curvature of the surfaces of the lens.

(ii) Nature of material of the lens.

Q.9 Does focal length of a lens depend upon u and v?

Ans. No, focal length of a lens does not depend upon u and v. When u is changed, v changes but f remains constant.

Q.10 When does a convex lens behave as a concave lens?

Ans. When a lens is placed inside a transparent medium of refractive index greater than that of its own material, it behaves as a concave lens.

Q.11 A combination of convex lens and a concave lens behaves as a convex lens. Which lens has longer focal length?

Ans. The combination of lenses behaves as a convex lens, thus the convex lens must have greater power. It means convex lens has a shorter focal length. Therefore, the concave lens must have a longer focal length.

Experiment 05

AIM

To determine the angle of minimum deviation for a given prism by plotting a graph between the angle of incidence and the angle of deviation.

Apparatus and Material Required

Drawing board, white paper sheet, triangular glass prism, meter scale, alpins, cellotape/drawing pins, graph paper, protractor and a sharp pencil.

Prism

A prism is a wedge shaped portion of a transparent refracting medium boundary by two plane refracting surfaces inclined to each other at a certain angle.

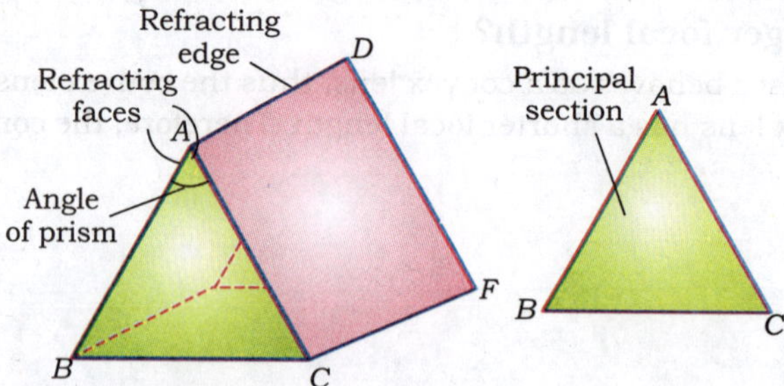

A ray of light entering through the first surface of the prism suffers refraction which on emerging out through the second surface suffers a further refraction. On drawing board, white sheet is fixed. Cellotape/drawing pins are used to fix the sheet on drawing board. Protractor is used to measure the angles drawn.

Theory/Principle

Determination of Angle of Minimum Deviation

Consider the principal section ABC of the prism. A ray of light PQ (say from air to glass) incident on the surface AB at an angle i is refracted at an angle r along QR and finally emerges out along RS as shown in the figure.

The dotted lines in the figure represent the normal to the surfaces. The angle of incidence at the second surface AC (or from glass to air) is r' and the angle of refraction or emergence be e. The **angle of deviation** δ is between the direction of incident ray PQ produced forward and the direction of emergent ray RS produced backward.

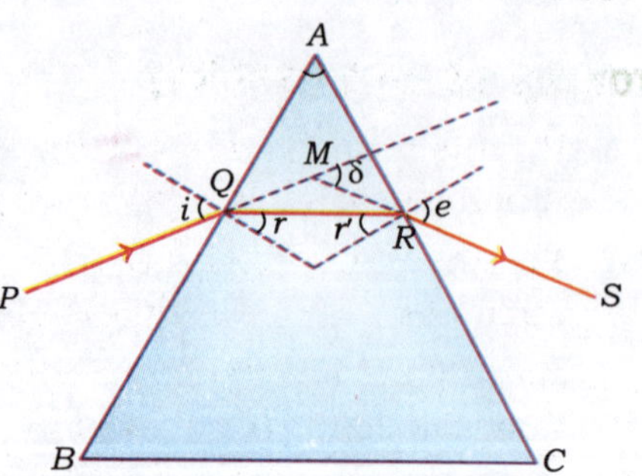

Refraction of light through a prism

From geometrical considerations, we have

$$A = r + r'$$

and

$$\delta = \angle MQR + \angle MRQ = (i - r) + (e - r')$$

$$\delta = i + e - A \quad \text{...(i)}$$

For minimum deviation δ_m, the light ray passes through the prism symmetrically, i.e. parallel to the base, so that

$$\delta = \delta_m, \; i = e \Rightarrow r = r'$$

Note At the minimum deviation of position of the prism, we get the brightest image of an object.

From Eq. (i), it is understood that by measuring the i, e and A, one can measure δ and hence can find the minimum angle of deviation.

Procedure

Drawing the Incident Ray

1. Fix a white sheet of paper on the drawing board with the help of cellotape or drawing pins.
2. By using a sharp pencil, draw a straight line XY in the middle and parallel to the length of the paper.
3. On the straight line XY mark the points, O_1, O_2, O_3, ...at suitable distances 10 to 12 cm and draw normals N_1O_1, N_2O_2, N_3O_3, ... on these points as shown in figure.

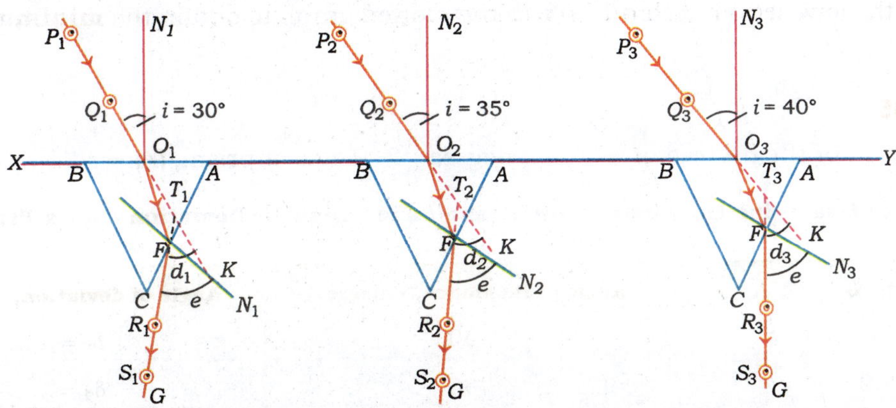

Determination of angle of minimum deviation

4. Draw straight lines P_1O_1, P_2O_2, P_3O_3, ...corresponding to the incident rays making angle of incidence at 30°, 35°, 40°, 45°, 50°, 55° respectively with the normals using a protractor. These lines represent the **incident rays.**
5. Note the values of the angles $\angle P_1O_1N_1$, $\angle P_2O_2N_2$, $\angle P_3O_3N_3$, ...on white sheet of paper.

Drawing the Emergent Ray

6. Put the prism with its refracting face AB on the line XY in such a way that point O_1 is in the middle of AB. Draw the boundary of the prism with a sharp pencil.
7. Fix two alpins P_1 and Q_1 with sharp tips vertically 12 cm apart, on the incident ray line P_1Q_1 such that pin Q_1 is close to point O_1.
8. Close your left eye and looking through the prism, bring your right eye in line with the images of the pins P_1 and Q_1.
9. Now, fix alpins R_1 and S_1 about 12 cm apart vertically on the white paper sheet with their tips in line with the tips of the images of pins P_1 and Q_1. Thus, pins R_1 and S_1 are collinear with the images of pins P_1 and Q_1.
10. Remove the pins R_1 and S_1 and encircle their pin pricks on the paper sheet with the help of sharp pencil. Also, remove the pins P_1 and Q_1 and encircle the pin pricks.

11. Join the pin pricks R_1 and S_1 with the help of sharp pencil and scale to obtain the **emergent ray** R_1S_1.

Measurement of Minimum Angle of Deviation

12. Keep on drawing the emergent ray R_1S_1 backwards and incident ray P_1Q_1 forward, so that they can meet at point T_1.
13. Draw arrow heads on P_1Q_1 and R_1S_1 to show the direction of incident and emergent rays respectively.
14. With help of protractor, measure the angle of deviation δ_1 and the $\angle BAC$ of the prism.
15. Repeat steps (6) to (14) by changing the values of angle of incidence, i.e. 35°, 40°, 45°, 50°, 55° and measure the corresponding angles of deviation δ_2, δ_3, δ_4, δ_5, δ_6...with protractor.

Note One can take more set of observations by suitably increasing the angle of incidence.

16. Note your observations in tabular form with proper units and significant figures.
17. Plot a graph between angle of incidence and angle of deviation by taking them along X and Y-axes respectively.
18. Choose the lowest point of the curve in the plotted graph to obtain the **minimum angle of deviation.**

Observations

1. Least count of the protractor = ... degree **2.** Angle of prism, (A) = ... degree

Table for Measuring the Angle of Incidence i and Angle of Deviation δ for a Prism

S. N.	Angle of incidence, i (degree)	Angle of deviation, δ (degree)
1	30	δ_1 = ...
2	35	δ_2 = ...
3	40	δ_3 = ...
4	45	δ_4 = ...
5	50	δ_5 = ...
6	55	δ_6 = ...

Note Even from the observation table, one can choose the minimum value of angle of deviation by taking two consecutive values of angle of incidence at which the readings of angle of deviation are observed minimum and then finding the mean of these two readings. After plotting the graph, this calculated value can be verified.

Plotting Graph

Choose angle of incidence i along X-axis and angle of deviation δ along Y-axis and suitable scales on these axes. Plot a graph between i and δ by drawing a free hand smooth curve passing practically through all the plotted points.

Draw a tangent on the lowest point of the graph parallel to X-axis, note the angle of minimum deviation δ_m on the Y-axis of the graph. Express your result with proper significant figures.

From graph, it can be said that the angle of deviation δ decreases with increase in angle of incidence i upto a certain value called **minimum angle of deviation** δ_m, then on increasing the angle of incidence, the angle of deviation also increases.

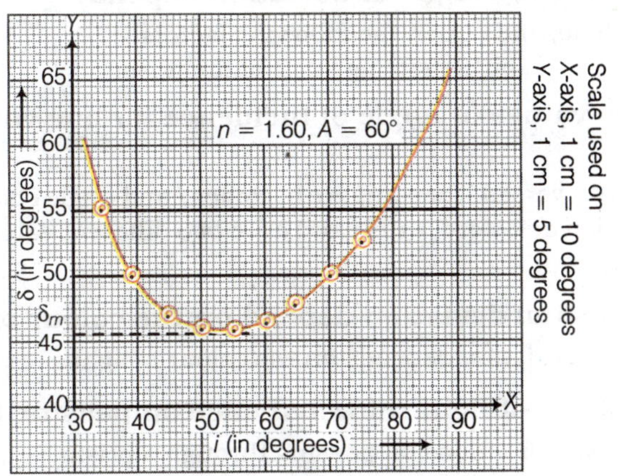

A graph between angle of incidence and angle of deviation

Result

The angle of minimum deviation, δ_m = ... degree.

PRECAUTIONS

1. *To locate the incident and emergent rays with greater accuracy, the distance PQ and RS should be about 12 cm.*
2. *To take various sets of observations, the angle of incidence should lie between 30° to 55°.*
3. *While fixing the alpins, it should be ensured that their tips must be in line.*
4. *The position of the prism should not be disturbed for a given set of observations.*
5. *The angle of incidence and the angle of deviation should be measured accurately by using protractor.*
6. *The same angle of incidence should be used for all observation.*

Sources of Error

1. The pins may not be fixed properly.
2. Pin pricks may be thick.
3. If all the three angles of refraction between adjacent pairs of faces are not equal, then
$$A + \delta \neq i + e$$
4. Errors may be created while measuring the values of the angles by using protractor.
5. The curve drawn may not be a smooth hand curve.
6. The incident ray pins and emergent ray pins may not be along the same straight line.

Viva-Voce

Q 1 On what factors does the angle of deviation depend?

Ans. The angle of deviation depends upon the following factors
(i) Angle of incidence (ii) Refracting angle of the prism (iii) Material of the prism

Q 2 Why there are two values of angle of incidence for one value of angle of deviation?

Ans. If the emergent ray be reversed, then angle e becomes i and angle i becomes e. The reversed ray will have same deviation as before, thus i and e are two different values for same angle of deviation.

Q 3 Does angle of minimum deviation depend on the colour of light?

Ans. Yes, angle of minimum deviation depends on the colour of light.

Q 4 How many times a ray of light refracted once on passing through a prism?

Ans. A ray of light suffers two refractions on passing through a prism.

Q 5 When is the deviation produced by a prism is maximum?

Ans. The deviation produced by a prism is maximum if the angle of incidence is 90°.

Q 6 What happens when a ray of light travels from a rarer medium to a denser medium of prism?

Ans. Since, the speed of light in denser medium is slower than that in rarer medium. So, a ray of light bends towards the normal while entering to a denser medium of prism.

Q 7 How does the refractive index of material change with addition of different colours?

Ans. Since, the refractive index is inversely proportional to the wavelength. Also, the wavelength of red colour is maximum and that of voilet colour is minimum.
So, $\mu_v > \mu_r$.

Q 8 Why is there no dispersion when white light is incident on a glass slab?

Ans. A glass slab can be thought of as two prisms with their reflecting angles oriented in opposite directions.
The dispersion caused by one "prism" is counteracted by the dispersion caused by the other, effectively cancelling out any separation of colours.

Q 9 When white light is incident on a prism, it splits into different colours. Why? [NCERT]

Ans. The refractive index of the prism's material varies for different wavelength, causing each colour to bend at a different angle. This variation in bending leads to the dispersion of light into its constituent colours.

Q 10 Interpret the graph i and δ. [NCERT]

Ans. The graph between i and δ indicates that there is only one unique value of angle of incidence for which the deviation is minimum.

Q 11 If the experiment is performed with angle of emergence taken as angle of incidence, will there be any change in the δ values? If yes, why? If not, why not? [NCERT]

Ans. During experiment, if angle of emergence is taken as angle of incidence, then as per symmetry the value of deviation remains the same as

$$\delta = i + e - A$$

$$\delta_{min} = 2i - A \qquad [\text{as, } \angle i = \angle e]$$

Experiment 06

AIM

To determine refractive index of a glass slab using a travelling microscope.

Apparatus and Material Required

A travelling microscope, a glass slab, lycopodium powder/chalk dust, a white sheet of paper, a marker and spirit level.

Travelling Microscope

A travelling microscope is an ordinary microscope (or a compound microscope) fixed on a stand in such a way that it may be made to travel in vertical as well as horizontal direction without disturbing its adjusted focus. The readings are recorded by means of main scale and vernier scale of high accuracy (0.001 cm) attached to the instrument.

Focusing an Object by Using the Travelling Microscope

The travelling microscope has two systems of converging lenses, i.e. objective *O* consisting of small aperture and small focal length and **eye-piece** *E* consisting of large aperture and large focal length. There are two separated tubes in which the objective and eye-piece are fitted.

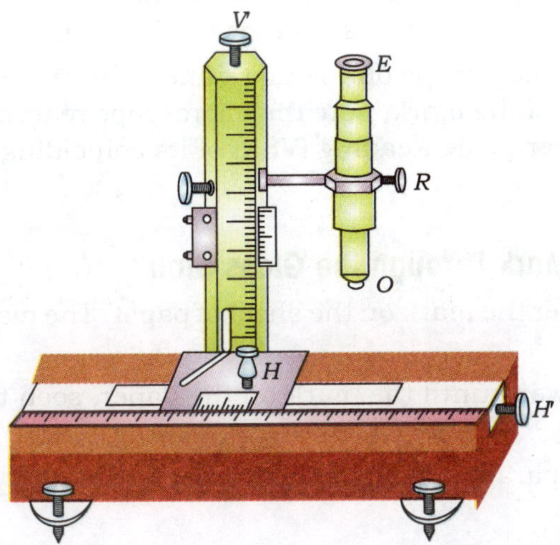

Theory/Principle

Refractive Index

The change in direction of light when it passes from one medium to another obliquely is called **refraction of light**. The ratio of velocity of light in first medium to the velocity of light in second medium is called **refractive index** of second medium with respect to first medium. It is represented by μ or n.

Determination of Refractive Index of a Glass Slab

On a horizontal surface, a glass slab is placed in air and its bottom surface is viewed from top, it appears to be elevated. The distance between this apparent bottom and the top surface of the slab gives the apparent thickness of the slab. The refractive index of glass with respect to the air medium is given by

$$^{g}\mu_{a} = \frac{\text{Real thickness of the slab}}{\text{Apparent thickness of the slab}} = \frac{t}{t'} = \frac{a_1 - a_3}{a_1 - a_2}$$

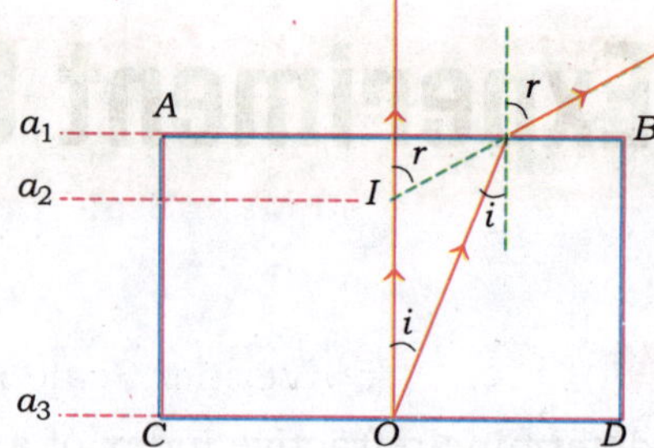

Formation of image *I* of a point mark *O* in a glass slab

Thus, by measuring the real thickness and apparent thickness of a glass slab, one can find the refractive index of a given glass slab.

Procedure

Setting up the Apparatus

1. Determine the least count of the microscope scale used.
2. Place the travelling microscope on the horizontal table. With the help of spirit level and levelling screws, level the base of the travelling microscope.
3. Set the travelling microscope exact vertically.

Focusing the Microscope on Mark

4. Put a mark on the sheet of paper by using a marker pen.
5. Now, place the sheet of paper on the horizontal platform of the microscope. Adjust the microscope in such a way that its lens system is vertically above the mark.
6. Next focus the travelling microscope on the mark and after removing the parallax between the cross-wire and image of the mark, note the microscope reading as a_1, using Main Scale Reading (MSR) and Vernier Scale Reading (VSR) of its coinciding division.

Focusing the Microscope on Mark Through the Glass Slab

7. Now, place a glass slab over the mark on the sheet of paper. The mark through the glass slab will appear to be raised.
8. Move the microscope upward until the mark on the paper, seen through the slab is sharp and clear.
9. Again after removing the parallax, note the microscope reading a_2 with the main scale and coinciding of vernier scale.

Focusing the Microscope on Particles of Lycopodium Powder

10. Sprinkle a little lycopodium powder over the top surface of glass slab. Ensure that thin layer of powder is spreaded over the surface of glass slab.
11. Raise the lens system of the microscope and focus it to see some of their particles clearly and note the microscope reading a_3.
12. Invert the glass slab and repeat the steps (6) to (11) two times more and take observations of a_1, a_2 and a_3.

Observations and Calculations

Least Count (LC) of the Travelling Microscope

20 Main Scale Division (MSD) = 1 cm (say)

$$\therefore \quad 1\text{ MSD} = \frac{1}{20}\text{ cm}$$

50 Vernier Scale Division (VSD) = 49 MSD (say)

$$\therefore \quad 1\text{ VSD} = \frac{49}{50}\text{ MSD} \Rightarrow 1\text{ VSD} = \frac{49}{50} \times \frac{1}{20}\text{ cm}$$

$$\therefore \quad \text{Least count of the travelling microscope} = 1\text{ MSD} - 1\text{ VSD} = \frac{1}{20} - \frac{49}{50} \times \frac{1}{20} = \frac{1}{20}\left[1 - \frac{49}{50}\right]$$

$$\text{LC} = 0.001\text{ cm}$$

Table for Refractive Index of Glass Slab

S. N.	Reading of the microscope when focused on						Particles on top of the glass surface		
	Mark made on paper			Mark on paper through the slab					
	MSR, M (cm)	VSR, N (cm)	a_1 = M+N × LC (cm)	MSR, M (cm)	VSR, N (cm)	a_2 = M+N × LC (cm)	MSR, M (cm)	VSR, N (cm)	a_3 = M+N × LC(cm)
1									
2									
3									

Refractive Index of Glass Slab

1. Refractive index, $^g\mu_a = \dfrac{\text{Real thickness of the slab}}{\text{Apparent thickness of the slab}} = \dfrac{a_1 - a_3}{a_1 - a_2} = \dfrac{t}{t'}$

   Find the refractive indices for all sets of observations.

2. Mean refractive index, $^g\mu_a = \dfrac{(^g\mu_a)_1 + (^g\mu_a)_2 + (^g\mu_a)_3}{3} = ...$

Error

The estimated uncertainty in the measurement of $^g\mu_a$ is given by

$$\Delta^g\mu_a = 2^g\mu_a\left[\frac{\Delta a}{t} + \frac{\Delta a}{t'}\right] \quad \text{[where, } \Delta a = \text{least count of microscope scale]}$$

The maximum of three values of $^g\mu_a$ will be reported for the error with result.

Result

The refractive index of glass of the slab is given by $^g\mu_a \pm \Delta^g\mu_a = ... \pm ...$

Here, $^g\mu_a$ is the mean refractive index.

1. *Least count of the scale of travelling microscope should be observed carefully.*
2. *The microscope should be levelled properly.*
3. *The screws used in focusing the microscope should be moved in one direction only to avoid backlash error.*
4. *If the microscope is focused for the first reading, i.e. a_1, then the focusing arrangement in the lens system should not be changed/altered for subsequent readings such as a_2 and a_3.*
5. *The glass slab should be placed on a horizontal surface.*
6. *Use hand lens/magnifying glass to read the vernier scale to avoid error in finding vernier coinciding division.*
7. *A very thin layer of lycopodium powder should be spread on the glass slab so that its particles can be easily seen.*

Sources of Error

1. The microscope scale may not be properly calibrated.
2. Position of the microscope may not be normal to the surface of the glass slab.
3. If the layer of lycopodium powder/chalk dust spread on the glass slab is thick, it will not actually represent the top of the glass slab and thus produces error in the result.
4. While taking the reading from microscope scale, error may occur.
5. The focusing arrangement may be changed after first reading.

Viva-Voce

Q 1 A lens of glass is immersed in water. How is the power of lens affected?

Ans. The power of a lens will decrease as ${}^{w}\mu_g < {}^{a}\mu_g$.

Q 2 How is lateral displacement of ray of light affected with increase in thickness of the slab?

Ans. The faces of the slab for incident ray and emergent ray are parallel. Therefore, the ray of light suffers lateral displacement which increases with gap between the two opposite faces of the slab.

Q 3 What lycopodium powder is spread over the glass surface?

Ans. Lycopodium powder is spread over the glass surface to focus the microscopeat the top surface accurately otherwise the bottom surface will be focused.

Q 4 On what factors does the apparent depth depend?

Ans. The apparent depth depends upon the following factors

(i) Nature of medium (ii) Thickness of medium (iii) Colour of light

Q 5 What is normal shift and write its causes?

Ans. Normal shift is the difference between actual depth and apparent depth. The main cause of normal shift is refraction of light.

Q 6 Will an object appear at a higher position or at a lower position to a fish under water?

Ans. An object will appear at a higher position to a fish under water.

Q 7 Why is the real thickness of a glass slab greater than the apparent thickness of the glass slab?

Ans. The real thickness of a glass slab is greater than the apparent thickness of the glass slab. Going from denser to a rarer medium, light ray bends away from the normal. That is why the image of the bottom point of slab appears to be raised.

Q 8 What is the least count of the vernier scale in travelling microscope?

Ans. The least count of the vernier scale in travelling microscope is 0.001 cm.

Q 9 In how many directions can you move your microscope?

Ans. We can move our microscope in two directions. They are as

(i) up and down vertically (ii) sideways horizontally

Q10 Why do we use the horizontal movement in the microscope?

Ans. We use the horizontal movement in the microscope to measure the diameter of very narrow tubes or wires.

Q11 Name the device used for measuring in the travelling microscope.

Ans. Vernier scale is the device used for measuring the travelling microscope.

Q12 Between which two points, the parallax is removed?

Ans. The parallax is removed between the cross-wire and the image of the mark.

Q13 How can you avoid backlash error?

Ans. The screws used in focusing the travelling microscope should be moved only in one direction to avoid backlash error.

Q14. Will a colourless slab be visible, if immersed in a transparent liquid of the same refractive index as that of the slab? State the reason for it. [NCERT]

Ans. No, because if a glass slab is put in a beaker containing a colourless liquid, the glass rod immediately seems to disappear as the glass slab and the liquid have the same refractive index.

Q15. You have three slabs of same dimensions the first one being hollow and completely filled with water, the second one is made of crown glass and the third of flint glass. If each of them has a coloured mark at the bottom, in which case will it appear to have risen the most? Given that $n_{flint} > n_{crown} > n_{water}$ [NCERT]

Ans. The glass slab containing water will have risen the most as the refractive index for the slab is given by $n = \frac{c}{v}$ and the value of n_{flint} is 1.6, n_{glass} is 1.5 and that n_{water} is 1.

Experiment 07

AIM

To find the refractive index of a liquid by using convex lens and plane mirror

Apparatus and Material Required

A convex lens of focal length about 20 cm, a plane mirror slightly bigger than the aperture of convex lens, a retort stand with clamp, a needle, clean water, a meter scale, plumb line, water dropper and a spherometer.

Theory/Principle

Determination of Focal Length of Convex Lens

When an object is placed on the point of principal focus of a convex lens, a real and inverted image coinciding with the object is formed. The figure below shows the formation of image $A'B'$ of an object AB by a convex lens placed at the reflecting surface of a plane mirror.

Consider a convex lens is placed on the reflecting surface of plane mirror. Now, an object needle (say AB) is placed at the distance as shown in figure, so that its real and inverted image $B'A'$ is formed at the same position.

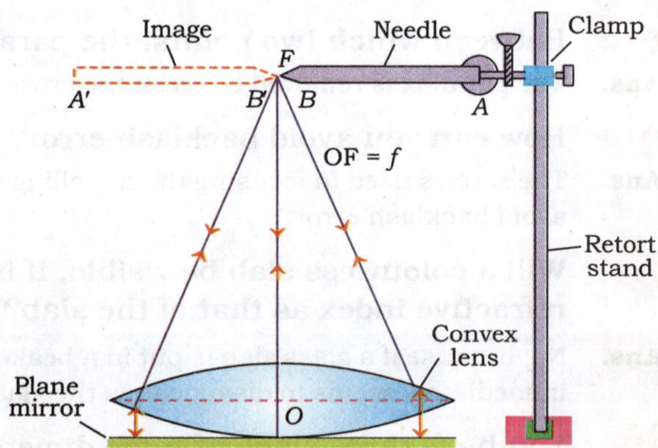

Fig.1 Determination of focal length of convex lens

The rays coming from tip of the needle placed at the principal focus F of convex lens emerge out parallel to its axis. These rays then fall normally on the plane mirror and retrace their path and form a real and inverted image at the principal focal plane of the lens. Here, the size of image is equal to the size of the needle. The tip of the needle gives the position of the second principal focus of the convex lens. Thus, $OF = f$ is the focal length of the convex lens having optical centre O.

Determination of Focal Length of Combination of Convex Lens and Plano-Concave Lens

If the space between the lens and plane mirror is filled with the clean water (or transparent liquid) having refractive index μ_w, a **plano-concave lens of water** will be formed. The needle has to be moved upward to a position F' to remove parallax between needle and its image formed.

In this case, the distance between the tip of needle and optical centre of the lens will be equal to the

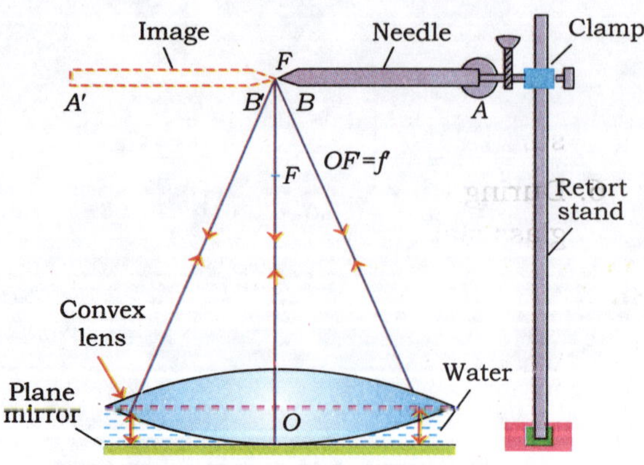

Fig.2 Focal length of plano-concave lens formed of water

focal length OF' (say f') of composite lens formed by convex lens and plano-concave lens of water. If f and f_w be the focal lengths of convex lens and water lens respectively, then the focal length f' of composite lens can be determined by using the following relation.

$$\frac{1}{f'} = \frac{1}{f} + \frac{1}{f_w}$$

$$\therefore \quad \frac{1}{f_w} = \frac{1}{f'} - \frac{1}{f} \Rightarrow f_w = \frac{ff'}{f - f'} \quad \ldots \text{(i)}$$

Determination of Refractive Index of Liquid (or water)

From lens maker's formula for a plano-concave lens,

$$\frac{1}{f} = (\mu - 1)\left(\frac{1}{R_1} - \frac{1}{R_2}\right)$$

Here, $f = f_w$ and $\mu = \mu_w$

$R_1 = R =$ radius of curvature of first surface of water lens

$R_2 = \infty =$ radius of curvature of second surface (touching the plane mirror) of water lens

$$\Rightarrow \quad \text{Refractive index of water, } \mu_w = \left(1 + \frac{R}{f_w}\right) \quad \ldots \text{(ii)}$$

The radius of curvature R of the spherical surface of convex lens can be determined by using a spherometer.

Hence, from Eq. (ii), it is understood that **by knowing the values of focal length of water lens and radius of curvature of spherical surface of convex lens, one can find the refractive index of water.**

Procedure to Determine the Radius of Curvature of Convex Lens

Initial Observations of Spherometer

1. First of all, take a spherometer and examine it properly, so that its legs and vertical scale are not shaky and screw at centre is not loose.
2. Note the value of one division on pitch scale of the given spherometer.
3. Note the number of divisions on circular scale.
4. After that, calculate the least count and pitch of the spherometer.

Setting Up the Three Legs and Screw of the Spherometer

5. Place the spherometer on a glass slab and move the central screw till its tip just touches the surface of glass slab.
6. During the motion of central screw, count the total number of rotations till it touches the glass slab.

Plane Surface (Sheet of Paper) Reading

7. Place the spherometer on a sheet of paper and press it lightly and take the impressions of the tips of its three legs.

8. Join the three impressions to make an equilateral triangle ABC and measure all the sides (i.e. AB, BC and CA) of ΔABC. Calculate the mean distance l between two legs of spherometer by using the following relation

$$l = \frac{AB + BC + CA}{3}$$

Note The term l^2 is used in determining the radius of curvature R, so one should take care of measuring the length l.

9. Read the main scale reading, i.e. equals to $m \times$ LC
   (m = number of complete main scale divisions below the edge of circular scale)
10. Read the circular scale reading, i.e. equals to $c \times$ LC
    (c = number of divisions in circular scale which coincides with the edge of main scale)
11. Now, calculate the total reading i.e. main scale reading + circular scale reading
    $\Rightarrow$ $m \times$ (LC of main scale) + $c \times$ (LC of spherometer)

Curved Surface (or Convex Mirror) Reading

12. Now, take convex mirror and set it on the horizontal surface, so that its convex surface is in upward direction.
13. Put the spherometer on the convex surface, so its legs rest on it as shown in the figure.
14. Now, move the central screw till it touches the surface of convex part. It is to be ensured that the screw touches the given spherical surface gently. One can observe its image formed due to reflection from the surface beneath it.
15. Again, note the reading of the circular scale, main scale and note whether the zero of the circular scale has moved down or up the zero of main scale.
16. The difference between two sets of observations with proper sign, i.e. (curved surface – plane surface) gives the value of h called **Sagitta**.
17. Repeat the steps (7) to (16) and calculate mean value of h.

Procedure to Determine the Refractive Index of Liquid (Water)

Determination of Rough Focal Length of Convex Lens

1. Estimate the rough focal length of convex lens (if it is not known) by following the same steps (1) to (3) given in Experiment (3).

Setting up the Apparatus

2. Place a plane mirror on the horizontal base, keeping its reflecting surface upward
3. Next place a convex lens of comparatively less aperture on the plane mirror.
4. Fix a small needle AB in the clamp of retort stand horizontally above the lens.
5. Adjust the position of the needle AB using plumb line and spirit level in such a way that its tip lies vertically above the optical centre of convex lens.

Determination of Focal Length of Convex Lens

6. Move the clamped needle AB gradually upward looking at the image and bring it to a height such that the tip of the needle AB exactly coincides with the tip of its image $A'B$.
7. Remove the parallax between both the tips.
8. When the parallax gets removed, both the tips coincide with each other. Note the distance (d_1) between the tip of the needle and upper surface of convex lens. Also, note the distance

(d_2) between the tip of the needle and upper surface of plane mirror. Then, take the average of both the distances as $OF = f$. This will give you the **focal length of convex lens.**

$$\text{Focal length, } f = \frac{d_1 + d_2}{2}$$

Determination of Focal Length of Plano-Concave Lens Formed of Water

9. Fill the open space between plane mirror and lens with clean water using dropper. Wait for few minutes, so that the water becomes stationary (as shown in figure 2).
10. Again adjust the position of needle by moving the clamp in upward direction, so that the parallax between needle and its inverted image is removed completely.
11. Measure the distances d_3 and d_4 of tip of the needle from top and bottom surface of lens respectively and take the average distance as $OF' = f'$. This will give you the **focal length of plano-concave lens.**

$$\text{Focal length, } f' = \frac{d_3 + d_4}{2}$$

12. Repeat the above procedures three more times and note the observations in the tabular form.

Determination of Refractive Index of Water

13. Determine the focal length of water lens by using the following relation

$$f_w = \frac{ff'}{f - f'}$$

where, f and f' are focal lengths determined in steps (8) and (11), respectively.

14. Now, after measuring the value of radius of curvature of the lens and focal length of water lens, determine the refractive index of water by using the following relation.

$$\mu_w = \left(1 + \frac{R}{f_w}\right)$$

Observations of Radius of Curvature of Convex Lens

Pitch of the Spherometer Screw

Value of smallest division on the vertical scale =......... mm

Distance (q) moved by the screw for complete rotations (p) of the circular disc =........ mm

Pitch of the screw (q/p) =........ mm

Least Count of Spherometer

Total number of divisions on the circular scale (N) =......... mm

$$\text{Least count (LC) of the spherometer} = \frac{\text{Pitch of the spherometer screw}}{\text{Number of divisions on the circular scale}}$$

$$= \frac{\text{Pitch of the screw}}{N} = \text{........ mm} = \text{........ cm.}$$

Table for Measurement of Sagitta (h)

S.N.	Curved surface reading				Plane surface reading				Mean corrected reading, $h = h_A - h_B$
	MSR x (cm)	CSD y	CSR $z = y \times LC$ (cm)	Curved surface total reading, $h_A = x + z$ (cm)	MSR x' (cm)	CSD y'	CSR $z' = y' \times LC$ (cm)	Plane surface total reading, $h_B = x' + z'$ (cm)	
1									$h_1 = \ldots$ cm
2									$h_2 = \ldots$ cm
3									$h_3 = \ldots$ cm
4									$h_4 = \ldots$ cm

Calculation for Radius of Curvature of Convex Lens

1. Mean distance between two legs of spherometer, $l = \frac{AB + BC + CA}{3} = \ldots\ldots\ldots$ cm

   where, AB, BC and CA are measured sides of equilateral triangle ABC.

2. Mean corrected value of Sagitta (h) $= \frac{h_1 + h_2 + h_3 + h_4}{4} = \ldots\ldots\ldots$ cm

3. Radius of curvature (R) $= \frac{l^2}{6h} + \frac{h}{2} = \ldots\ldots\ldots$ cm

Observations for Focal Length of Water Lens

Table for Calculation of Focal Length of Convex Lens (f) and Plano-concave Lens of Water (f') and Refractive Index of Water (μ_w)

S.N.	Position of tip of the needle w.r.t. optical centre O						$f_w = \frac{ff'}{f - f'}$ (cm)	Δf_w (cm)	μ_w	$\Delta \mu_w$
	Without water ($OF = f$)			With water ($OF' = f'$)						
	Distance of the needle from			Distance of the needle from						
	Upper surface of the lens, d_1 (cm)	Lower surface of the lens, d_2 (cm)	Average distance, $f = \frac{d_1 + d_2}{2}$ (cm)	Upper surface of the lens, d_3 (cm)	Lower surface of the lens, d_4 (cm)	Average distance, $f' = \frac{d_3 + d_4}{2}$ (cm)				
1										
2										
3										
4										

Calculation for Refractive index of Water

Mean value of focal length of water lens, $f_w = \frac{f_{w_1} + f_{w_2} + f_{w_3} + f_{w_4}}{4} = \ldots\ldots$ cm

Refractive index of water, $\mu_w - 1 + \frac{R}{f_w}$

Find the mean of different values of refractive index. $\mu_w = \frac{\mu_{w_1} + \mu_{w_2} + \mu_{w_3} + \mu_{w_4}}{4} = \ldots\ldots$

Error

As we have determined refractive index of water by using formula

$$\mu_w = \left(1 + \frac{R}{f_w}\right)$$

So error will be estimated in the value of refractive index as

$$\Delta\mu_w = \mu_w \left[\frac{\Delta R}{R} + \frac{\Delta f_w}{f_w}\right], \quad \Delta f_w = f_w^2 \left[\frac{\Delta f}{f^2} + \frac{\Delta f'}{f'^2}\right]$$

where, Δf, Δf_w and ΔR are the least counts of the measuring scales with the help of which they are measured and f_w is the mean focal length of water lens.

The maximum of four values $\Delta\mu_w$ will be reported with the result as experimental error.

Result

The refractive index of clean water w.r.t. air is $\mu_w \pm \Delta\mu_w = \ldots \pm \ldots$

where, μ_w = mean of four readings of refractive index

$\Delta\mu_w$ = maximum of four values of error.

PRECAUTIONS

In Determining the Radius of Curvature of Convex Lens

1. *The screw should be moved in one direction only to avoid the backlash error.*
2. *Legs of spherometer must touch the spherical surface.*
3. *Screw present at centre must touch the curved or plane surface.*

In Determining the Refractive Index of Water

4. *The convex lens should be so adjusted on the mirror so that its principal axis is vertical with respect to mirror.*
5. *Thin lens should be used, so that the distance measured from the surface of lens is nearly equal to the distance measured from optical centre.*
6. *Water should be poured slowly using a dropper so that the position of the lens on the mirror does not change.*
7. *The thin lens should be used so that the distance measured from the optical surface is nearly equal to the distance measured from its surface. However, it is better to measure distance from both surfaces and take the average for f or f'.*

Sources of Error

In Determining the Radius of Curvature of Convex Lens

1. Graduations may not be uniform on scale.
2. There may be instrumental and human errors.
3. Parallax error may arise while reading the pitch scale corresponding to the level of the circular scale.

In Determining the Refractive Index of Water

4. The radius of curvature of plano-concave lens of water may not be equal to that of convex lens.
5. The needle fixed in the clamp may not be horizontal.

Viva-Voce

Q 1 What is the effect of placing a liquid between the lens and the mirror on the effective focal length?

Ans. The focal length decreases due to increased refraction, making the lens system more converging.

Q 2 For what purpose, we use spherometer?

Ans. A spherometer is a device used to measure the radii of curvatures of spherical surfaces like concave mirror, convex lens, etc.

Q 3 In this experiment, at which condition the parallax is removed completely?

Ans. The parallax is removed completely when the sharp end of needle is exactly at the principal focus of the needle.

Q 4 Find the refractive index of glass with respect to water (μ_{gw}).

Ans. Since, $\mu_w = \frac{4}{3}$ and $\mu_g = \frac{3}{2}$ so, $\mu_{gw} = \frac{\mu_g}{\mu_w} = \frac{3/2}{4/3} = \frac{9}{8}$

Q 5 On which factors does the refractive index of a material depend?

Ans. The refractive index of a material depends on

(i) The wavelength of light (colour)

(ii) Temperature

Q 6 Write the value of refractive index of water and glass w.r.t. air.

Ans. Refractive index of water w.r.t. air = $\mu_w = \frac{4}{3}$

Refractive index of glass w.r.t. air = $\mu_g = \frac{3}{2}$

Q 7 Define refractive index.

Ans. The refractive index of a medium is defined as the ratio of velocity of light in vacuum to that in medium.

i.e. $$\mu = \frac{\text{Velocity of light in vacuum}}{\text{Velocity of light in medium}} = \frac{c}{v}$$

Q 8 Why should we move the needle upward after filling water between lens and plane mirror?

Ans. The water and convex lens both will work as a combined lens and the image formation would be at larger distance from the optical centre, so we move the needle upward to get the image at the same position.

Experiment 08

AIM

To find the refractive index of a liquid using a concave mirror and a plane mirror.

Apparatus and Material Required

A concave mirror, water, an optical needle, a clamp stand, one meter scale, plumb line and a spirit level.

Theory/Principle

If the tip of object needle is the centre of curvature *C*, then the tip of image will exactly coincide with it (principal axis is vertical to the plane). When water is filled in concave mirror, object needle is shifted at *C* to remove parallax between tips of object needle and its image.

A ray starting from *C* will reach at *E* without deviation because it is along radius of curvature. Due to water in the concave mirror, the position of object and image shifts to *C*, *i.e.* now ray starting from *C* after refraction moves along *ED* and then *DC* to make apparent image of centre of curvature.

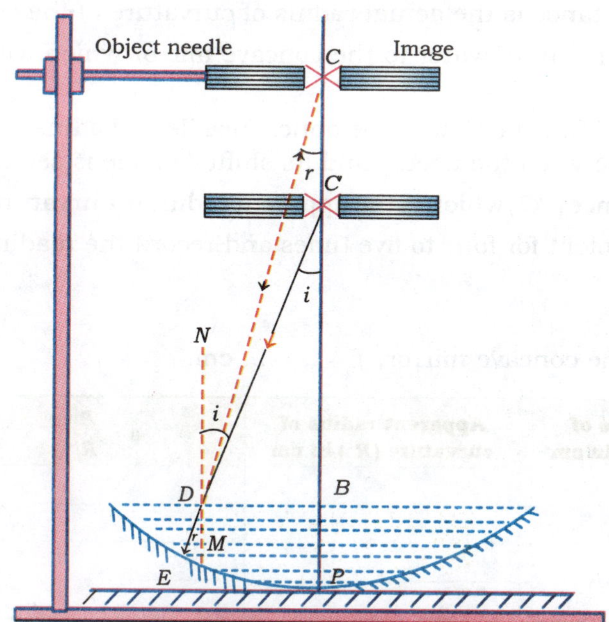

Refractive index of liquid

$$\therefore \quad \angle NDC = i \text{ (Angle of incidence)} = \angle BCD$$

$$\angle MDE = r \text{ (Angle of refraction)} = \angle BCD$$

$$\therefore \quad {}_a\mu_w = \frac{\sin i}{\sin r} = \frac{DB/DC}{DB/DC} = \frac{DC}{DC}$$

In $\quad \Delta BCD, \sin i = \dfrac{DB}{DC'}$

and ΔBCD, $\sin r = \frac{DB}{DC}$

For normal view, D will be near B.

Therefore, ${}_a\mu_w = \frac{BC}{BC'}$

If small quantity of water in concave mirror B will be very near to P, *i.e.*

$$BC \simeq PC \text{ and } BC' \simeq PC'$$

$$\therefore \quad {}_a\mu_w = \frac{PC}{PC'} = \frac{\text{Real radius of curvature of mirror}}{\text{Apparent radius of curvature of mirror}}$$

Procedure

(i) Place the concave mirror on a horizontal surface (use a spirit level to ensure that the surface is horizontal), so that its principal axis is along vertical.

(ii) Hold the optical needle horizontally in a clamp stand, so that its tip lies just above the pole P and at a distance equal to $2f$ (f is focal length) as shown in figure.

(iii) Remove the parallax between the needle and its image.

(iv) Mark the real and inverted image of the optical needle in the mirror. Note the reading of this image.

(v) Measure the distance (PC) using plumb line and meter scale.

(vi) This measured distance is the actual radius of curvature of the concave mirror.

(vii) Now, add small amount of water to the concave mirror which will change the position of image needle.

(viii) Adjust the screw to upper or lower, the optical needle and adjust its position from C to C to remove parallax between the needle and its shifted image is seen.

(ix) Measure the distance (PC) which is the apparent radius of curvature of the concave mirror.

(x) Repeat the experiment for four to five times and record the readings.

Observations

Rough focal length of the concave mirror, f = ... cm.

S.N.	Actual radius of curvature (R) in cm	Apparent radius of curvature (R') in cm	$\mu = \frac{R}{R'}$	Mean (μ)
1.				
2.				
3.				
4.				

Calculations

Putting the observed values of actual radius R and apparent radius R' in $\mu = \frac{R}{R'}$, and calculate the value of refractive index of the given medium.

Result

Refractive index of water, μ = ...

PRECAUTIONS

1. Parallax should be removed from tip-to-tip.

2. The bench correction should be applied.

3. The upright may be vertical.

4. The mirror and surface of the water should be very clean.

5. The distance should be measured from the centre of the mirror, not from the surface of water.

Sources of Error

1. The object needle may not be horizontal.
2. The principal axis may not be vertical.
3. Parallax may occur.

Viva-Voce

Q 1 What do you mean by absolute refractive index of a medium?

Ans. It is defined as the ratio of the velocity of light in vacuum to the velocity of light in the medium.

Q 2 What is the relative refractive index?

Ans. It is defined as the ratio of the speed of light in medium 1 to its speed in medium 2.

Q 3 The refractive index of a medium is found to be 1.5. What do you mean by this statement?

Ans. This statement means the speed of light in vacuum is 1.5 times faster than that in the medium.

Q 4 What is the relation between refractive index, relative permeability and relative permittivity?

Ans. Refractive index = $(\mu_r \varepsilon_r)^{1/2}$

Q 5 Why is the speed of light of all colours same in air?

Ans. Vacuum is space which does not resist the speed of light, hence all colours or wavelength of light ray travel at same speed. i.e. Speed of light is 3×10^8 m/s.

Q 6 Which colour of white light travels with least speed in a transparent medium?

Ans. Violet colour

Q 7 An object is placed at a distance of $2f$ from a concave mirror of focal length f. Where is the image formed?

Ans. It is formed at $2f$.

Q 8 **For what position of an object, a concave mirror forms an enlarged virtual image?**

Ans. A concave mirror forms an enlarged virtual image when the object is kept between focus and pole.

Q 9 **If an object is at infinity infront of a concave mirror, where is the image formed?**

Ans. The image is formed at the focus.

Q10 **If colours are added to water keeping its transparency, would this alter the value of refractive index and intensity of the image?** [NCERT]

Ans. The refractive index will change and the intensity of image decreases because dyes used for colouring absorb specific wavelengths of light, even if overall transparency is maintained.

Q11 **If you gradually increase the quantity of water in the mirror, starting with a few drops, do you expect any change in the position or brightness of the image?** [NCERT]

Ans. The image will shift away from the mirror but brightness will not change.

Q12 **If a small quantity of some transparent liquid (like kerosene) lighter than water is added such that it forms a thin film on the water surface, can the experiment still be performed? If so, would the value of refractive index change?** [NCERT]

Ans. Yes, experiment can be performed. The position of the image will be approximately same and we will get approximately same value of refractive index because the layer of kerosene is very thin.

Experiment 09

AIM

To draw the *I-V* characteristic curve for a *p-n* junction in forward and reverse bias.

Apparatus and Material Required

A *p-n* junction diode (or semiconductor diode), a resistor of value 3Ω, a variable voltage power supply (0-12 V), a voltmeter (0-12 V), a milliammeter (0-200 mA), a microammeter (0-200 μA), a one-way key, connecting wires and a piece of sand paper.

Theory/Principle

p-n Junction Diode

When a *p*-type semiconductor is grown over an *n*-type semiconductor, the compound crystal forms a device called *p-n* junction diode.

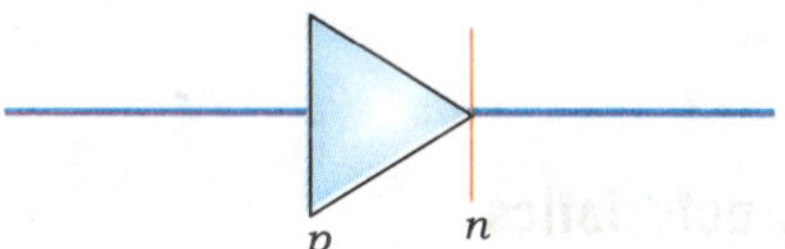

Symbol of *p-n* junction diode

Forward and Reverse Biasing of Diode

When an external potential difference is applied to a *p-n* junction, then two types of biasing may take place.

(i) A diode is said to be **forward biased**, if its *p*-region is connected to the positive terminal of the battery and *n*-region to the negative terminal of the battery.

(ii) A diode is said to be **reverse biased**, if its *p*-region is connected to the negative terminal of the battery and *n*-region to the positive terminal of the battery.

Circuit Diagram to Draw Forward Bias Characteristic

The circuit diagram for a *p-n* junction diode in forward bias mode is as shown in the figure.

With increase in bias voltage, the negligible forward current flows until the applied voltage crosses a certain value. After a characteristic voltage (about 0.7V for Si and 0.3V for Ge), the diode current increases suddenly exponentially even for small increase in bias voltage.

The value of bias voltage at which the forward current increases rapidly is called **threshold voltage** or **cut-in voltage** (V_{th}).

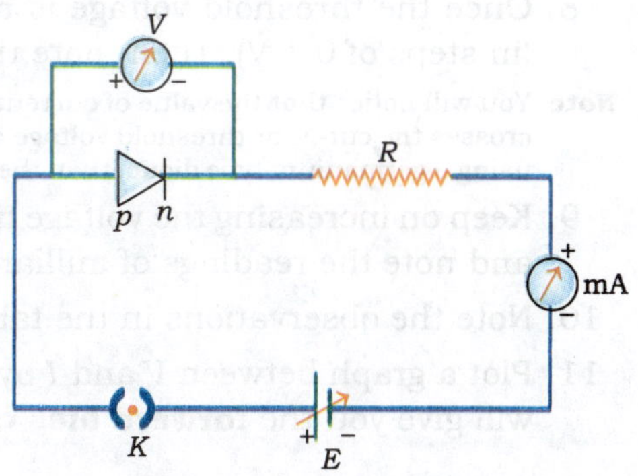

Fig. (a) Forward biasing of *p-n* junction

Circuit Diagram to Draw Reverse Bias Characteristic

The circuit diagram for a *p-n* junction diode in reverse bias mode is given in the figure below.

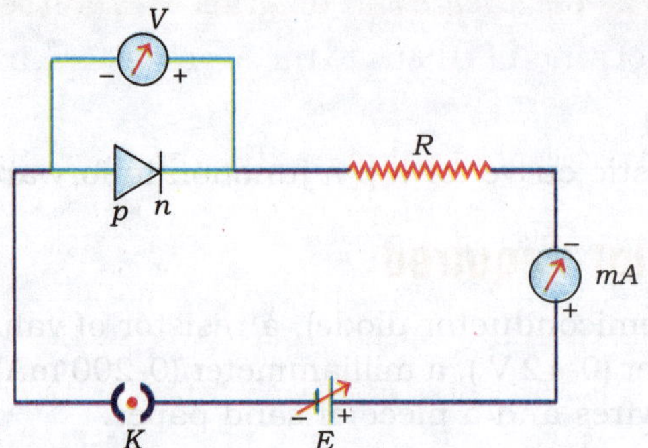

Fig. (b) Reverse biasing of *p-n* junction

As the applied voltage is increased in reverse bias condition, initially very small reverse current of the order of microamperes) flows. At the moment when reverse bias voltage increases to sufficiently high value, the reverse current suddenly increases to a large value and becomes constant. This constant current (in range of μA) is called **reverse saturation current**.

Procedure

(i) To Draw Forward Bias Characteristics

1. Draw a neat circuit diagram of forward bias characteristic as shown in Fig.(a).
2. Note the range and least count of given voltmeter (*V*) and milliammeter (*mA*).
3. Remove the insulating layers from the leads of diode and connecting wires by using a sand paper.
4. Connect the variable voltage power supply, voltmeter, *p-n* junction diode, milliammeter, resistor and a plug key as per the circuit diagram of forward bias characteristic of diode.

Note It should be ensured that the positive terminal of the battery is connected to the *p*-section and negative terminal to *n*-section of diode.

5. Give a small voltage to the circuit by gently turning the knob of power supply.
6. Note down the voltmeter reading across the diode and corresponding milliammeter reading.
7. Now, increase the applied voltage gradually in stepwise manner and note the corresponding voltmeter and milliammeter readings in each step.
8. Once the threshold voltage is reached, increase the voltage across the diode very slowly (in steps of 0.1 V). Then, note the corresponding current flowing through the diode.

Note You will notice that the value of current flowing through the diode will be negligibly small till the applied voltage crosses the cut-in or threshold voltage after which the current suddenly increases with the rapid rate. If you are using a germanium type diode, then the threshold voltage will be 0.3 V and for silicon type diode, it will be 0.7 V.

9. Keep on increasing the voltage till the current reaches the maximum value of milliammeter and note the readings of milliammeter and voltmeter.
10. Note the observations in the tabular form.
11. Plot a graph between *V* and *I* by taking them along *X* and *Y*-axes respectively. This graph will give you the **forward bias characteristic of diode.**

(ii) To Draw Reverse Bias Characteristics

1. Draw a neat circuit diagram of reverse bias characteristic as shown in Fig.(b).
2. Make the connections as per the circuit diagram for reverse bias characteristic.
3. Connect the *p*-section of junction diode to the negative terminal of power supply and remove the milliammeter with a microammeter.
4. Note the range and least count of voltmeter (V) and microammeter (μA).

Note In case of reverse biasing, we use micrometer and power supply of 15 V instead of milliammeter and power supply of 3 V as used in forward biasing.

5. With the help of variable voltage power supply, gradually, increase the applied voltage in steps and note the corresponding voltmeter reading in the tabular form.
6. Continue increasing the voltage until the reverse current becomes nearly constant, indicating saturation. Note the final reading of the voltmeter and microammeter.
7. Plot a graph between V and I by taking them along negative X-axis and negative Y-axis, respectively. This graph will give you the **reverse bias characteristic of diode.**

Observations

(i) For Forward Biasing

1. Range of voltmeter = (...... to ......) V
2. Least count of voltmeter scale = ... V
3. Range of milliammeter = (...... to ......) mA
4. Least count of milliammeter scale = ... mA

Table for Forward Bias Voltage and Current

S. N.	Forward voltage, V_f (V)	Forward current, I_f (mA)
1		
2		
3		
⋮		
10		

(ii) For Reverse Biasing

1. Range of voltmeter = (..... to .....) V
2. Least count of voltmeter scale = ... V
3. Range of microammeter = (.... to ....) μA
4. Least count of microammeter scale = ... μA

Table for Reverse Bias Voltage and Current

S. No.	Reverse voltage, V_r (V)	Reverse current, I_r (μA)
1		
2		
3		
⋮		
10		

Plotting Graph

1. Plot a graph between forward voltage (V_f) along positive X-axis and forward current (I_f) along the positive Y-axis. Locate the knee and determine the threshold voltage. The point where the current starts increasing suddenly is called **knee point** in the forward bias characteristic.
2. Plot the reverse voltage (V_r) along the negative X-axis and the corresponding current along the negative Y-axis. Locate the breakdown voltage (V_{br}) and determine the reverse saturation current (I_{sat}).

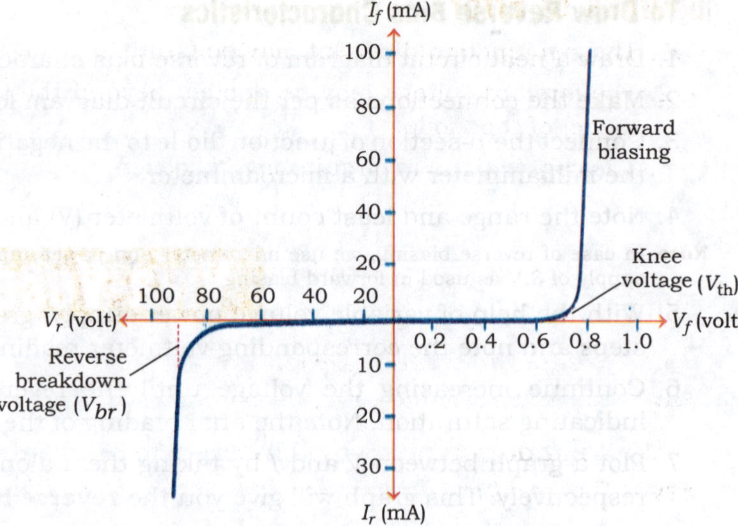

Current-voltage (I-V) characteristic curve for *p-n* junction diode in forward bias and reverse bias

Note When there is a sudden increase in reverse saturation current, this phenomenon is called **breakdown of *p-n* junction diode** and the corresponding voltage is called **reverse breakdown voltage**. The current is called saturation current because it gets saturated as its value is not affected by increase in applied voltage.

Result

1. The value of threshold voltage for given diode, V_{th} = ... V
2. The reverse saturation current for the given diode, I_{sat} = ... μA

PRECAUTIONS

1. *Before connecting the wires, their ends should be cleaned with the help of sand paper to remove the insulation.*
2. *All connections in circuit should be neat and clean.*
3. *The voltmeter, milliammeter and microammeter should be of suitable range and the current and voltage should not be exceeded beyond their limits.*
4. *Terminals of Voltmeters and ammeter should be connected to the battery in the right manner.*
5. *The key should be opened when the circuit is not being in use and it should be closed only at the time of taking observations.*
6. *Find out manufacturer's specification for maximum current through the diode in forward bias voltage. Never exceed this limit else the diode may get damaged.*
7. *Find out manufacturer's specification for maximum reverse voltage to be applied to the diode in reverse bias. Never exceed this limit.*
8. *The potential difference (V) across the diode should be increased gradually in small steps (0.1 V). Take care that the current should not be exceeded beyond the specified limit.*

Sources of Error

1. The *p-n* junction diode kit may be faulty.
2. The forward voltage may be applied beyond the tolerance limit (or a limit specified on a diode) of the diode.
3. The connections in circuit may be loosen.

Viva-Voce

Q 1 Define the term depletion layer.

Ans. The region near the *p-n* junction free from electrons and holes is called depletion layer.

Q 2 What do you mean by the term potential barrier?

Ans. The potential difference developed across the junction of *p*-type and *n*-type semiconductor in the diode is called potential barrier. It prevents further diffusion of charge carriers across the junction.

Q 3 The diode connected to the battery is not conducting. What is the reason behind it?

Ans. When the diode is connected in reverse bias, i.e. by connecting the positive terminal of the battery to *n*-side and negative terminal of the battery to *p*-side, then no current flows through the diode.

Q 4. Define the term biasing of junction.

Ans. The process of applying an external potential difference across a p-n junction is called biasing. It can be either forward or reverse bias depending on the polarity.

Q 5 What do you mean by the characteristics of a junction diode?

Ans. The characteristics of a junction diode reveal the way of behaviour of junction diode. It is a graph drawn between circuit current and bias voltage of a junction diode.

Q 6 Define doping.

Ans. The process of adding a suitable impurity to an intrinsic semiconductor is called doping. When a trivalent impurity is added, then the pure semiconductor becomes *p*-type semiconductor and it becomes *n*-type when pentavalent impurity is added.

Q 7 Name three trivalent impurities.

Ans. (i) Boron (B_5) (ii) Aluminium (Al_{13}) (iii) Indium (In_{49})

Q 8 Name four pentavalent impurities.

Ans. (i) Arsenic (As_{33}) (ii) Antimony (Sb_{51}) (iii) Bismuth (Bi_{83}) (iv) Phosphorous (P_{15})

Q 9 Name the majority charge carriers in *n*-type semiconductor and *p*-type semiconductor.

Ans. Free electrons in *n*-type semiconductor and holes in *p*-type semiconductor.

Q 10 Give the definition of extrinsic semiconductor and intrinsic semiconductor.

Ans. (i) A semiconductor doped with suitable impurity is called extrinsic semiconductor.
(ii) A semiconductor in its pure form is called intrinsic semiconductor.

Q 11 Define cut-in voltage.

Ans. The forward characteristic curve of a *p-n* junction shows a rise in forward current only beyond a certain forward voltage. This value of forward voltage is known as cut-in voltage.

Q 12 What is the order of forward current and reverse current?

Ans. The order of forward current is milliampere (mA), whereas of reverse current is microampere (μA).

Q 13 When is a *p-n* junction diode said to be in forward biased?

Ans. A *p-n* junction diode is said to be in forward biasing mode when *p*-type semiconductor is connected to positive terminal of the battery and *n*-type semiconductor is connected to the negative terminal of the battery.

Q 14 What do you mean by hole?

Ans. The deficiency or vacancy of an electron is called as a hole. Holes act as positive charge carriers.

Q 15 What is the principle of working of *p-n* junction diode as a rectifier?

Ans. The resistance of the junction diode becomes low when forward biased and high when reverse biased.

Q 16 What are acceptor and donor impurities?

Ans. Acceptor impurities are trivalent elements, such as indium and boron. These impurities accept one electron and convert the semiconductor material into *p*-type. Donor impurities, such as arsenic and phosphorus, donate one electron when added to an intrinsic semiconductor, transforming it into an *n*-type crystal.

Q 17 How can you operate the *p-n* junction diode as switch? [NCERT]

Ans. An ideal junction diode acts as closed switch when operated in forward bias, whereas it acts as an open switch when operated in reverse bias.

Q 18 How does bias affect the thickness of the depletion layer? [NCERT]

Ans. Forward bias reduces the thickness of the depletion layer, while reverse bias increase it.

Activity 01

AIM

To identify a diode, an LED, a resistor and a capacitor from a mixed collection of such items.

Apparatus and Material Required

A multimeter, an LED, a junction diode, a resistor and a capacitor.

Theory/Principle

Diode It is a two-terminal device which conducts only when it is forward biased and does not conduct when it is reverse biased. It does not emit light, while conducting.

LED (Light Emitting Diode) It is a special type of diode having two terminals. An LED conducts when it is forward biased and does not conduct when it is reverse biased. It emits light while conducting. The LEDs are of different colours like red, green, white, etc.

Resistor It is a two-terminal device used to control the current flow by offering the opposition in its path.

Capacitor It is a two-terminal device which does not conduct but stores charge when DC voltage is applied.

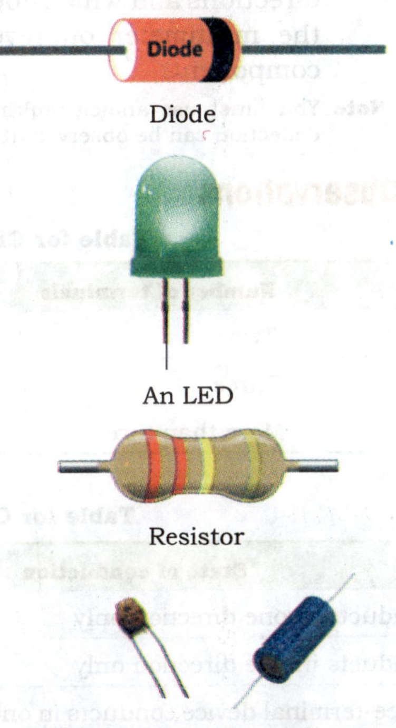

Diode

An LED

Resistor

Different types of capacitor

Procedure

Identifying the Diode, Resistor and LED (A two Terminal Component)

1. Pick a component having two terminals from the given mixed collection of items. It could be a resistor, a capacitor, a diode or an LED.
   (i) Look for the component having colour bands of three set of colours followed by a silver or gold band. This component is a resistor. One can verify the component by using multimeter only.
   (ii) Ensure that the multimeter is set-up in the resistance mode of highest range. Connect or touch the multimeter terminals to the component terminals and watch for multimeter deflection. Also, repeat it by reversing the component terminals.
   (iii) In both the cases, if equal deflection is shown in the multimeter scale, then the component is a resistor.

(iv) If on connecting the terminals, the large deflection in the multimeter scale is observed which gradually returns back to zero, then the component is a capacitor of large value of capacitance.

Note If a capacitor having small value of capacitance is given, then there is no deflection in the multimeter scale rather the pointer remains at zero position.

(v) If the multimeter shows some deflection in one direction with the emission of light from the component and much less or zero deflection in other direction (or an unequal deflection with emission of light), then the component is LED.

(vi) If the multimeter shows some deflection in one direction but with no emission of light from the component and much less or zero deflection in other direction, then the component is a diode.

2. Record your observations by writing the name of the device having two, three and more than three terminals and label each component by a different alphabet e.g. *A*, *B*, *C*, *D*, *E*, ... Also, write the name of the device or component which conducts in one direction, in two directions and which does not conduct. One can take an idea by observing the deflection of the multimeter on reversing the terminals of multimeter touching the terminals of component.

Note You must use analog multimeter instead of digital multimeter. If digital multimeter is being used, then deflection can be observed from the reading.

Observations

Table for Checking the Number of Terminals

S. N.	Number of terminals	Alphabet marked on the device	Name of device
1	Two		
2	Three		
3	More than three		

Table for Checking the State of Conduction

S. N.	State of conduction	Emission of light	Device code	Name of the device
1	Conducts in one direction only	Yes/No		
2	Conducts in one direction only	Yes/No		
3	Three-terminal device conducts in one direction only between central terminal and either of the remaining terminals.	Yes/No		
4	Conducts in both directions.	Yes/No		
5	Does not conduct, gives an initial deflection which decays to zero.	Yes/No		

Result

A diode, an LED, a resistor and a capacitor are identified one-by-one from a given mixed collection of such items.

PRECAUTIONS

In addition to general precautions which are necessary while using a multimeter, some are discussed below.

1. *While checking out any component clean its leads properly by using sand paper, so that the insulation can be removed.*
2. *Preferably use analog multimeter and not the digital multimeter, so that the deflection shown by the pointer can be observed.*
3. *The current should be observed with the reverse polarity every time.*

Sources of Error

1. When the metal ends of a multimeter leads are touched, the multimeter should show zero resistance. If it does not show, bring the pointer to zero using 'Zero Adj Knob' on the multimeter.
2. While checking resistance of a component, avoid touching either of the metal ends of the multimeter leads. Body resistance in parallel with component resistance can affect the resistance measurement.

Viva-Voce

Q 1 **Define LED.**

Ans. LED means Light Emitting Diode. This diode emits light when connected in forward bias.

Q 2 **How an LED emits light?**

Ans. When an LED is connected in forward biasing mode then recombination of electrons and holes takes place at junction and energy is released in the form of light.

Q 3 **How can you say that the resistor is a component that conducts in both directions?**

Ans. As the resistance offered by a resistor does not change even when the polarity of battery gets reversed and the deflection in the multimeter is shown equally in both directions, so we can say that the resistance is a component that conducts in both directions.

Q 4 **What do you mean by a capacitor?**

Ans. A two-terminal device which does not conduct either in forward biasing mode or in reverse biasing mode is called a capacitor.

Q 5 **Which allow AC current to pass through it, either a capacitor or an inductor?**

Ans. Capacitor

Q 6 **Why does a diode conduct only in one direction?**

Ans. A diode conducts current only in one direction due to the nature of its p-n junction and the way it responds to biasing (voltage applied across it).

Q 7 **Why is no light emitted in a diode but an LED emits?**

Ans. In a regular diode, when electrons and holes recombine, the energy is released as heat. However, in a LED, the energy released at the junction is in the form of light.

Activity 02

AIM

Use of multimeter to see the unidirectional flow of current in case of a diode and an LED and check whether a given electronic component (e.g. diode) is in working order.

Apparatus and Material Required

A multimeter, a diode, an LED, plug key, a battery, a resistance box, connecting wires and a piece of sand paper.

Theory/Principle

Analog Multimeter Used in Resistance Mode

Multimeter is an instrument used for measuring current in amperes, voltage in volts and resistance in ohm. Therefore, it is also known as AVO meter. The figure shows a circuit for multimeter used to measure the resistance.

To Check the Unidirectional Flow of Current in Junction Diode and LED

When a diode is in forward bias mode, a substantial current in order of mA will flow in the circuit. But when it is in reverse bias mode, almost negligible current of the order of μA will flow in the circuit.

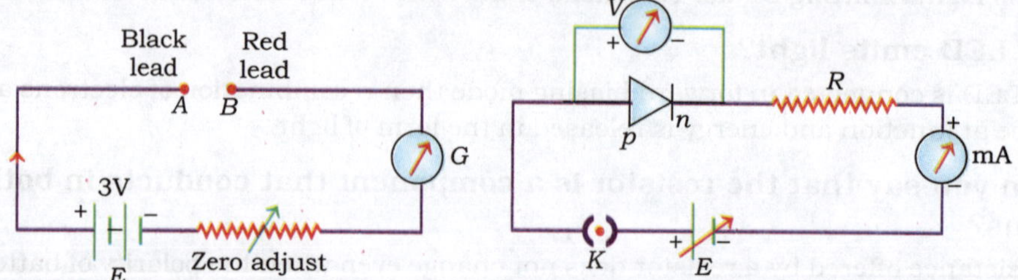

Multimeter in resistance mode

Circuit diagram to check the unidirectional flow of current in diode and LED

Checking the Working Order of Given Electronic Component

A diode or LED is in working order, if it allows the current to flow when it is in forward biased. A transistor conducts only when base-emitter junction is forward biased and does not conduct when the junction is reverse biased. If the current flows or does not flow in both biasing, then the transistor is damaged. An IC has minimum of eight legs on a single silicon chip but its working function can be tested out by an IC tester only, instead of multimeter.

Procedure

1. If the diodes, transistors and connecting wires are not used for a long time, then they may have some insulating layers on their surface. In order to remove insulation, clean their ends with the help of a sand paper till they shine.

Adjustment of the Multimeter

2. Touch the two metal ends or probes of multimeter with each other.
3. Observe that multimeter shows zero resistance. If it is not so, adjust the **zero adjust knob** to bring the pointer on zero reading.
4. Now, set the multimeter to the high range of resistance by using selector switch.

Identification of Diode to Check its Working Order and Unidirectional Flow of Current

5. Touch the positive lead or probe of the multimeter to the one terminal (say 1) of diode and the negative probe to the other terminal (say 2) of diode. Observe the value of resistance whether it is high or low.
6. If high value of resistance is observed, it shows that the diode is in reverse bias mode and the terminal connected to the negative probe of the multimeter is *p*-type of diode and the other terminal is *n*-type. In this way, the diode is in proper working condition.
7. Interchange of probe touching the terminals 1 and 2 of diode indicates that it is in forward bias offering a low value of resistance. Observe the low value of resistance. This shows the unidirectional flow of current.
8. If in both the cases of steps (5) and (7), the low value of resistances is observed then the diode is damaged. On the other hand, if the high value of resistances is observed, this indicates the diode is discontinuous or open.
9. Now, replace the diode by an LED and repeat steps (5) to (8) to know whether it is in proper working condition or not and further check for the unidirectional flow of current. Here, you find that an LED also allows the flow of current when it is forward biased and emits light as well.

10 A multimeter is not used to check an IC. An IC tester is used for this purpose.

Result

1. The given diode's working order has been checked using multimeter.
2. The unidirectional flow of current in a junction diode and LED has been realised.

PRECAUTIONS

1. *While obtaining resistance of any component, clean its leads properly.*
2. *Set the multimeter using selector switch for appropriate range.*
3. *Allow a suitable range of electric current through the electronic component otherwise they may get damaged.*

Sources of Error

1. Before using the multimeter, its zero adjust knob should be adjusted to give zero reading.
2. While checking the resistance of a component, avoid touching both the metal ends of multimeter leads. There may be some error in the measurement of resistance due to presence of body resistance in parallel with component resistance.

Viva-Voce

Q 1 An electronic component has two pins. How will you identify them?

Ans.

(i) If the component passes electric current in one direction only without emitting any light, then it is a diode.

(ii) If the component passes electric current in one direction only and emits light also, it is an LED.

(iii) If the component passes current in both the directions, it is a resistor.

(iv) If the component does not pass direct current at all, it is a capacitor.

Q 2 Define a diode.

Ans. A two-terminal device which conducts when it is forward biased and does not conduct when it is reverse biased is known as a diode.

Q 3 Can we pass AC through a resistor?

Ans. Yes

Q 4 A multimeter shows infinite resistance even the terminals a of a diode are interchanged. What does it indicates?

Ans. The diode is damaged.

Q 5 How does temperature effect the performance of a diode?

Ans. As temperature increases the forward voltage drop of a diode decreases and reverse saturation current increases. This can affect the performance and reliability of the diode.

Q 6 Explain the effect of diode's breakdown voltage on its application in high voltage circuits.

Ans. The breakdown voltage determines how much reverse voltage the diode can handle before it starts conducting significantly. In high voltage circuits, diodes with high breakdown voltage are used to prevent accidental damage.

Activity 03

AIM

To study the effect of intensity of light (by varying distance of the source) on an LDR.

Apparatus and Material Required

An LDR, two power supplies (12 V each), key, a milliammeter of range 0-500 mA, a voltmeter of range 0-10 V, a 12 V lamp, a 47 Ω resistor, connecting wires and sand paper.

Theory/Principle

A device sensitive to light is called Light Dependent Resistor (LDR) or **photoresistor**. The resistance of an LDR is proportional to the intensity of light falling on it. LDR is made up of semiconductor materials like cadmium-sulphide (CdS). The resistance of LDR decreases as the intensity of light falling on the LDR increases.

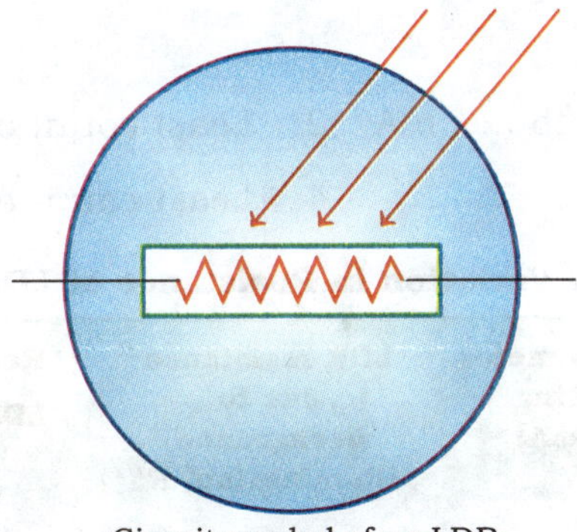

Circuit symbol of an LDR

Procedure

Setting up the Elements in a Circuit

1. Before using the connecting wires, clean their ends with the help of sand paper to remove the insulation.
2. Assemble the components as shown in the circuit diagram in figure.
3. Connect a voltmeter in parallel with LDR and a milliammeter in series with it.
4. Connect the combination with a 47Ω resistor *via* a one-way key *K*.
5. Open the key *K* by pulling out the plug from it.
6. Set up a 12 V lamp fixed in clamp vertically facing LDR. Adjust LDR normally below the lamp at about 10 cm (say). Keep the lamp in switch OFF mode.

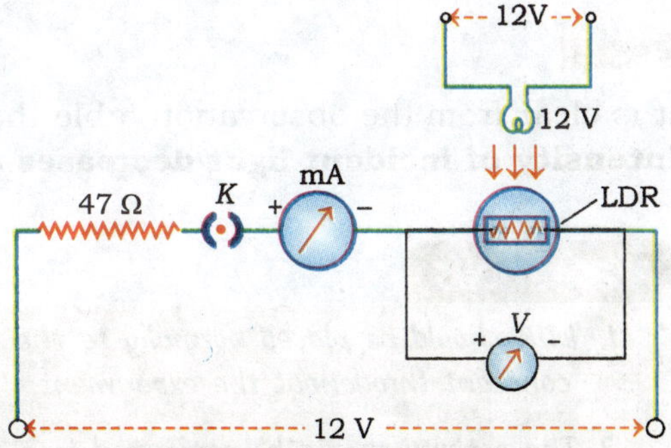

Circuit diagram for the working of an LDR when a light falls on it

Determination of Resistance of LDR

7. Now close the key K by inserting the plug into it.
8. The milliammeter and voltmeter indicate some deflection. The deflections in these measuring instruments are shown due to background illumination.
9. By using voltmeter and milliammeter readings, find the value of resistance R' of LDR due to background illumination.
10. Now, switch ON the lamp and observe the readings of voltmeter and milliammeter. Find the value of resistance R of LDR.
11. Add R' (calculated in step 9) to this measured value of R. This shows that background illumination has been taken into account.
12. Change (or increase) the distance between lamp and LDR by 5 cm and repeat the steps (10) and (11) to measure the value of LDR resistance.
13. Note the observations and calculate the resistance of LDR at successive distances (or by increasing the distance 5 cm each time). Add the resistance R' each time to the measured value of R.

Note It is to be ensured that this time the larger value of resistance of *LDR* is measured than that measured in step (10).

Observations

1. Range of milliammeter = 0 to ......mA
2. Least count of milliammeter = ...mA
3. Range of voltmeter = 0 to V
4. Least count of voltmeter = ...V

Table for Variation in Resistance of LDR with Distance

S. N.	Distance between LDR and source d (cm)	Voltmeter reading, V (V)	Milliammeter reading, I (mA)	LDR resistance due to background illumination, R'	Resistance of LDR, $R = \frac{V}{I}$ (Ω)	Actual value of resistance $(R + R')$Ω
1						
2						
3						
4						

Result

It is clear from the observation table that as the distance of the lamp from the LDR increases, **intensity of incident light decreases and resistance of LDR increases.**

PRECAUTIONS

1. *LDR should be placed normally to the light source, so that angle of incidence of light remains constant throughout the experiment.*
2. *The activity should be performed in a dark room. Yet, the resistance due to background illumination should be taken into account.*
3. *One should add the resistance due to background illumination to the final resistance for each set of observations.*
4. *The connections of LDR with voltmeter and ammeter should be tightened. The 47 Ω resistor should also be tightened with milliammeter via a key K.*

Viva-Voce

Q 1 Can we use an LDR for comparing the illuminating power of two bulbs? Why?

Ans. Yes, The luminous intensity depends on the intensity of the source. Also, the resistance of LDR depends on the intensity of light falling on it. So, we use an LDR to compare the illuminating, power of two bulbs.

Q 2 What is the SI unit of luminous intensity?

Ans. candela (cd)

Q 3 When light falls on the surface of an LDR, what effect will be on its resistance?

Ans. As light falls on the surface of an LDR, the resistance of LDR decreases.

Q 4 An LDR is a kind of sensing device. What do you mean by a sensor?

Ans. A sensor is a detector that measures a physical quantity and converts it into a signal which can be read by humans or by an instrument. Mostly sensors are used to sense light, sound, heat, pressure, image, etc., LDR is light sensitive resistor while thermistor is a temperature sensitive resistor.

Q 5 Why does the conductivity of an LDR increase with intensity?

Ans. The photons incident on the semiconductor are absorbed by the bound electrons causing them to jump to the conduction band. This results in an increase in conductivity.

Q 6 Where are LDR's used?

Ans. LDR's are commonly used in light sensitive circuits such as solar cells, photographic light meters, street lights and automatic lighting systems.

Q 7 Why does the resistance of LDR not remain constant? [NCERT]

Ans. The name itself indicates that it is a type of resistor which depends on the light falling on it. The resistance of LDR depends on the intensity of light falling on it. As intensity increases, resistance decreases and *vice-versa.*

Q 8 Why a resistance is connected in series with LDR?

Ans. We use a suitable resistance in series with LDR in order to protect the LDR from damage.

Q 9 How is an LDR is different from a thermistor?

Ans. The resistance, of an LDR varies with the intensity of light falling on it, while a thermistor's resistance changes with temperature.

Activity 04

AIM

To observe refraction and lateral deviation of a beam of light incident obliquely on a glass slab.

Apparatus and Material Required

A rectangular glass slab, a drawing board, white sheet of paper, drawing pins, alpins, adhesive tape or cello-tape, a half meter scale, a protractor and a sharply pointed pencil.

Theory/Principle

When a ray of light is incident on a rectangular glass slab, then the light ray gets refracted. Also, the light ray emerges out of the slab parallel to the direction of incident ray.

The angle which the emergent ray makes with the normal at the point of emergence is called the angle of emergence ($\angle e$). The emergent ray suffers a lateral displacement which is proportional to the thickness of glass slab.

Lateral Deviation

When a ray of light is incident obliquely on a glass slab having parallel faces, the perpendicular distance between the incident ray and the emergent ray which emerges out from the other face is called lateral deviation.

The lateral deviation produced by the glass slab is given by the following relation

$$d = \frac{t}{\cos r}\sin(i - r) \quad \text{...(i)}$$

where, t = thickness of the glass slab, i = angle of incidence and r = angle of refraction.

Thus, by measuring the thickness of the glass slab, angle of incidence and angle of refraction of light ray, one can find its lateral displacement.

From Eq. (i), it is understood that

$$d \propto t$$

$\therefore$ The lateral displacement is directly proportional to the thickness of the glass slab.

Procedure

Drawing the Incident Ray

1. Fix a sheet of white paper on a drawing board with the help of drawing pins or cello-tape.
2. Place the given glass slab nearly in the middle of the sheet.
3. Mark the boundary of glass slab with sharp pencil, then remove the slab and label it as *PQRS*.
4. On the line *PQ*, mark a point *E* and draw a normal N_1EN_2 at it.
5. Draw a line *AE* making angle AEN_1, with the normal. This line **AE represents the incident ray**.
6. Now, place the glass slab again on its boundary *PQRS* and fix two alpins *A* and *B* vertically at 8 to 10 cm distance apart on the line *AE* you have drawn.

Drawing the Emergent Ray

7. Look through the glass slab along the plane of paper from the side *SR*. Close your one eye and adjust the position of your head in such a way that the images of pins *A* and *B* will be seen by other eye clearly along the same straight line (practically only one pin is seen and the other pin will be covered by first one).
8. At the images of pins *A* and *B* fix two other pins *C* and *D* vertically in such a way that all the four pins, i.e. pins *A*, *B*, *C* and *D* lie in the same straight line.
9. Remove the glass slab and all the pins (*A*, *B*, *C* and *D*) from the board and encircle the pin-pricks on the paper with a sharp pencil.
10. Join the pricks made by pins *D* and *C* and extend the line *DC* towards the slab, so that it meets the boundary line *RS* at point *F*. The line **FD represents the emergent ray**.

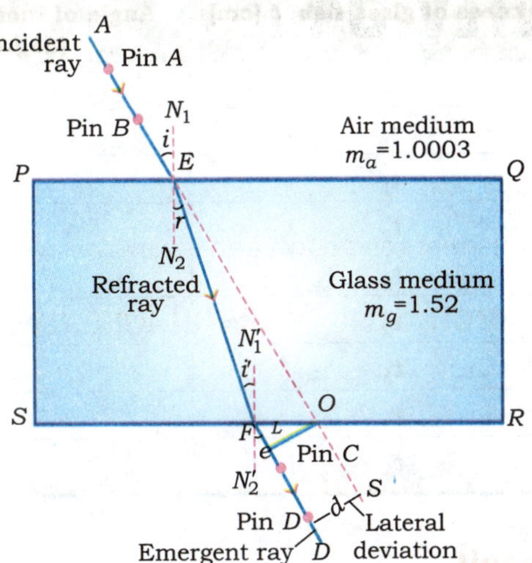

Measurement of Lateral Deviation

11. Now, join *E* and *F*, so that for incident ray *AE*, the refracted ray and emergent ray are *EF* and *FD* respectively.
12. On the line *RS*, draw a normal $N_1' FN_2'$ at point *F*. With the help of protractor, measure $\angle AEN_1$, $\angle FEN_2$ and $\angle DFN_2'$ labelled as $\angle i$, $\angle r$ and $\angle e$, respectively.
13. Find the thickness t_1 of the glass slab by measuring the breadth *PS* of the glass slab.
14. Find the lateral deviation *d* by using the following relation

$$\text{Lateral deviation, } d = \frac{t_1}{\cos r}\sin(i-r)$$

Here, t_1 is the thickness of the glass slab which you have measured in step (13) and *i* and *r* are angles of incidence and refraction which have been measured in step (12).

15. Now, fix another sheet of paper on the board and repeat all the above steps taking different angles of incidence. Again measure $\angle i$, $\angle e$ and lateral deviation *d*. Repeat it for two more times.
16. Repeat the steps (1) to (15) but use another slab of different thickness (say t_2 this time).
17. Find the lateral deviation *d* for this glass slab of thickness t_2.
18. Similarly, one can take the glass slab of thickness t_3 to measure the lateral deviation *d*.
19. Note your observations in the tabular form with proper units and significant figures.

Observations

Least count of protractor = ...(degree)

Least count of half meter scale = ... mm = ... cm

Table for Measurement of $\angle i$, $\angle e$ and Lateral Deviation d

S. N.	Thickness of glass slab, t (cm)	Angle of incidence, $\angle i$ (degree)	Angle of emergence, $\angle e$ (degree)	Lateral deviation, d (cm)
1	t_1			
2	t_1			
3	t_1			
4	t_2			
5	t_2			
6	t_2			
7	t_3			
8	t_3			
9	t_3			

Result

1. The ray of light emerging out from a glass slab is parallel to the direction of incident ray but is laterally deviated.
2. Within the experimental error, the angle of incidence is equal to the angle of emergence. i.e. $\angle i = \angle e$.
3. The lateral deviation of emergent ray w.r.t. incident ray is directly proportional to the thickness of glass slab.

PRECAUTIONS

1. To locate the incident and emergent rays with greater accuracy, the distance between pins should be 8 to 10 cm.

2. Take care that the feet of all the pins A, B, C and D should lie on the same straight line.

3. The glass slab should be of uniform thickness.

4. The angle of incidence and refraction should be measured accurately thereby, the lateral deviation can be measured with greater accuracy.

5. While viewing the pins, never see with both the eyes. Close one eye and see by another eye so that the rays coming to retina should lie on the same straight line. Thus, our view purely becomes a straight line and the exact position of images of pins can be estimated.

Viva-Voce

Q 1 Define lateral shift.

Ans. The perpendicular shift in the path of incident ray when it emerges out from denser medium is called the lateral shift.

Q 2 If the thickness of glass slab increases then what difference we observe in lateral shift?

Ans. Since, the lateral shift is directly proportional to the thickness of glass slab so, with increase in thickness, the lateral shift increases.

Q 3 Define denser and rarer media.

Ans. For a pair of media, the medium having large refractive index and low velocity of light is called denser medium, whereas the medium having small refractive index and large velocity of light is called rarer medium.

Q 4 Define angle of emergence.

Ans. The angle which the emergent ray makes with the normal at the point of emergence is called the angle of emergence ($\angle e$).

Q 5 What do you mean by refraction of light?

Ans. The phenomenon of bending of light when a light ray changes its medium is called refraction of light.

Q 6 What are the laws of refraction?

Ans. There are two laws of refraction

(i) The incident ray, the refracted ray and the normal at the point of incidence, all lie in the same plane.

(ii) The ratio of sine of angle of incidence (sin i) to the sine of angle of refraction (sin r) is always constant.

i.e. $$\frac{\sin i}{\sin r} = \mu = \text{constant}$$

Q 7 Define refractive index of a medium.

Ans. The ratio of velocity of light in vacuum to the velocity of light in medium is called the refractive index of the medium.

i.e. $$\mu = \frac{c}{v}$$

Q 8 What is the relation between angle of incidence ($\angle i$) and angle of emergence ($\angle e$) for a rectangular glass slab?

Ans. The angle of emergence is always equal to the angle of incidence for a rectangular glass slab, i.e. $\angle e = \angle i$.

Q 9 What do you mean by Snell's law?

Ans. The ratio of sine of angle of incidence to the sine of angle of refraction for a pair of media is constant which is called as refractive index of medium 2 w.r.t. medium 1.

i.e. $$\mu_{21} = \frac{\sin i}{\sin r}$$

Q10 A ray of light is travelling from glass to air. Will the angle of refraction be greater or less than the angle of incidence?

Ans. The angle of refraction will be greater than the angle of incidence because the ray is travelling from a denser medium (glass) to a rarer medium (air).

Q 11 What factors influence the lateral displacement produced by a slab?

Ans. It depends upon the following factors

(i) Refractive index of the slab

(ii) Angle of incidence

(iii) Thickness of the slab

Activity 05

AIM

To observe the diffraction of light due to a thin slit.

Apparatus and Material Required

Two razor blades, a source of light (sodium lamp), one adhesive tape, a piece of black paper, a screen, two glass slides.

Theory/Principle

Diffraction of Light

The phenomenon of bending of light around a small hole and spreading into the region of geometric shadow is called the **diffraction of light**. Diffraction is an evidence of wave nature of light. The diffraction pattern arises due to interference of light waves from different points of same wavefront.

Observing the Diffraction of Light

Take two razor blades and hold them in such a way that their edges are parallel and form a narrow slit (separation being of the order of wavelength of light λ) in between. Look through the slit on the glass bulb. With slight adjustment of slit, a diffraction pattern of central bright band having alternate bright and dark bands of decreasing intensity and fringe width is observed.

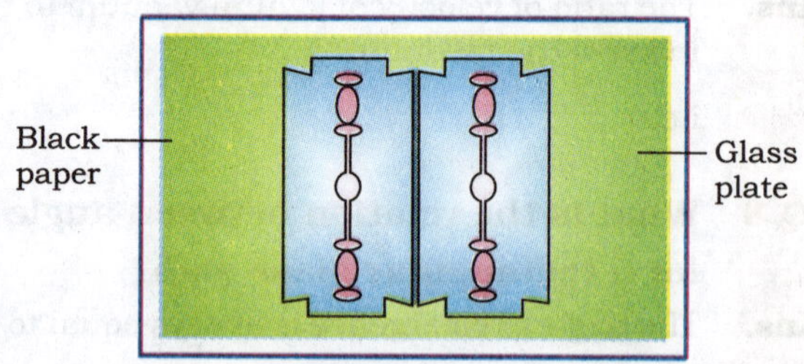

To observe the diffraction of light through thin slit using two razor blades

Procedure

1. Take a glass plate and fix a black paper on the top surface of it by using adhesive tape.
2. Cut out a narrow slit in the central part of the black paper.
3. Place two razor blades side by side quite close to each other over the narrow slit. Next, place a sodium lamp with a straight filament at a distance about 2 m behind the fine slit of the blades.
4. Place a screen nearly 15 cm ahead from the slit and by the adjusting the blades placed over the slit, observe the light falling on the screen from the narrow slit.The light coming from the slit will spread and it bends around the corners and dark and bright fringes will be observed.
5. Repeat the steps 4 and 5 for a laser pencil. Note the changes observed in the fringes.

Result

Light waves incident on very small apertures bend around the corners which indicates the phenomenon of diffraction.

PRECAUTIONS

1. *The slit should be fixed at a minimum distance of 2 m from the source of light.*
2. *Always use monochromatic light for diffraction pattern.*
3. *The space between the edges of blade should be minimum and the blades should be held parallel to each other. The paper pasted on the glass plate should be dark black.*

Viva-Voce

Q 1 Define diffraction of light.

Ans. The phenomenon of bending of light around the edges of an obstacle is known as diffraction of light.

Q 2 When a white light illuminates a slit, then what do we observe on a screen placed in front of the slit?

Ans. On the screen, we observe a central bright fringe having alternate dark and bright fringes.

Q 3 What is the essential condition for diffraction of light to occur?

Ans. Diffraction of light occurs when size of the obstacle or the aperture is comparable to the wavelength of light.

Q 4 How is the width of central maximum varies with the width of slit?

Ans. The width of central maximum increases with the decrease in slit width.

Q 5 What do you mean by the limit of resolution?

Ans. The smallest linear or angular separation between two point objects at which they can be just separately seen by an optical instrument, is known as the limit of resolution of the optical instrument.

Q 6 What makes the centre of the diffraction pattern bright?

Ans. The waves from the two halves of the wavefront reach the centre in the same phase, hence the centre of diffraction pattern is bright.

Q 7 The diffraction pattern is observed for slit widths of the order of wavelength λ of light used. What happens when the slit width is few times the wavelength of light λ? [NCERT]

Ans. If there is slight increase in slit width, light will be diffracted.

Q 8 If we place a screen in front of a very narrow slit illuminated by a white light, then what will we observe?

Ans. We will observe a central bright fringe having alternate dark and bright fringes of decreasing intensity on both sides of the central bright fringe.

Q 9 If light bends around the obstacles, then why we cannot see around a building?

Ans. Since, the wavelength of light is much smaller than the size of the wall. So, the diffraction of light around the edge of the wall is very poor. Thus, we cannot see around a building.

Activity 6a

AIM

To study the nature and the size of the image formed by a convex lens for different distances of candle from the lens.

Apparatus and Material Required

A convex lens of small focal length and known thickness, a candle, optical bench with three uprights, a match box, a V-shaped stand, a meter scale, a screen and a spirit level.

Theory/Principle

Nature and Size of Image Formed by a Convex Lens

A convex lens is also called as converging lens. The position, nature and size of the image of an object formed by a thin convex lens depends upon the position of object w.r.t. converging lens.

1. If an object is placed at infinity, i.e. $u = \infty$, a real , inverted and highly diminished image is formed at the second principal focus F_2 on the other side of the lens, i.e. $v = f$.
2. If an object is placed in between infinity and $2F_1$ of the lens (or beyond the $2F_1$ of the lens), i.e. $\infty > u > 2f$, a real, inverted and diminished image of the object is formed in between F_2 and $2F_2$ on the other side of the lens, i.e. $f < v < 2f$.
3. If an object is placed exactly at the $2F_1$ of the lens, i.e. $u = 2f_1$, a real and inverted image of the object is formed at $2F_2$ on the other side of the lens, i.e. $v = 2f$. In this situation, the size of the image is equal to the size of the object.
4. If an object is placed in between the $2F_1$ and F_1 of the lens, i.e. $f < u < 2f$, a real, inverted and enlarged image beyond the $2F_2$ (or in between $2F_2$ and infinity) on the other side of lens is formed.
   i.e. $$2f < v < \infty.$$
5. If an object is placed at the first principal focus F_1 of the lens, i.e. $u = f$, a highly enlarged, real and inverted image is formed at the infinity on the other side of the lens, i.e. $v = \infty$.
6. If an object is placed in between the first principal focus F_1 and optical centre O of the lens, i.e. $f > u > 0$, an enlarged, virtual and erect image of the lens is formed on the same side of the lens.

Note In all the six cases , we have seen that the rays coming from the object converge at a single point. For both real and virtual images, the same mechanism is involved. Therefore, the convex lens is also called as **converging lens.**

Procedure

Determination of Rough Focal Length of Convex Lens

1. First of all find the rough or approximate focal length of convex lens by following the steps (1) to (3) given in Experiment 3 of section B.

Setting up the Apparatus

2. Place the optical bench on a horizontal table and check the level of the optical bench whether it is horizontal or not. If it is not so then set it horizontally by using levelling screws and spirit level.
3. Fix an upright holding a convex lens LL' and adjust it approximately in the middle of the optical bench, such that its principal axis is horizontal and parallel to the meter scale of the optical bench. In this position, the lens would lie in a plane perpendicular to the table.
4. Now, fix another upright holding the lighted candle vertically over the optical bench. Place this upright on the left hand side of the lens.
5. Adjust the height of upright holding the candle such that the tip of the lighted candle lies on the principal axis of the lens. At this position, the height of the tip of the flame of lighted candle becomes equal to the height of the optical centre of the lens.
6. On the other side of the lens, fix an upright holding a screen (or cardboard screen).
7. Also adjust the height of the upright holding a screen so that the tip of the lighted candle, optical centre of the convex lens and centre of the screen lie in a same horizontal line.

Observing the Nature and Size of the Image of the Lighted Candle

8. As it is not possible to place the upright holding the lighted candle at the infinite distance from the convex lens so adjust the upright holding the lighted candle (from left side of the lens) to a point slightly away from $2F_1$ (i.e. to a distance slightly more than $2f$ from the point O, where f is the focal length of the lens determined in step 1).
9. Now, observe the screen, the image of lighted candle will be formed at a position closer to the second principal focus F_2 on the right hand side of the lens.
10. Over the optical bench, adjust the position of the screen near to the second principal focus F_2 of the lens.
11. Make final adjustments to get a sharp image of the lighted candle on the screen. Observe the nature of the image. A real, inverted and highly diminished image will be formed.

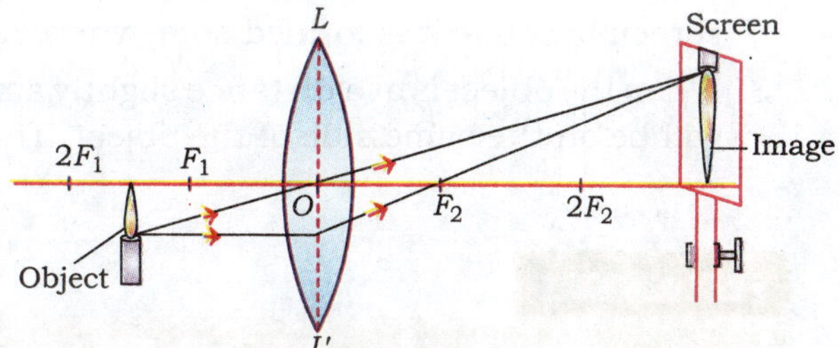

Real image of a lighted candle formed by a thin convex lens

12. Measure the height of the flame of the lighted candle using a small plane mirror strip with a graph paper strip pasted on it. Also measure the height of the image of the flame being formed on the screen. For this, fix a small graph paper on the screen. Alternatively, fix a white paper on the screen and mark the positions of the top and bottom of the image and determine the height of the image using a meter scale.
13. Shift the lighted candle towards the lens by a small distance (say by 5 cm or 3 cm). Repeat the steps (11) and (12) and record observations. In this manner, take at least six sets of observations.
14. Keep on adjusting the upright holding the lighted candle, when it lies in between $2F$ and F of the lens, then the real, inverted and magnified image of the candle will be formed beyond $2F$ on the other side of the lens provided the position of the upright holding the convex lens is not disturbed.

    If you further keep on adjusting the lighted candle and it comes to the position F, then the image of the candle will not be seen on the screen so that it is assumed to be formed at infinity.

15. Set the upright holding the lighted candle between F and optical centre of the lens. At this position of the candle, an enlarged, virtual and erect image will be formed beyond $2F$ of the lens on the same side of the lens, where the lighted candle is placed.

Observations

1. Rough focal length of the convex lens = ...cm.
2. Size of the candle flame ≈ ......cm.

Table for Characteristics of Image with Different Positions of Object

S.N.	Position of lens (cm)	Position of candle (cm)	Position of image on the screen (cm)	Nature of image	Size of image relative to the object (cm)
1					
2					
3					
4					
5					
6					

Result

1. As the object is moved towards the focus of the lens, the size of image increases and it moves away from the focus. The images formed are on the other side of the lens. These images are real and inverted.
2. At the moment, when the object is too close to the lens, the image cannot be found on the screen because it is formed somewhere at infinity.
3. When the object is at a distance slightly smaller than the focal length, then the image formed will be on the same side of the object. The image will be virtual, enlarged and erect.

PRECAUTIONS

1. *Perform this activity at shaded place otherwise the images may not be distinctly visible.*
2. *While measuring the rough focal length of lens by focusing the sun, do not look on the image of the sun directly as it may hurt your eyes.*
3. *The optical bench on which the uprights holding lighted candle, lens and screen are mounted should be levelled horizontally.*
4. *The tip of the candle flame, optical centre of the lens and centre of the screen should lie in a horizontal line.*
5. *The position of the uprights holding the lens should not be disturbed throughout the experiment.*
6. *The aperture of the lens must be small otherwise the image formed will not be distinct.*
7. *Eye should be kept at a distance more than 25 cm from the image formed on the screen.*

Viva-Voce

Q 1 Define refraction of light.

Ans. When a ray of light passes from one medium to the other, it bends from its path. This phenomenon of bending of light is called refraction of light.

Q 2 What do you mean by a convex lens?

Ans. A lens which is thick at the centre but thinner at the edges is called convex lens.

Q 3 If an object is placed at the infinity from a convex lens, then where is the image formed?

Ans. At the principal focus on the other side of the lens.

Q 4 Out of convex lens and concave lens, which lens is converging?

Ans. Convex lens is converging in nature.

Q 5 Why is a convex mirror preferred as a rear view mirror?

Ans. It provides a wider field of view compared to a plane mirror.

Q 6 How is a convex mirror different from a concave mirror?

Ans. The concave mirror is polished on the side facing the centre of curvature, while the convex mirror is polished on the side opposite to the centre of curvature.

Q 7 How does the size of image formed by convex lens vary as the burning candle is moved from one end of the table to the lens? [NCERT]

Ans. The size of image is inversely proportional to the distance of object from the optical centre of convex lens. So, as the burning candle is moved from one end of the table towards the lens, the size of image increases gradually.

Q 8 What should be the position of the object to get the image on the same side of the lens as the object? [NCERT]

Ans. The object should be placed between F and optical centre of the lens.

Q 9 Where should the object be placed to get a virtual and erect image of the object? [NCERT]

Ans. The object should be placed between F and optical centre of the lens.

Q 10 How does the position of image formed by a convex lens vary as the burning candle is moved along the principal axis of the lens from infinity to its focus? [NCERT]

Ans. The position of image w.r.t. lens goes on increasing as the burning candle is moved from infinity to the focus of lens along the principal axis.

Q 11 What will be the position of the object to get a real image having the same size as that of object? [NCERT]

Ans. The object must be placed at $2F$, so that its image formed on the other side of the lens should have same size as that of object.

Activity 6b

AIM

To study the nature and size of an image formed by a concave mirror on a screen by using a candle and a screen (for different distances of candle from the mirror).

Apparatus and Material Required

A concave mirror of focal length nearly 25 cm, a candle, optical bench with three uprights, a match box, spirit level, a meter scale and a cardboard screen having rectangular slot.

Theory/Principle

Nature and Size of Image Formed by a Concave Mirror

The characteristics of the images formed by a concave mirror depend upon the position of object from the reflecting surface of the mirror. The following are the cases of images formed of an object placed at different distances from the concave mirror.

1. When an object is placed at infinity, i.e. $u = \infty$, a real, inverted and highly diminished image is formed at the principal focus of the concave mirror, i.e. $v = f$.
2. When an object is placed in between infinity and centre of curvature of the concave mirror, i.e. $\infty > u > 2f$, a real, inverted and diminished image is formed in between the centre of curvature C and principal focus F of the concave mirror, i.e. $2f > v > f$.
3. When an object is placed at the centre of curvature of the concave mirror, i.e. $u = 2f$, a real and inverted image of same size as that of the object is formed at the centre of curvature of the concave mirror, i.e. $v = 2f$.
4. When an object is placed in between the centre of curvature and principal focus of the concave mirror, i.e. $2f > u > f$, a real, enlarged and inverted image of the object is formed in between the infinity and centre of curvature of the concave mirror, i.e. $\infty > v > 2f$.
5. When an object is placed at the principal focus of the concave mirror, i.e. $u = f$, a highly enlarged, real and inverted image of the object is formed at infinity, i.e. $v = \infty$.
6. When an object is placed in between the principal focus and centre or pole of the concave mirror, i.e. $f > u > 0$, an enlarged, virtual and erect image is formed behind the mirror.

Note A real image is one through which the rays of light actually pass after reflection from concave mirror. It is always inverted and can be formed on the screen. A virtual image is one through which the rays do not actually pass, although they appear to come from it. A virtual image is always erect.

Procedure

Determination of Rough Focal Length of Concave Mirror

1. First of all find the rough or approximate focal length of concave mirror by following the steps (1) and (2) given in Experiment 1.

Setting up the Apparatus

2. Place the optical bench on a horizontal table and by using spirit level, check the level of optical bench whether it is horizontal or not. If it is not so, then set it horizontally by using levelling screws.

3. Fix an upright holding the concave mirror over the optical bench and adjust this upright near the zero mark of the scale of the optical bench (or on the one end of the optical bench).
4. Now, fix an another upright holding a lighted candle near the other end of the optical bench.
5. Place the third upright holding the cardboard screen having rectangular slot in between the lighted candle and concave mirror.
6. Adjust the heights of three uprights so that the tip of the flame of the candle, upper edge of the cardboard screen and centre or pole of the concave mirror lie in a horizontal line and parallel to the length of the optical bench.

Note It should be ensured that all uprights must be placed vertically over the optical bench.

When Lighted Candle is Placed at Infinity Position

7. As it not possible to find the infinite position of lighted candle, so place the lighted candle on the extreme position of the optical bench, i.e. beyond $2F$ of the concave mirror.
8. Now, observe the screen, the image of lighted candle will be formed at a position closer to the principal focus F of the concave mirror.
9. Shift the position of the screen near to the principal focus. When the screen comes to the position F (or principal focus) of the concave mirror exactly, a real, inverted and highly diminished image of the lighted candle is formed on the screen.
10. Read the position of the mirror, screen and lighted candle uprights on the optical bench meter scale and record the readings in the observation table.
11. Measure the height of the lighted candle and its image by following the step (12) of Activity 6(a).

When the Candle Lies Beyond the Centre of Curvature of the Mirror

12. Now, move the lighted candle towards the mirror and also move the screen away from the mirror. When the lighted candle lies beyond the centre of curvature C of the mirror and the screen lies in between C and F, a real, inverted and diminished image of the candle is formed on the screen.

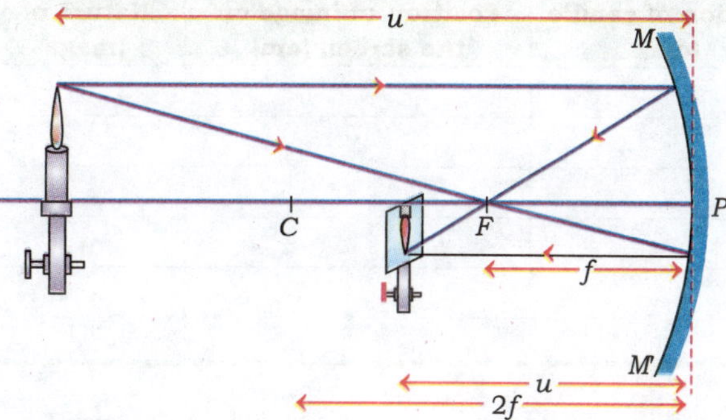

Formation of image of the lighted candle when it lies beyond the centre of curvature of the mirror

13. Adjust the position of the screen to get a sharp image. Repeat the steps (10) and (11) and note your observations.

When Candle Lies at Centre of Curvature of the Mirror

14. Bring the lighted candle at C (or centre of curvature of the mirror). Shift the position of the screen from the principal focus F on the optical bench. One has to use the rough value of focal length measured in step (1).

15. Make final adjustments to get a sharp image of the lighted candle on the screen. When the screen comes to the point F, a real and inverted image of same size as that of the lighted candle is formed.

Note When the lighted candle is placed at point C, its image is formed at the same point. But it is not possible to observe the image at the same point (or point where the candle itself has been placed), so one can use a tabular bulb parallel to the upper edge of the slot of the cardboard screen.

16. By repeating the steps (10) and (11), note your observations.

When Candle Lies in between Centre of Curvature and Principal Focus of the Mirror

17. Bring the candle in between C and F, the image of the candle will be formed beyond the point C. At this time, the image is not formed in between the candle and the mirror, so that an ordinary cardboard may be used to observe the image of the candle. A real, inverted and enlarged image is formed on the screen beyond the centre of curvature of the mirror.
18. Repeat the steps (10) and (11) and note your observations.

When Candle Lies in between Principal Focus and Pole of the Mirror

19. Place the candle at point F (or principal focus of the mirror). The image of the lighted candle cannot be studied at this position of the candle, so that the image is assumed to be formed at infinity.

When Candle Lies at Principal Focus of the Mirror

20. Bring the candle in between F and P (or principal focus and pole) of the mirror, a virtual image of the candle is formed behind the concave mirror. As the image is virtual, so that it cannot be taken on the screen.
21. Note your observations in the tabular form.

Observations

Rough focal length of concave mirror = ... cm

Table for Characteristics of Image for Different Positions of Object

S.N.	Position of concave mirror (cm)	Position of candle (cm)	Position of image on the screen (cm)	Nature of image	Size of image relative to the object (cm)
1					
2					
3					
4					
5					
6					

Result

Observations on the nature, size and position of image show that

1. As the position of candle changes, the change in characteristics of image is observed.
2. As the object moves towards the focus, its image is moved away from the focus.
3. The size of image increases as it moves away from the concave mirror.
4. If the object is placed between infinity and principal focus of mirror, then the image formed by the concave mirror is real and inverted.

5. If the object is placed between focus and pole of concave mirror, then the image is formed behind the concave mirror and it is virtual, erect and enlarged.

PRECAUTIONS

1. While measuring the rough focal length of the mirror by focusing the sun, do not look on the image directly, it may hurt your eyes.
2. The tip of the flame of the candle, upper edge of the cardboard screen and centre of the mirror should lie on a same horizontal line.
3. The aperture of mirror should be small otherwise the image formed will not be distinct.
4. The concave mirror should be front-coated otherwise multiple reflections may take place which may confuse in estimating the position of image.
5. All uprights must be vertical.

Viva-Voce

Q. 1 Define spherical mirror.

Ans. A reflecting portion which is cut from a hollow sphere of glass whose one surface is polished is called a spherical mirror.

Q. 2 How many types a spherical mirror has?

Ans. A spherical mirror has two types

(i) concave mirror

(ii) convex mirror

Q.3 How can we identify a spherical mirror as convex mirror?

Ans. When the reflecting surface of a spherical mirror is bulging out, then the mirror is said to be a convex one.

Q 4 What do you mean by a real image?

Ans. A real image is formed due to actual intersection of reflected light. A real image can be formed on the screen.

Q 5 The focal length of concave mirror is 20 cm, what is the radius of curvature? [NCERT]

Ans. $\because$ $R = 2f$ and $f = 20$ cm (given)

$\therefore$ $R = 2 \times 20 = 40$ cm

Q 6 What is the effect on the size and intensity of the image formed when the lower half of concave mirror is painted black? [NCERT]

Ans. The size of image will be same while the intensity reduces to half of the original one.

Q 7 Is it possible to get virtual image on the screen? [NCERT]

Ans. No

Q 8 In a similar experiment using lenses, the images look a little coloured unlike this experiment? Mention its reason. [NCERT]

Ans. Because the lens is assumed to be made up of infinite number of prisms, so the phenomenon of splitting of light may create some colour in the image.

Activity 07

AIM

To obtain a lens combination with the specified focal length by using two lenses from a given set of lenses.

Apparatus and Material Required

A set of thin convex lenses of known powers, optical bench with uprights, screen, a collimator to provide a parallel beam of light, spirit level and a half meter scale.

Theory/Principle

Focal Length of the Lens

The distance between principal focus and optical centre of the lens is called the focal length of the lens (f).

Power of the Lens

The ability of a lens to converge or diverge the rays passing through it, is called the power of the lens (P). Mathematically, the power of the lens is defined as the reciprocal of its focal length.

$$\therefore \quad \text{Power, } P = \frac{1}{f}$$

Focal Length and Power of Lens Combination

Two or more lenses placed in contact together so that their principal axes is common, then this arrangement is called the **lens combination**. If $f_1, f_2, f_3, \ldots, f_n$ be the focal lengths of individual lenses and f be the focal length of their combination, then

$$\frac{1}{f} = \frac{1}{f_1} + \frac{1}{f_2} + \frac{1}{f_3} + \ldots + \frac{1}{f_n}$$

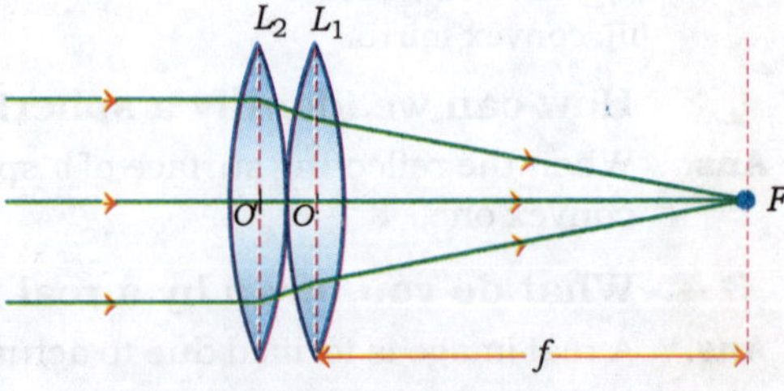

Parallel beam of light focusing on the combination of two lenses

So, the power of lens combination is given by

$$P = P_1 + P_2 + P_3 + \ldots + P_n$$

where, $P_1, P_2, P_3, \ldots, P_n$ are the powers of individual lenses.

If two lenses are combined together, then focal length of combination is $\frac{1}{f} = \frac{1}{f_1} + \frac{1}{f_2}$

The power of this combination is given by $P = P_1 + P_2$

Procedure

Selection of Convex Lenses

1. First of all, calculate the power of the combination of two lenses corresponding to the required focal length. Select a convex lens from a given set of convex lenses whose power is smaller than that of the combination of lenses.

2. Calculate the power of unknown convex lens to be kept in contact with lens of known focal length to obtain a combination of lenses of desired focal length. From the given set of lenses, select the lens whose power is close to the calculated power.

Note If the focal length of an individual lens is not known, then one does not need to get confused because the power of a lens can be calculated by using the relation $P = \frac{1}{f}$, where f is the focal length of a lens which can be roughly measured by focusing the image of a distant object such as building, tree, etc., on a plane wall or a sheet of paper placed on the other side of the lens.

Setting up the Apparatus

3. Set up the optical bench on a horizontal table. By using spirit level, check the level of the table whether it is horizontal or not. If it is not so, then with the help of levelling screws, set it horizontally.
4. Place the upright holding a collimator on the one end of the optical bench and ensure that a parallel beam of light will be directed along the optical bench.

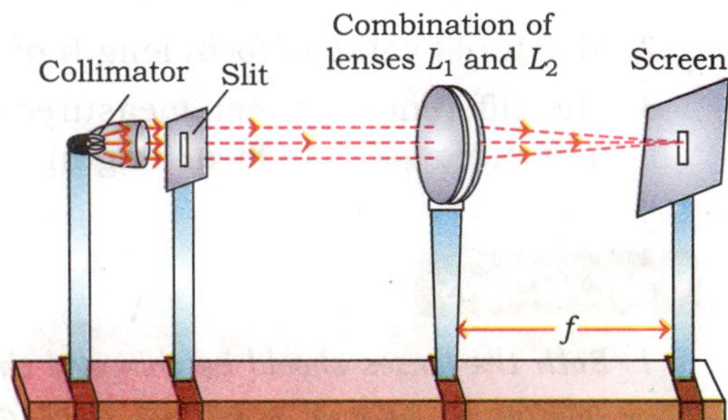

Experimental setup for finding the focal length of combination of two convex lenses

5. Place an upright holding the two selected convex lenses L_1 and L_2 on the middle of the optical bench. Ensure that the two lenses are in contact with each other.
6. Now, place an another upright holding a slit in between collimator and lenses in such a way that a parallel beam of light can easily pass through the slit. Place an upright holding a screen on the other side of the lenses (or on the other end of the optical bench).

Determination of Focal Length of Lens Combination

7. Switch ON the collimator, so that the parallel beam of light can be directed on the combination of lenses *via* a narrow slit.
8. Observe the screen placed on the other side of the lenses. An image is formed on the screen.
9. Adjust the distance between the combination of lenses and screen, thereby a sharply focused image can be obtained. Measure the distance of screen from both the lenses and calculate their mean. This mean distance will give you the **focal length of lens combination**.
10. Repeat the steps (7) to (9) at least three times by changing the position of upright holding the lens combination (say 2-3 cm each time) on the optical bench.

Observations and Calculations

1. Least count of scale of optical bench = ... mm
2. Focal length of first lens $L_1 = f_1 = \ldots$ cm
3. Focal length of second lens $L_2 = f_2 = \ldots$cm
4. Focal length of lens combination, $f = \frac{f_1 f_2}{f_1 + f_2}$

Table for Focal Length of Combination of Two Convex Lenses

S.N.	Distance of lens L_1 from the screen, d_1 (cm)	Distance of lens L_2 from the screen, d_2 (cm)	Mean distance, $d = \frac{d_1 + d_2}{2} = f$ (cm)
1			$f_1 = \ldots$cm
2			$f_2 = \ldots$cm
3			$f_3 = \ldots$cm

Find the focal length for each set of observation then take the mean of all values of focal length.

Focal length, $f = \dfrac{f_1 + f_2 + f_3}{3} = ...\text{cm}$

Result

1. Focal length of combination of two lenses having focal lengths of f_1 and f_2 in contact, $f = \dfrac{f_1 f_2}{f_1 + f_2} = ...\text{ cm}$
2. Measured value of focal length of lens combination = ... cm
3. The difference between measured value and calculated value of focal length (or error in the measured value of focal length) = ... cm

PRECAUTIONS

1. *Both the lenses should be thin and they should have same aperture. Also, the lenses should be placed in such a way that their axes lie on the same straight line. Before using the optical bench, it should be set horizontally by using spirit level and levelling screws.*
2. *For each set of observations, the change in position of upright holding the lens should be very small (say 2 to 3 cm only).*
3. *The power of the selected convex lens should be smaller than that of the combination of lenses.*
4. *The incident beam must be parallel beam of Light.*
5. *The combination of the two lenses must be converging.*
6. *The image formed by the individual lenses or combination on the screen must be sharp.*

Viva-Voce

Q 1 Differentiate thick convex lens and thin convex lens on the basis of their focal lengths.

Ans. The focal length of thin convex lens is greater than that of a thick one.

Q 2 What are the factors on which the focal length of a lens depends?

Ans. The factors on which the focal length of a lens depends are

(i) Radii of curvature of surface of the lens

(ii) Refractive index of material of the lens

(iii) Colour of incident light

Q 3 If a convex lens is dipped completely in the water, what will be the effect on its focal length?

Ans. If the convex lens is dipped completely in water, the focal length of convex lens becomes four times than that in air medium.

Q 4 If two lenses of focal lengths f_1 and f_2 are placed at a distance d apart, then what will be the formula for effective focal length?

Ans. $\dfrac{1}{f} = \dfrac{1}{f_1} + \dfrac{1}{f_2} - \dfrac{d}{f_1 f_2}$

This focal length is greater than the focal length obtained by lenses in contact.

Project 01

AIM

To study various factors on which the internal resistance or emf of a cell depends.

Apparatus and Material Required

A potentiometer, a battery, three one-way keys, a rheostat of low resistance, a high resistance box (0 -10 kΩ), a fractional resistance box, a galvanometer, a jockey, an ammeter, a voltmeter, a voltaic cell (primary cell), electrolytes of different concentrations, connecting wires and sand paper.

Terms Related To Project

Internal Resistance (r) It is the resistance offered by the electrolyte of a cell to the flow of current through it.

Electromotive Force (E) It is the potential difference of a cell in an open circuit, i.e. when no current is drawn from it. It is type of force that causes or tends to cause a current to flow in a circuit. It is equivalent to the potential difference between the terminals and is commonly measured in volts.

Theory/Principle

Principle of Potentiometer

If a steady current I is flowing through a wire of uniform cross-section, then the potential difference across any portion of the wire is directly proportional to the length of that portion.

i.e. $$V \propto l \Rightarrow \frac{V}{l} = K$$

where, K = potential gradient (i.e. potential per unit length of wire).
The internal resistance of a cell depends on

(a) distance between the plates (electrodes)
(b) common area of the electrodes immersed in the electrolyte
(c) concentration of the electrolyte

Procedure

1. Prepare a cell filled with an electrolyte of given concentration as shown in the figure 1.
2. Arrange the circuit diagram to determine the internal resistance of a primary cell as shown in the figure 1.

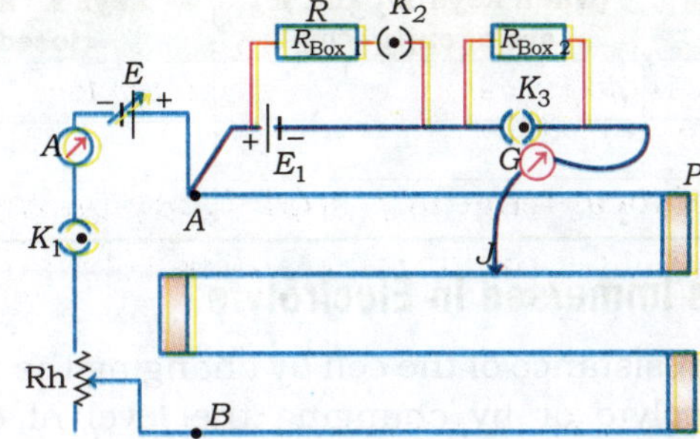

Fig.1 Circuit to measure internal resistance of a primary cell

Determination of Internal Resistance of a Cell

3. After checking the circuit connections close key K_1.
4. Keep keys K_2 and K_3 open and remove a high resistance key from resistance box $R_{Box\,2}$. Find the position of balance point l_2.
5. Now, close key K_3 to short circuit the resistance p and find the balanced point l_1.
6. Take $R = 10\Omega$ from $R_{Box\,1}$, close the key K_2 and quickly measure the new balance point l_2. Open key K_2 as soon as this has been done.
7. Keep the ammeter reading constant through out the above observation.
8. Reduce the value of R in steps of $1\,\Omega$ and for each value of R obtain the balanced point l_2.
9. Substitute the value of l_1, l_2 and R in equaiton

$$r = \frac{l_1 - l_2}{l} R$$

and calculate the internal resistance.

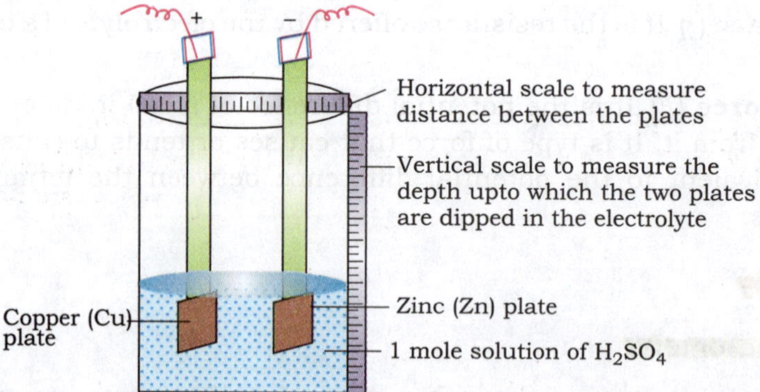

Fig. 2 Voltaic cell with an electrolyte of given concentration

Observations and Calculations

Effect of Separation Between the Plates

Determine the internal resistance of the cell for different separations between the plates with the same electrolyte. Keep the same area of plate immersed in the electrolyte throughout the observations. Record the observations in the following table.

Table for Effect on Internal Resistance by Changing the Separation between the Plates

S.N.	Separation between the plates (cm)	Resistance, $R\,(\Omega)$	Balancing length		Internal resistance, $r = \left(\frac{l_1 - l_2}{l_2}\right) R\,(\Omega)$
			Open circuit (when keys K_2 and K_3 are open) l_1 (cm)	Closed circuit (when keys K_2 and K_3 are closed) l_2 (cm)	
1					
2					
3					

Effect of Area of Plates Immersed in Electrolyte

Determine the internal resistance of the cell by changing the depth upto which the two plates are immersed in the electrolyte or by changing the level of electrolyte in the cell. Record the observations in the below table.

Table for Effect on the Internal Resistance of the Cell by Changing the Area of the Plates Immersed in the Electrolyte

S.N.	Length of the plates immersed in the electrolyte (cm)	Resistance, R (Ω)	Balancing length		Internal resistance, $r = \left(\frac{l_1 - l_2}{l_2}\right) R$ (Ω)
			Open circuit (when keys K_2 and K_3 are open) l_1 (cm)	Closed circuit (when keys K_2 and K_3 are closed) l_2 (cm)	
1					
2					
3					

Effect of Concentration of Electrolyte

Determine the internal resistance of the cell by filling it with the electrolyte of given concentration. Maintain a constant distance between two plates for the same area immersed in the electrolyte. Repeat the procedure with electrolytes of varying concentrations by keeping the level of electrolyte constant in each case. Record the observations in the below table.

Table for the Effect on the Internal Resistance of the Cell with Varying Concentration of Electrolyte

S.N.	Concentration of electrolyte (mole)	Resistance, R (Ω)	Balancing length		Internal resistance, $r = \left(\frac{l_1 - l_2}{l_2}\right) R$ (Ω)
			Open circuit (when keys K_2 and K_3 are open) l_1 (cm)	Closed circuit (when keys K_2 and K_3 are closed) l_2 (cm)	
1					
2					
3					

Result

1. The internal resistance of a cell increases with increase in distance between the electrodes.
2. Internal resistance increases with decrease in common area of plates immersed in the electrolyte.
3. Internal resistance increases with decrease in concentration of electrolyte.

PRECAUTIONS

1. *Before using the connecting wires, their ends should be cleaned with the help of sand paper.*
2. *All the connections should be tight.*
3. *The emf of cell (E_l) should not be greater than the emf of battery (E). Always $E > E_l$.*
4. *Positive terminal of both E and E_l should be connected to the zero end, i.e. end A of potentiometer wire. Do not pass the current for long time, so as to avoid heating effect. The heating of wire may cause a change in the resistance.*

Viva-Voce

Q 1 Why do we use rheostat in the main circuit?

Ans. By adjusting the rheostat slider, a null point is obtained in the last segment of potentiometer wire. Thus, we get a large balancing length which increases the accuracy of measurement.

Q 2 If the galvanometer pointer deflects in one direction only, then what would be the reason behind it?

Ans. The pointer deflects in one direction only due to the reason that either the positive terminal of the battery and cell are not connected to the zero end of the wire or the potential drop across the wire is less than the emf to be balanced.

Q 3 Why alkali accumulator is better than the lead accumulator?

Ans. Alkali accumulator is better because of the following reasons

(i) It can withstand rough heating.

(ii) It is lighter, stronger and more durable than the lead accumulator.

(iii) It is not damaged due to over charging or over discharging.

Q 4 Why should the emf of primary cell E_1 be less than the emf of auxiliary battery E?

Ans. If E_1 will be greater than E, then the balance point will not be obtained.

Q 5 In what way, we can increase the sensitivity of potentiometer?

Ans. By reducing the potential drop per unit length of potentiometer wire, we can increase the sensitivity of potentiometer.

Q 6 Define the sensitivity of a potentiometer.

Ans. A potentiometer is considered more sensitive, if it can accurately measure a small fall in potential difference.

Q 7 Why do we keep the temperature of electrolyte constant throughout the experiment?

Ans. The temperature of the electrolyte is kept constant because the internal resistance of the cell varies with temperature.

Q 8 You are given with cells *A* and *B*. Cell *A* is freshly prepared and cell *B* has been in use for some time. Which of the two has less internal resistance? [NCERT]

Ans. Cell *A* is freshly prepared and cell *B* has been in use for some time. Here the electrolyte of cell *B* is less than that of cell *A*. So, the internal resistance of cell *B* is greater than that of cell *A*, because the internal resistance is inversely proportional to the concentration of electrolyte.

Project 02

AIM

To study the variation in current flowing in a circuit containing an LDR because of a variation in

(i) the power of incandescent lamp, used to illuminate the LDR (keeping all the lamps at fixed distance).

(ii) the distance of incandescent lamp (of fixed power) used to illuminate the LDR.

Apparatus and Material Required

LDR, a source of light (as bulbs of 20 W, 40 W, 60 W and 100 W), a 6 V battery, a multimeter, a meter scale, two clamps.

Theory/Principle

Same as Activity 3 of Section B.

Procedure

1. To study the variation in current flowing in a circuit containing an LDR because of a variation in the distance of incandescent lamp used to illuminate the LDR, refer the same procedure given in Activity 3 of Section B.
2. Now use a 20W bulb in lamp clamped vertically facing LDR.
3. Switch ON the lamp and measure the resistance of LDR by following the steps (7) to (11) given in Activity 3 of Section B.
4. Repeat the steps (2) and (3) by placing bulb of 40 W, 60 W, 80 W and 100 W.
5. Note your observations in the tabular form.

Observations and Calculations

1. Range of milliammeter = 0 to ......mA 2. Least count of milliammeter = ...mA

3. Range of voltmeter = 0 to ......V 4. Least count of voltmeter = ...V

Table for Variation in Resistance of LDR with Distance

S. N.	Distance between LDR and source d (cm)	Voltmeter reading, V (V)	Milliammeter reading, I (mA)	LDR resistance due to background illumination, R' (Ω)	Resistance of LDR, $R = \frac{V}{I}$ (Ω)	Actual value of resistance, $(R + R')$Ω
1						
2						
3						
4						

Table for Determination of Current and Resistance for Different Power Bulbs having Constant Distance from LDR

S.No.	Power of the bulb	Current, I (mA)	LDR resistance due to background illumination, R'	Resistance, $R = \frac{V}{I}$ (Ω)	Actual value of resistance, $(R + R')$Ω
1	20 W				
2	40 W				
3	60 W				
4	80 W				
5	100 W				

Result

1. The electric current flowing through a circuit containing LDR increases with decrease in distance between bulb and LDR as concluded from first table.
2. The electric current flowing through a circuit containing LDR increases with increase in power (thus intensity) of bulb as concluded from second table.

PRECAUTIONS

Same as Activity 3 of Section B.

Sources of Error

Same as Activity 3 of Section B.

Q 1 What do you mean by an LDR?

Ans. LDR stands for light dependent resistor. The resistance of LDR vary with the intensity of light falling on it.

Q 2 What are the materials required for preparing an LDR?

Ans. Generally, we use cadmium sulphide (CdS) to prepare LDR. Also, cadmium selenide, thallium sulphide, etc., are used for making LDR depending on their applications.

Q 3 An LDR has a high resistance. Why?

Ans. The presence of high resistance will lock the majority of electrons into the crystal lattice, so the electrons are not free to move from the crystal lattice.

Q 4 How is the intensity of incident light varied?

Ans. The intensity of incident light can be varied in the following ways

(i) By changing the distance of source from the exposed surface.

(ii) By changing the power of source of light.

Q 5 What should be the resistance of a typical LDR in total darkness?

Ans. Few megaohms (~10 MΩ)

Q 6 What happens when light falls on an LDR?

Ans. When a light falls on the surface of a LDR, some of the electrons get sufficient energy to break free from crystal lattice and hence, the electrons are free to move across the crystal lattice to conduct electricity.

Project 03

AIM

To find the refractive indices of

(a) water

(b) oil (transparent)

using a plane mirror, an equiconvex lens (made from a glass of known refractive index) and an adjustable object needle.

Apparatus and Material Required

A plane mirror, a convex lens, clean water, transparent oil (kerosene oil), retort stand with clamp, optical needle, plumb line, a half meter scale, a dropper.

Theory/Principle

Same as Experiment 7.

Procedure

1. To determine the radius of curvature of convex lens, follow the procedure given in Experiment 7 (Section B).
2. To determine the focal length of water lens and hence to find the refractive index of water, follow the procedure given in Experiment 7 (Section B).
3. Next, follow the same procedure but use transparent oil this time instead of water.

Observations

Same as Experiment 7 (Section B).

Calculations

Same as Experiment 7 (Section B).

Result

1. Refractive index of water, $\mu_w = 1 + \frac{R}{f_w} = \ldots$

2. Refractive index of kerosene oil, $\mu_o = 1 + \frac{R}{f_o} = \ldots$

where, f_w = focal length of water lens, f_o = focal length of oil lens

PRECAUTIONS

Same as Experiment 7.

Sources of Error

Same as Experiment 7.

Viva-Voce

Q 1 What do you mean by refractive index?

Ans. It is defined as the ratio of velocity of light in vacuum to that in medium.

$$\mu = \frac{\text{Velocity of light in vacuum}}{\text{Velocity of light in medium}}$$

Q 2 Name the device used to measure the refractive index of a liquid directly.

Ans. Refractometer

Q 3 What is the relation between refractive index and critical angle?

Ans. $\mu = \frac{1}{\sin C}$, where

C = critical angle.

Q 4 How can we identify a liquid?

Ans. The refractive index is a characteristic property of substance. If we know the exact value of refractive index of any material, then we can easily identify the substance .

Q 5 Which instrument is used to measure the radius of curvature of lens?

Ans. The radius of curvature of lens is measured by using spherometer.

Q 6 Which factors influence the refractive index of a medium?

Ans. It depends upon

(i) wavelength of light

(ii) nature of medium

(iii) temperature.

Q 7 Which medium allows light to travel faster, water or glass?

Ans. Light travels faster in water because it has a lower refractive index (μ = 1.33 for water, compared to μ = 1.5 for glass).

Project 04

AIM

To investigate the relation between the ratio of (i) output and input voltage and (ii) number of turns in the secondary coil and primary coil of self-designed transformer.

Apparatus and Material Required

A soft iron rod, copper wires of different cross-sections, two AC ammeters and two AC voltmeters.

Theory/Principle

Transformer

A transformer is an electrical device used for changing the AC voltage. A transformer which increases the AC voltage is called step-up transformer, whereas a transformer which decreases AC voltage is called step-down transformer.

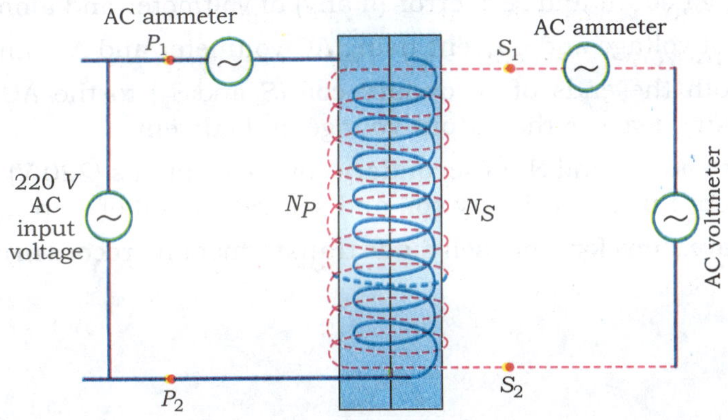

A self designed transformer

Working Principle of Transformer

A transformer is based on the principle of mutual induction, i.e. the alternating current passing through the primary coil creates a continuous changing flux through the core. This changing flux induces an alternating emf in the secondary coil. Consider an ideal transformer whose all the flux is linked with the primary and secondary windings of the core as shown in the figure.

The emf induced in the primary coil is given by

$$E_P = -N_P \frac{d\phi}{dt} \quad \text{...(i)}$$

The emf induced in the secondary coil is given by

$$E_S = -N_S \frac{d\phi}{dt} \quad \text{...(ii)}$$

where, ϕ is the magnetic flux linked with each turn of primary and secondary coil at a time t.

Dividing Eq. (ii) by Eq. (i), we get transformer ratio (K).

$$\therefore \quad \frac{E_S}{E_P} = \frac{N_S}{N_P} = K \quad \text{...(iii)}$$

For an ideal transformer there is no loss of energy. So, the output power should be equal to the input power.

$$\therefore \quad I_P E_P = I_S E_S$$

$$\frac{I_P}{I_S} = \frac{E_S}{E_P} = K \qquad \text{...(iv)}$$

Procedure

Making of Transformer

1. Take a soft iron rod and cover it with a thick paper.
2. Wound a large number of turns of thin copper wire around thick paper, so as to prepare a primary coil of transformer.
3. With the help of sheet of paper, cover the primary coil and wound relatively smaller number of turns of thick copper wire on it, so as to prepare a secondary coil of step-down transformer.

Testing the Working of Transformer

4. Connect both the ends of primary coil (P_1 and P_2) to a 220 V AC mains.
5. Note down the least count and zero error (if any) of voltmeter and ammeter.
6. Measure the input voltage and current using AC voltmeter and AC ammeter respectively.
7. Next, connect both the ends of secondary coil (S_1 and S_2) to the AC voltmeter and AC ammeter and again measure the output voltage and current.
8. Now, connect the ends S_1 and S_2 of secondary coil to AC mains (220 V) and again measure voltage and current through primary coil and secondary coil of step-up transformer.
9. Repeat all the above steps for other self made transformer and record in observation table.

Observations

For Voltmeter

1. AC voltage = ... V
2. LC (Least Count) of AC voltmeter = ... V
3. Zero error of voltmeter = ... V
4. Range of voltmeter = 0 to ... V

For Ammeter

5. LC (Least Count) of AC ammeter = ... A
6. Zero error of ammeter = ... A
7. Range of ammeter = 0 to ... A

Table to Investigate the Relation between E_S and E_P and N_S and N_P

S.N.	Number of turns in the primary coil (N_P)	Number of turns in the secondary coil (N_S)	Voltage in primary coil (E_P)	Voltage in secondary coil (E_S)	Current in primary coil (I_P)	Current in secondary coil (I_S)	Power loss
1							
2							
3							
4							
5							

Result

1. The output voltage of the transformer across the secondary coil with respect to input voltage depends on the turn ratio $\frac{N_S}{N_P}$.
2. The output current of the transformer across the secondary coil with respect to input current depends upon the turn ratio $\frac{N_S}{N_P}$.
3. Some loss of power between input and output coil of a transformer is observed.

PRECAUTIONS

1. *The improvised transformer may not have very high efficiency otherwise it may get hot very soon.*
2. *Some special care should be taken while working with AC mains.*
3. *Before winding the turns on iron rod, it should be covered with a sheet of paper.*
4. *The zero error of voltmeter and ammeter should be taken into account.*
5. *Connect transformer to AC mains for short intervals only, otherwise the coil may be burnt due to over-heating.*

Q 1 What do you mean by a transformer?

Ans. A transformer is a device used for converting a low AC voltage to a high AC voltage or *vice-versa*.

Q 2 On which principle, the transformer works?

Ans. A transformer works on the principle of mutual induction.

Q 3 What is step-up transformer?

Ans A transformer which increases the AC voltage is called a step-up transformer.

Q 4 What is a step-down transformer?

Ans. A transformer which decreases the AC voltage is called a step-down transformer.

Q 5 **Define efficiency of a transformer.**

Ans. The efficiency of a transformer is defined as the ratio of output power to the input power,

i.e. efficiency (η) = $\frac{P_{out}}{P_{in}} = \frac{E_s I_s}{E_P I_P}$

Q 6 **What is an ideal transformer?**

Ans. An ideal transformer is one where there is no power loss. For this output, power is equal to the input power. Thus, $\eta = 1$ for ideal transformer.

Q 7 **Define transformer ratio.**

Ans. The ratio of output voltage to the input voltage is the measure of turns ratio or transformer ratio (K).

i.e., $$K = \frac{V_{out}}{V_{in}} = \frac{N_s}{N_P}$$

where, N_s and N_P are number of turns in the secondary and primary coils respectively.

Q 8 **Where do we use a step-up transformer?**

Ans. A step-up transformer is used for production of X-rays and neon advertisement.

Q 9 **Which type of transformer is used for welding purpose?**

Ans. Step-down transformer.

Q 10 **Name the energy losses in transformer.**

Ans. Copper losses, iron losses and flux leakage are the losses in transformer which reduces the efficiency of transformer.

Project 05

AIM

To investigate the dependence of the angle of deviation on the angle of incidence using a hollow prism filled one by one, with different transparent fluids.

Apparatus and Material Required

A drawing board, white sheets of paper, a hollow prism, drawing pins, a pencil, a meter scale, a protractor, graph papers, different liquids such as water, kerosene oil, spirit, etc.

Terms Related to Project

Refer to Experiment 5 given in Section B

Theory/Principle

From Experiment 5 given in Section B, we have $\delta = i + e - A$

where, δ = angle of deviation, i = angle of incidence, A = angle of prism

e = angle of emergence

The minimum value of the angle of deviation suffered by a ray on passing through a prism is called the **angle of minimum deviation** (δ_m). When a prism is in the position of minimum deviation, a ray of light passes symmetrically through the prism, so that

$$i = e, \quad r = r' \quad \text{and} \quad \delta = \delta_m$$

$$\therefore \quad A + \delta_m = i + i \quad \Rightarrow \quad i = \frac{A + \delta_m}{2}$$

Also, $$A = r + r' = 2r \quad \Rightarrow \quad r = \frac{A}{2}$$

From Snell's law, the refractive index of the material of the prism will be

$$\mu = \frac{\sin i}{\sin r} = \frac{\sin\left(\frac{A + \delta_m}{2}\right)}{\sin\left(\frac{A}{2}\right)}$$

Procedure

Follow the steps (1) to (18) given in Experiment 5 of Section B to measure the angle of deviation and to investigate the dependence of angle of deviation on the angle of incidence but with the difference that use a hollow prism filled with a water. Similarly, follow the same procedure by using kerosene oil, spirit and turpentine oil one by one in place of water or liquid.

Observations

Least count of protractor =... degree.

Angle of hollow prism, A =... degree.

Table to Investigate the Dependence of Angle of Deviation on the Angle of Incidence

S. N.	Angle of incidence, i (°)	Angle of deviation δ (°)			
		Water	Kerosene oil	Spirit	Turpentine oil
1	30°				
2	35°				
3	40°				
4	45°				
5	50°				
6	55°				

Plotting Graph

Same as Experiment 5 given in Section B.

Calculation

1. From the graph, find the value of angle of minimum deviation δ_m corresponding to the lowest point of the graph.
2. The refractive index of the transparent medium, $\mu = \dfrac{\sin[(A+\delta_m)/2]}{\sin(A/2)}$
3. The speed of light in a transparent medium, $v = \dfrac{c}{\mu}$

   where, c is speed of light in vacuum= 3×10^8 m/s.

Result

1. The graph between i and δ indicates that as the angle of incidence i increases, the angle of deviation δ first decreases, attains a minimum value δ_m and then starts increasing for further increase in angle of incidence.
2. The angle of minimum deviation for
   (i) Water, δ_m =..... degree (ii) Kerosene oil, δ_m =...... degree
   (iii) Spirit, δ_m =...... degree (iv) Turpentine oil, δ_m =...... degree
3. The refractive indices of
   (i) Water, μ =...... (ii) Kerosene oil, μ =.........
   (iii) Spirit, μ =......... (iv) Turpentine oil, μ =.........
4. Speed of light in
   (i) Water, v =......... m/s (ii) Kerosene oil, v =...... m/s
   (iii) Spirit, v =......... m/s (iv) Turpentine oil, v =......m/s

PRECAUTIONS

Same as given in Experiment 5, Section B.

Q 1 Name the factors on which angle of deviation depends.

Ans. The angle of deviation depends on the following factors

(i) Refractive index of the material of prism (μ)

(ii) Angle of prism (A)

(iii) Angle of incidence (i)

Q 2 Write the formula for refractive index of material of prism in terms of angle of prism and minimum deviation.

Ans. $$\mu = \frac{\sin\,[(A - \delta_m)/2]}{\sin\,(-A/2)}$$

Q 3 Why we use prism having equiangular triangle base?

Ans. Because this provides a much wider range for the variation of angle of incidence.

Q 4 Does the value of angle of deviation also depend on the wavelength of light used?

Ans. Yes, as the angle of deviation depends on refractive index and refractive index depends on wavelength. Therefore, angle of deviation also depends on wavelength.

Q 5 What is the angle of minimum deviation?

Ans. The angle of deviation varies with the angle of incidence. At a specific angle of incidence, the deviation reaches its lowest value.This is known as the angle of minimum deviation.

Project 06

AIM

To estimate the charge induced on each one of the two identical styrofoam (or pith) balls suspended in a vertical plane by making use of Coulomb's law.

Apparatus and Material Required

Two identical styrofoam balls with metal coating, physical balance or electronic balance, meter scale, teflon thread, glass rod, silk/wool cloth, clamp stand/rigid support.

Theory /Principle

Coulomb's Law

Coulomb's law states that

"The force of interaction (F) between any two point charges is directly proportional to the product of the charges (q_1 and q_2) and inversely proportional to the square of the distance (r) between them".

Mathematically, it is expressed as

$$F = \frac{Kq_1q_2}{r^2}$$

or

$$F = \frac{1}{4\pi\varepsilon_0} \cdot \frac{q_1q_2}{r^2}$$

where, K is constant of proportionality called **Coulomb constant** and its value is $9 \times 10^9 \text{N-m}^2/\text{C}^2$, ε_0 is permittivity of free space and its value is $8.85 \times 10^{-12}\ \text{C}^2/\text{N-m}^2$.

Determination of Charge Induced on Each Styrofoam Ball

Consider two small identical styrofoam balls suspended through teflon threads of equal lengths (l) from a rigid support (at point O). These balls will stay in contact hanging almost vertically but when these balls are charged, then the charged balls having charge q exert repulsive forces on each other.

The magnitude of this force is given by

$$\text{Force, } F = \frac{Kq^2}{x^2} \quad \text{....(i)}$$

where, x = separation between the charged balls after repulsion

The weight of each ball is $w = mg$ which acts vertically downward

Also, restoring force on each ball is $F_{rest} = mg \sin\theta$ which acts towards mean or rest position of the balls.

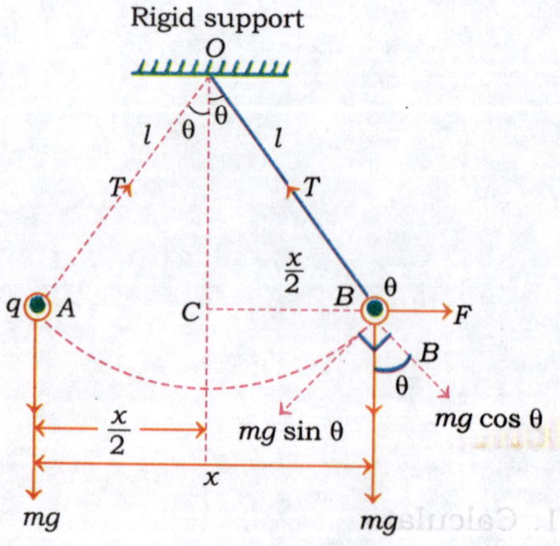

Determination of charge Induced on each styrofoam ball

Thus, by knowing the value of mass (m), separation between balls (x) and length (l) of thc thread, the charge induced on the each ball can be estimated.

Procedure

Setting up the Apparatus

1. Take two identical small styrofoam balls coated with metal paint. Measure the mass of each ball using physical balance.
2. Now, tie the balls with teflon thread and suspend at a point on a clamp stand or a rigid support.
3. Measure the length of threads by meter scale and ensure that it should be equal.

To Estimate the Charge Induced on Each Ball

4. Now, take a glass rod and rub it with silk/wool, so that it can be charged.
5. Touch the charged glass rod to both the balls together, so that they can acquire charge equally.
6. The balls which are suspended freely stay away a certain distance apart due to repulsive force acting between them.
7. Measure the distance between the balls when they become stationary and note the distance.
8. Touch any one suspended ball with other uncharged third ball and take the third ball away and repeat step (5).

Note On touching the balls together, almost half of charge is transferred from charged ball to uncharged ball.

9. Touch other suspended ball with other uncharged fourth ball and take the fourth ball away and repeat the step (5).
10. Note the distance between balls each time and determine the charge in each case. Thereafter, take the mean of different values of charge.

Observations

1. Mass of each ball, m =........... g   2. Radius of each ball, r =........... mm
3. Length of each thread, l = ... cm

Table for Measuring the Charges on Balls *A* and *B* and Distance Between the Balls

S.N.	Charge on ball *A*	Charge on ball *B*	Distance between the balls, *x* (cm)
1	0	0	0
2	q	q	x_1 = ... cm
3	q	$q/2$	x_2 = ... cm
4	$q/2$	$q/2$	x_3 = ... cm

Calculations

1. Calculate the charge in each case using the relation $q = \sqrt{\dfrac{mgx^3}{2lK}}$
2. Find the mean value of charge, $q = \dfrac{q_1 + q_2 + q_3 + q_4}{4}$ = ... C

Result

The charge on each ball = ... C

PRECAUTIONS

1. The length of the thread with which the balls are suspended should be equal.
2. Do not touch the suspended balls by any conducting body.
3. The glass rod should be rubbed properly with the silk cloth.
4. Measure the mass of the balls accurately.

Viva-Voce

Q 1 Why do the two styrofoam balls repel each other after charging?

Ans. Because they acquire like charges due to identical rubbing or contact, leading to electrostatic repulsion.

Q 2 Why is Coulomb's law suitable for this experiment?

Ans. Because it quantifies the force between two point charges, allowing estimation of charge from measured force and distance.

Q 3 How many types of charges are possible? Name these types.

Ans. There are two types of charges, i.e. positive charge and negative charge.

Q 4 State the law of conservation of charge.

Ans. According to the law of conservation of charge, charge can neither be created nor be destroyed , it can be transferred from one body to another body.

Q 5 What happens when two similar charges are brought together?

Ans. Repulsion between them takes place.

Q 6 What should be the polarity of two charges for attraction?

Ans. Opposite to each other, i.e. if one is positive, then the other charge must be negative.

Q 7 Why is it important that both balls are of equal mass and suspended by equal-length threads?

Ans. To ensure symmetric deflection and equal charge distribution for accurate calculation.

Q 8 Why is a rigid support necessary for this setup?

Ans. To ensure the suspension point remains fixed and symmetrical displacement occurs.

Q 9 What do you mean by a negatively charged body?

Ans. A body which gains electrons becomes negatively charged.

Q 10 What do you mean by a positively charged body?

Ans. A body is said to be positively charged when it loses electrons.

Q 11 If an object is charged, will there be any change in its mass?

Ans. Yes, because electrons that are transferred do have mass. This change in mass is barely noticeable because the mass of an electron is extremely small approximately 9.1×10^{-31} kg.

Project 07

AIM

To study the factor on which the self-inductance of a coil depends by observing the effect of this coil, when put in series with a resistor/bulb in a circuit fed up by an AC source of adjustable frequency.

Apparatus and Material Required

AC source of adjustable frequency, connecting wires, an electric bulb or resistor, rheostat, AC ammeter, an one-way key, soft iron rod, a coil of large turns and a piece of sand paper.

Theory/Principle

Self-Inductance

Self-induction is the property of a coil by virtue of which the coil opposes any change in the strength of current flowing through it by inducing an emf in itself. The induced emf is given by

$$e = -\frac{LdI}{dt}$$

where, e is induced emf, $\frac{dI}{dt}$ is rate of change of current through the coil and L is the self-inductance of the coil.

The self-inductance of a coil is given by, $L = \frac{\mu_0 \mu_r N^2 A}{l}$

where, μ_r = relative permeability of magnetic material, $\mu_r = \frac{\mu}{\mu_0}$,
N = total number of turns in the the coil, A = area of cross-section of the coil and l = length of the coil.

Thus, the self-inductance of the coil depends upon the following factors

(i) Number of turns (N) in the coil
(ii) Length of the coil
(iii) Area of cross-section of the coil
(iv) Permeability of material of the coil
(v) Shape of the coil

Procedure

Setting up the Elements in a Circuit

1. Before using the connecting wires clean their ends with the help of sand paper. Connect all the components as shown in the circuit diagram.
2. Switch OFF the key K by pulling out the plug from it.
3. Note the least count and zero error of AC ammeter.
4. Switch ON the AC supply and insert the plug into the key.

5. Maintain the constant current in the circuit by using the rheostat Rh.

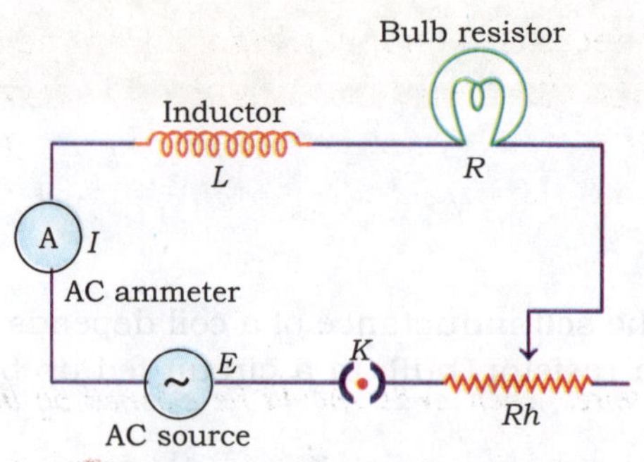

Circuit diagram to study the factors on which the self-inductance of a coil depends

When AC Source of 60Hz

6. Consider the frequency of source to be 60 Hz and voltage be 6 V.
7. Note the reading of current in AC ammeter and observe the brightness of the bulb.
8. Put a soft iron rod inside the inductor core and note the reading of current in AC ammeter and check the brightness of the bulb again. This time, the current in AC ammeter and brightness of bulb both are decreased.

When AC Source of 50Hz

9. Now switch OFF the supply and decrease the frequency of AC source say 50 Hz.
10. Again, switch ON the supply and adjust the same constant voltage 6 V by using the variable resistor or rheostat. Note reading of current in the ammeter and brightness of the bulb. The current and brightness both are increased.
11. Insert an iron rod in the core of coil again and record the current and brightness. The current and brightness both are decreased. Repeat the steps 9 and 10 by adjusting the frequency of AC source such as 40 Hz, 30 Hz and 20 Hz.

Observations

1. Least count of ammeter = ...A
2. Zero error of ammeter = ...A
3. Range of ammeter = 0 to..............A

Table to Study the Factors Affecting Self-Inductance of a Coil

S. No.	Frequency of applied voltage, *f* (Hz)	Current in ammeter without iron rod in the coil (A)	Current in ammeter with iron rod in the coil (A)
1	60		
2	50		
3	40		
4	30		

Result

1. The current in the circuit decreases on inserting the iron rod in the core of coil at constant frequency of applied voltage and brightness of bulb also decreases and *vice-versa.*
2. The current in the circuit increases on decreasing the frequency of applied voltage and *vice-versa*, which shows that the brightness of bulb increases.

PRECAUTIONS

1. *Before using the connecting wires, their ends should be cleaned by using sand paper.*
2. *The coil used must have large number of turns. The current should be passed for small time to avoid excessive heating.*
3. *The experiment should be performed at low voltages only. To take two consecutive observations, the difference in frequency should not be quite large.*

Viva-Voce

Q 1 Why do we use an inductor in an electric circuit?

Ans. We use an inductor in an electric circuit because it delays the growth and decay of current in the circuit.

Q 2 Is the reactance of coil equal to the resistance?

Ans. No, because a coil offers reactance in AC circuit only resistance is the hindrance to the flow of current in DC circuit.

Q 3 Which is responsible for dissipation of energy either resistance or reactance?

Ans. Resistance

Project 08

AIM

To study the earth's magnetic field using a compass needle-bar magnet by plotting magnetic field lines and tangent galvanometer.

Apparatus and Material Required

Tangent galvanometer, a battery or battery eliminator (0 to 6 V), a rheostat, spirit level, a reversing key, an ordinary key, an ammeter, connecting wires, a piece of sand paper and a meter scale.

Theory/principle

Tangent Galvanometer

It is an early measuring instrument for small electric current.

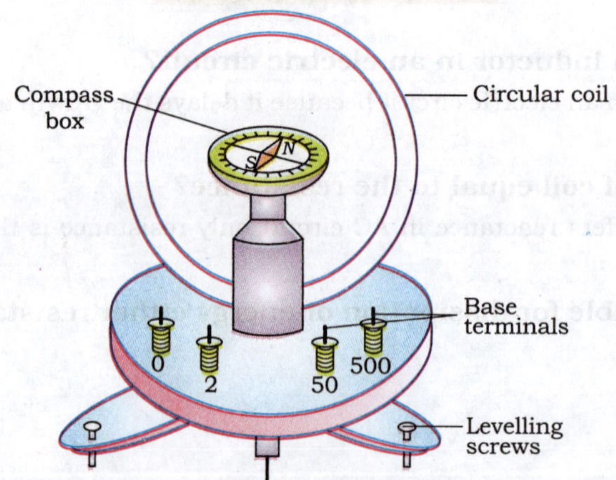

A tangent galvanometer

Working Principle of Tangent Galvanometer

The tangent galvanometer works on **magnetic effect of electric current** and the **tangent law**. It works on the principle that when the coil of the tangent galvanometer is kept in magnetic meridian and current passes through any of the coil, then the magnetic needle at the centre gets deflected and comes to an equilibrium position under the action of two perpendicular fields : one due to horizontal component of earth (B_H) and the other due to the field (B) set up by the coil due to current.

In equilibrium, $B = B_H \tan\theta$

This relation is known as tangent law but magnetic field at the centre of coil, $B = \dfrac{\mu_0 NI}{2R}$

where, N = number of turns, R = radius of tangent galvanometer or coil,

I = current to be measured

and θ = angle made by needle from the direction of B_H in equilibrium.

Hence, $\frac{\mu_0 NI}{2R} = B_H \tan\theta$ or $I = \frac{2RB_H \tan\theta}{\mu_0 N}$ $\Rightarrow$ $I = K \tan\theta$

where, $K\left(=\frac{2RB_H}{\mu_0 N}\right)$ is called **reduction factor.**

$$\therefore \qquad I \propto \tan\theta$$

This is the principle of tangent galvanometer i.e.

"The current to be measured by tangent galvanometer is directly proportional to tangent of deflection of the magnetic needle of tangent galvanometer". This is known as **tangent law.**

Thus, if we plot a graph between *I* and $\tan\theta$ **by taking them along *X* and *Y*-axes respectively, then we will get a straight line.**

From the slope of the graph, the value of horizontal component of earth's magnetic field can be obtained.

Procedure

Setting up the Elements in the Circuit

1. Before using the connecting wires, clean their ends by using sand paper so that the insulation deposited on them can be removed.
2. Connect the components as per the circuit diagram.

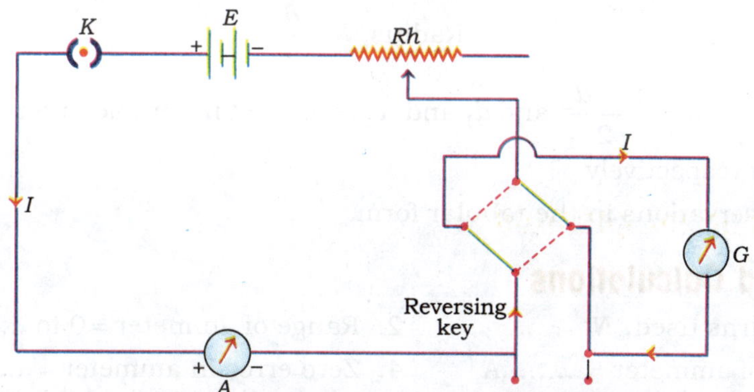

Circuit diagram to study the earth's magnetic field using a tangent galvanometer *G*

Setting up the Tangent Galvanometer

3. With the help of spirit level, set the level of the base and the compass needle in compass box of tangent galvanometer by adjusting the levelling screw.
4. Rotate the coil of the galvanometer about its vertical axis, till the magnetic needle, its image in the plane mirror fixed at the base of the compass box and the coil, i.e. all lie in the same vertical plane. At this position, the ends of the aluminium pointer should read 0-0. If this is not possible, then rotate the box without disturbing the position of the coil, till at least one of the ends of the pointer stands at the zero marks.
5. Close the key *K*, so that the current can flow in the galvanometer. Read both ends of pointer and take the mean of values shown by both the ends.
6. Now, with the help of reversing key or commutator, reverse the direction of current. Read both the ends of pointer again and take the mean of values shown by both the ends.

7. Take the difference between two mean values measured in steps (5) and (6) and observe the difference, if it is differ by more than 1°, then turn the coil slightly until the two values agree. This will set the plane of the coil exactly in the magnetic meridian.

Variation in Deflection (or θ) due to Current

8. Bring the deflection in galvanometer around 45° by adjusting the sliding contact of rheostat. By adjusting the rheostat, the current is adjusted so that the deflection shown in the galvanometer gets changed. Take care that the deflection should be in the range 30° to 60°.
9. Note the readings of the ammeter and the deflection of the compass needle in the box shown by two ends of pointer on the circular scale.
10. Next reverse the direction of current in the coil of galvanometer. Again note the readings of current and deflection of needle.
11. Take the mean of four values of deflection (two values by each end of the pointer) and then find the value of tan θ, where θ is the mean value of deflection.
12. Take four more sets of reading by changing the value of current.
13. Plot the graph between I and tan θ by taking them along X and Y-axes, respectively. One can find that the graph will be a straight line.

Determination of Radius of Tangent Galvanometer

14. Measure the inner and outer diameters of the coil with the help of meter scale at least three times and then find the radius of the tangent galvanometer by using the following relation

$$\text{Radius, } R = \frac{d}{2}$$

where, diameter, $d = \frac{d_1 + d_2}{2}$ and d_1 and d_2 represent inner and outer diameters of tangent galvanometer respectively.

15. Note your observations in the tabular form.

Observations and Calculations

1. Number of turns used, N = ...
2. Range of ammeter = 0 to ....A
3. Least count of ammeter = ...A
4. Zero error in ammeter = ...A

Table for Variation of θ With I

S. N.	Value of deflection θ (degree)				Mean θ (degree)	tan θ (degree)	Ammeter reading, I (A)	
	For current in one direction		For current in reverse direction					
	θ_1	θ_2	θ_3	θ_4			Observed	Corrected
1								
2								
3								
4								
5								

Table for Radius of Tangent Galvanometer (R)

S. N.	Inner diameter, d_1 (cm)	Outer diameter, d_2 (cm)	Mean diameter, $d = \frac{d_1 + d_2}{2}$ (cm)	Radius, $R = \frac{d}{2}$ (cm)
1				R_1 = ……… cm
2				R_2 = ……… cm
3				R_3 = ……… cm

5. Mean radius of the coil, $R = \frac{R_1 + R_2 + R_3}{3}$ = ……cm

Plotting Graph

Plot the graph between I and $\tan\theta$ by taking them along X- and Y-axes, respectively. The graph shows a straight line.

From graph,

Slope of the straight line, $m = \frac{BC}{AC}$

$$m = \frac{\tan\theta}{I} = \frac{\tan\theta}{1} \times \frac{\mu_0 N}{2RB_H \tan\theta}$$

$$m = \frac{\mu_0 N}{2RB_H}$$

$$B_H = \frac{\mu_0}{4\pi}\frac{2\pi N}{Rm} = 10^{-7} \times \frac{2\pi N}{Rm}$$

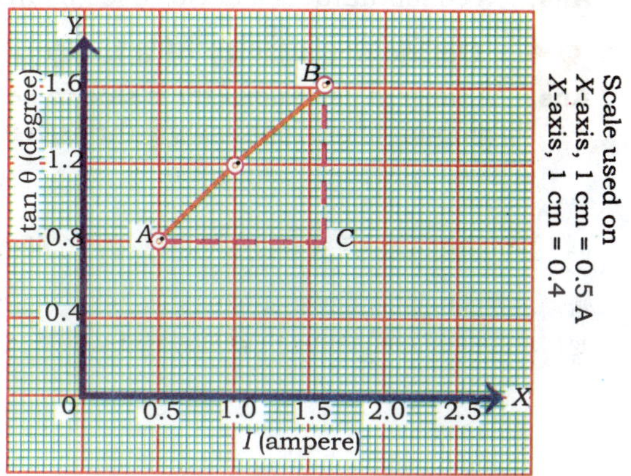

Graph showing relation between current and deflection of tangent galvanometer

Result

1. Experimental value of horizontal component of the earth's magnetic field, B_H = ………T
2. Theoretical value of horizontal component of the earth's magnetic field, $B'_H = 0.32 \times 10^{-4}$ T
3. Percentage error = $\frac{B'_H - B_H}{H} \times 100$ = ……%

PRECAUTIONS

1. *The reversing key should be switched OFF when readings are not being taken.*
2. *The magnetic needle should swing freely in the horizontal plane.*
3. *The plane of the coil should be set in the magnetic meridian.*
4. *All the readings should be taken for deflection in between 30° and 60°.*
5. *Keep the tangent galvanometer at a large distance from the rest of the apparatus.*
6. *The tangent galvanometer set accurately in the magnetic meridian and the plane of the coil should be vertical.*
7. *While reading the ends of the pointer, error due to parallex should be avoided.*

Viva-Voce

Q 1 Name the law on which, the principle of working of a tangent galvanometer depends.

Ans. A tangent galvanometer works on the principle of tangent law.

Q 2 What should be the unit of reduction factor?

Ans. $\because$ $K = I \tan \theta$

Also $\tan \theta$ is the ratio, so there is no unit for $\tan \theta$. Thus, the unit of reduction factor K is same as the unit of current I, i.e. ampere (A).

Q 3 What do you mean by a commutator or reversing key?

Ans. A commutator is a device used in an electric circuit to reverse the direction of current.

Q 4 Define sensitivity of a tangent galvanometer.

Ans. A tangent galvanometer is said to be more sensitive, if it produces a large deflection for small amount of current flowing through it.

Appendices

APPENDIX 1

LOGARITHMS

	0′	6′	12′	18′	14′	30′	36′	42′	48′	54′	Mean Differences				
	0°.0	0°.1	0°.2	0°.3	0°.4	0°.5	0°.6	0°.7	0°.8	0°.9	1′	2′	3′	4′	5′
0	.0000	0017	0035	0052	0070	0087	0105	0122	0140	0157	3	6	9	12	15
1	.0175	0192	0209	0227	0244	0262	0279	0297	0314	0332	3	6	9	12	15
2	.0349	0366	0384	0401	0419	0436	0454	0471	0488	0506	3	6	9	12	15
3	.0523	0541	0558	0576	0593	0610	0628	0645	0663	0680	3	6	9	12	15
4	.0698	0715	0732	0750	0767	0785	0802	0819	0837	0854	3	6	9	12	15
5	.0872	0889	0906	0924	0941	0958	0976	0993	1011	1028	3	6	9	12	14
6	.1045	1063	1080	1097	1115	1132	1149	1167	1184	1201	3	6	9	12	14
7	.1219	1236	1253	1271	1288	1305	1323	1340	1357	1374	3	6	9	12	14
8	.1392	1409	1426	1444	1461	1478	1495	1513	1530	1547	3	6	9	12	14
9	.1564	1582	1599	1616	1633	1650	1668	1685	1702	1719	3	6	9	12	14
10	.1736	1654	1771	1788	1805	1822	1840	1857	1874	1891	3	6	9	12	14
11	.1908	1925	1942	1959	1977	1994	2011	2028	2045	2062	3	6	9	11	14
12	.2079	2096	2113	2130	2147	2164	2181	2198	2215	2232	3	6	9	11	14
13	.2250	2267	2284	2300	2317	2334	2351	2368	2385	2402	3	6	8	11	14
14	.2419	2436	2453	2470	2487	2504	2521	2538	2554	2571	3	6	8	11	14
15	.2588	2605	2622	2639	2656	2672	2689	2706	2723	2749	3	6	8	11	14
16	.2756	2773	2790	2807	2823	2840	2857	2874	2890	2907	3	6	8	11	14
17	.2924	2940	2957	2974	2990	3007	3024	3040	3057	3074	3	6	8	11	14
18	.3090	3107	3123	3140	3156	3173	3190	3206	3223	3239	3	6	8	11	14
19	.3256	3272	3289	3305	3322	3338	3355	3371	3387	3404	3	5	8	11	14
20	.3420	3437	3453	3469	3486	3502	3518	3535	3551	4567	3	5	8	11	14
21	.3584	3600	3616	3633	3649	3665	3681	3697	3714	3730	3	5	8	11	14
22	.3746	3762	3778	3795	3811	3827	3843	3859	3875	3891	3	5	8	11	14
23	.3907	3923	3939	3955	3971	3987	4003	4019	4035	4051	3	5	8	11	14
24	.4067	4083	4099	4115	4131	4147	4163	4179	4195	4210	3	5	8	11	13
25	.4226	4242	4258	4274	4289	4305	4321	4337	4352	4368	3	5	8	11	13
26	.4384	4399	4415	4431	4446	4462	4478	4493	4509	4524	3	5	8	10	13
27	.4540	4555	4571	4586	4602	4617	4633	4648	4664	4679	3	5	8	10	13
28	.4695	4710	4726	4741	4756	4772	4787	4802	4818	4833	3	5	8	10	13
29	.4848	4863	4879	4894	4909	4924	4939	4955	4970	4985	3	5	8	10	13
30	.5000	5015	5030	5045	5060	5075	5090	5105	5120	5135	3	5	8	10	13
31	.5150	5165	5180	5195	5210	5225	5240	5255	5270	5284	2	5	7	10	12
32	.5299	5314	5329	5344	5358	5373	5388	5402	5417	5432	2	5	7	10	12
33	.5446	5461	5476	5490	5505	5519	5534	5548	5563	5577	2	5	7	10	12
34	.5592	5606	5621	5635	5650	5664	5678	5693	5707	5721	2	5	7	10	12
35	.5736	5750	5764	5779	5793	5807	5821	5835	5850	5864	2	5	7	10	12
36	.5878	5892	5906	5920	5934	5948	5962	5976	5990	6004	2	5	7	9	12
37	.6018	6032	6046	6060	6074	6088	6101	6115	6129	6143	2	5	7	9	11
38	.6157	6170	6184	6198	6211	6225	6239	6252	6266	6280	2	5	7	9	11
39	.6293	6307	6320	6334	6347	6361	6374	6388	6401	6414	2	4	7	9	11
40	.6428	6441	6455	6468	6481	6494	6508	6521	6534	6547	2	4	7	9	11
41	.6561	6574	6587	6600	6613	6626	6639	6652	6665	6678	2	4	7	9	11
42	.6691	6704	6717	6730	6743	6756	6769	6782	6794	6807	2	4	6	9	11

	0′	6′	12′	18′	14′	30′	36′	42′	48′	54′	Mean Differences				
	0°.0	0°.1	0°.2	0°.3	0°.4	0°.5	0°.6	0°.7	0°.8	0°.9	1′	2′	3′	4′	5′
43	.6820	6833	6845	6858	6871	6884	6896	6909	6921	6934	2	4	6	8	11
44	.6947	6959	6972	6984	6997	7009	7022	7034	7046	7059	2	4	6	8	10
45	.7071	7083	7096	7108	7120	7133	7145	7157	7169	7181	2	4	6	8	10
46	.7193	7206	7218	7230	7242	7254	7266	7278	7290	7302	2	4	6	8	10
47	.7314	7325	7337	7349	7361	7373	7385	7396	7408	7420	2	4	6	8	10
48	.7431	7443	7455	7466	7478	7490	7501	7513	7524	7536	2	4	6	8	10
49	.7547	7558	7570	7581	7593	7694	7615	6727	7638	7649	2	4	6	8	9
50	.7660	7672	7683	7694	7705	7716	7727	7738	7749	7760	2	4	6	7	9
51	.7771	7782	7793	7804	7815	7826	7837	7848	7859	7869	2	4	5	7	9
52	.7880	7891	7902	7912	7923	7934	7944	7955	7965	7976	2	4	5	7	9
53	.7986	7997	8007	8018	8028	8039	8049	8059	8070	8080	2	3	5	7	9
54	.8090	8100	8111	8121	8131	8141	8151	8161	8171	8181	2	3	5	7	8
55	.8192	8202	8211	8221	8231	8241	8251	8261	8271	8281	2	3	5	7	8
56	.8290	8300	8310	8320	8329	8339	8348	8358	8368	8377	2	3	5	6	8
57	.8387	8396	8406	8415	8425	8434	8443	8453	8462	8471	2	3	5	6	8
58	.8480	8490	8499	8508	8517	8526	8536	8545	8554	8563	2	3	5	6	8
59	.8572	8581	8590	8599	8607	8616	8625	8634	8643	8652	1	3	4	6	7
60	.8660	8669	8678	8686	8695	8704	8712	8721	8729	8738	1	3	4	6	7
61	.8746	8755	8763	8771	8780	8788	8796	8805	8813	8821	1	3	4	6	7
62	.8829	8838	8846	8854	8862	8870	8878	8886	8894	8902	1	3	4	5	7
63	.8910	8918	8926	8934	8942	8949	8957	8965	8973	8980	1	3	4	5	6
64	.8988	8996	9003	9011	9018	9026	9033	9041	9048	9056	1	3	4	5	6
65	.9063	9070	9078	9085	9092	9100	9107	9114	9121	9128	1	2	4	5	6
66	.9135	9143	9150	9157	9164	9171	9178	9184	9191	9198	1	2	3	5	6
67	.9205	9212	9219	9225	9232	9239	9245	9252	9259	9265	1	2	3	4	6
68	.9272	9278	9285	9291	9298	9304	9311	9317	9323	9330	1	2	3	4	5
69	.9336	9342	9348	9354	9361	9367	9373	9379	9385	9391	1	2	3	4	5
70	.9397	9403	9409	9415	9421	9426	9432	9438	9444	9449	1	2	3	4	5
71	.9455	9461	9466	9472	9478	9483	9489	9494	9500	9505	1	2	3	4	5
72	.9511	9516	9521	9527	9532	9537	9542	9548	9553	9558	1	2	3	4	5
73	.9563	9568	9573	9578	9583	9588	9593	9558	9603	9608	1	2	3	3	4
74	.9613	9617	9622	9627	9632	9636	9641	9646	9650	9655	1	2	2	3	4
75	.9659	9664	9668	9673	9677	9681	9686	9690	9694	9699	1	1	2	3	4
76	.9703	9707	9711	9715	9720	9724	9728	9732	9736	9740	1	1	2	3	3
77	.9744	9748	9751	9755	9759	9763	9768	9770	9774	9778	1	1	2	2	3
78	.9781	9785	9789	9792	9696	9799	9803	9806	9810	9813	1	1	2	2	3
79	.9816	9820	9823	9826	9829	9833	9836	9839	9842	9845	1	1	2	2	3
80	.9848	9851	9854	9857	9860	9863	9866	9869	9871	9874	0	1	1	2	2
81	.9877	9880	9882	9885	9888	9890	9893	9895	9898	9900	0	1	1	2	2
82	.9903	9905	9907	9910	9912	9914	9917	9919	9921	9923	0	1	1	2	2
83	.9925	9928	9930	9932	9934	9936	9938	9940	9942	9943	0	1	1	1	2
84	.9945	9947	9949	9951	9952	9954	9956	9957	9959	9960	0	1	1	1	2
85	.9962	9963	9965	9966	9968	9969	9971	9972	9973	9974	0	0	1	1	1
86	.9976	9977	9978	9979	9980	9981	9982	9983	9984	9985	0	0	1	1	1
87	.9986	9987	9988	9989	9990	9990	9991	9992	9993	9993	0	0	0	1	1
88	.9994	9995	9995	9996	9996	9997	9997	9997	9998	9998	0	0	0	0	0
89	.9998	9999	9999	9999	9999	1.000	1.000	1.000	1.000	1.000	0	0	0	0	0
90	1.000														

APPENDIX 2

ANTILOGARITHMS

	0	1	2	3	4	5	6	7	8	9	Mean Differences								
											1	2	3	4	5	6	7	8	9
.00	1000	1002	1005	1007	1009	1012	1014	1016	1019	1021	0	0	1	1	1	1	2	2	2
.01	1023	1026	1028	1030	1033	1035	1038	1040	1042	1045	0	0	1	1	1	1	2	2	2
.02	1047	1050	1052	1054	1057	1059	1062	1064	1067	1069	0	0	1	1	1	1	2	2	2
.03	1072	1074	1076	1079	1081	1084	1086	1089	1091	1094	0	0	1	1	1	1	2	2	2
.04	1096	1099	1102	1104	1107	1109	1112	1114	1117	1119	0	1	1	1	1	2	2	2	2
.05	1122	1125	1127	1130	1132	1135	1138	1140	1143	1146	0	1	1	1	1	2	2	2	2
.06	1148	1151	1153	1156	1159	1161	1164	1167	1169	1172	0	1	1	1	1	2	2	2	2
.07	1175	1178	1180	1183	1186	1189	1191	1194	1197	1199	0	1	1	1	1	2	2	2	2
.08	1202	1205	1208	1211	1213	1216	1219	1222	1225	1227	0	1	1	1	1	2	2	2	3
.09	1230	1233	1236	1239	1242	1245	1247	1250	1253	1256	0	1	1	1	1	2	2	2	3
.10	1259	1262	1265	1268	1271	1274	1276	1279	1282	1285	0	1	1	1	1	2	2	2	3
.11	1288	1291	1294	1297	1300	1303	1306	1309	1312	1315	0	1	1	1	2	2	2	2	3
.12	1318	1321	1324	1327	1330	1334	1337	1340	1343	1346	0	1	1	1	2	2	2	2	3
.13	1349	1352	1355	1358	1361	1365	1368	1371	1374	1377	0	1	1	1	2	2	2	3	3
.14	1380	1384	1387	1390	1393	1396	1400	1403	1406	1409	0	1	1	1	2	2	2	3	3
.15	1413	1416	1419	1422	1426	1429	1432	1435	1439	1442	0	1	1	1	2	2	2	3	3
.16	1445	1449	1452	1455	1459	1462	1466	1469	1472	1476	0	1	1	1	2	2	2	3	3
.17	1479	1483	1486	1489	1493	1496	1500	1503	1507	1510	0	1	1	1	2	2	2	3	3
.18	1514	1517	1521	1524	1528	1531	1535	1538	1542	1545	0	1	1	1	2	2	2	3	3
.19	1549	1552	1556	1560	1563	1567	1570	1574	1578	1581	0	1	1	1	2	2	3	3	3
.20	1585	1589	1592	1596	1600	1603	1607	1611	1614	1618	0	1	1	1	2	2	3	3	3
.21	1622	1626	1629	1633	1637	1641	1644	1648	1652	1656	0	1	1	2	2	2	3	3	3
.22	1660	1663	1667	1671	1675	1679	1683	1687	1690	1694	0	1	1	2	2	2	3	3	3
.23	1698	1702	1706	1710	1714	1718	1722	1726	1730	1734	0	1	1	2	2	2	3	3	4
.24	1738	1742	1746	1750	1754	1758	1762	1766	1770	1774	0	1	1	2	2	2	3	3	4
.25	1778	1782	1786	1791	1795	1799	1803	1807	1811	1816	0	1	1	2	2	2	3	3	4
.26	1820	1824	1828	1832	1837	1841	1845	1849	1854	1858	0	1	1	2	2	3	3	3	4
.27	1862	1866	1871	1875	1879	1884	1888	1892	1897	1901	0	1	1	2	2	3	3	3	4
.28	1905	1910	1914	1919	1923	1928	1932	1936	1941	1945	0	1	1	2	2	3	3	4	4
.29	1950	1954	1959	1963	1968	1972	1977	1982	1986	1991	0	1	1	2	2	3	3	4	4
.30	1995	2000	2004	2009	2014	2018	2023	2028	2032	2037	0	1	1	2	2	3	3	4	4
.31	2042	2046	2051	2056	2061	2065	2070	2075	2080	2084	0	1	1	2	2	3	3	4	4
.32	2089	2094	2099	2104	2109	2113	2118	2123	2128	2133	0	1	1	2	2	3	3	4	4
.33	2138	2143	2148	2153	2158	2163	2168	2173	2178	2183	0	1	1	2	2	3	3	4	4
.34	2188	2193	2198	2203	2208	2213	2218	2223	2228	2234	1	1	2	2	3	3	4	4	5
.35	2239	2244	2249	2254	2259	2265	2270	2275	2280	2286	1	1	2	2	3	3	4	4	5
.36	2291	2296	2301	2307	2312	2317	2323	2328	2333	2339	1	1	2	2	3	3	4	4	5
.37	2344	2350	2355	2360	2366	2371	2377	2382	2388	2393	1	1	2	2	3	3	4	4	5
.38	2399	2404	2410	2415	2421	2427	2432	2438	2443	2449	1	1	2	2	3	3	4	4	5
.39	2455	2460	2466	2472	2477	2483	2489	2495	2500	2506	1	1	2	2	3	3	4	5	5
.40	2512	2518	2523	2529	2535	2541	2547	2553	2559	2564	1	1	2	2	3	4	4	5	5
.41	2570	2576	2582	2588	2594	2600	2696	2612	2618	2624	1	1	2	2	3	4	4	5	5
.42	2630	2636	2642	2649	2655	2661	2667	2673	2679	2685	1	1	2	2	3	4	4	5	6
.43	2692	2698	2704	2710	2716	2723	2729	2735	2742	2748	1	1	2	3	3	4	4	5	6
.44	2754	2761	2767	2773	2780	2786	2793	2799	2805	2812	1	1	2	3	3	4	4	5	6
.45	2818	2825	2831	2838	2844	2851	2858	2864	2871	2877	1	1	2	3	3	4	5	5	6
.46	2884	2891	2897	2904	2911	2917	2924	2931	2938	2944	1	1	2	3	3	4	5	5	6
.47	2951	2958	2965	2972	2979	2985	2992	2999	3006	3013	1	1	2	3	3	4	5	5	6
.48	3020	3027	3034	3041	3048	3055	3062	3069	3076	3083	1	1	2	3	4	4	5	6	6
.49	3090	3097	3105	3112	3119	3126	3133	3141	3148	3155	1	1	2	3	4	4	5	6	6

ANTILOGARITHMS (Contd.)

	0	1	2	3	4	5	6	7	8	9	Mean Differences								
											1	2	3	4	5	6	7	8	9
.50	3162	3170	3177	3184	3192	3199	3206	3214	3221	3228	1	1	2	3	4	4	5	6	7
.51	3236	3243	3251	3258	3266	3273	3281	3289	3296	3304	1	2	2	3	4	5	5	6	7
.52	3311	3319	3327	3334	3342	3350	3357	3365	3373	3381	1	2	2	3	4	5	5	6	7
.53	3388	3396	3404	3412	3420	3428	3436	3443	3451	3459	1	2	2	3	4	5	6	6	7
.54	3467	3475	3483	3491	3499	3508	3516	3524	3532	3540	1	2	2	3	4	5	6	6	7
.55	3548	3556	3565	3573	3581	3589	3597	3606	3614	3622	1	2	2	3	4	5	6	7	7
.56	3631	3639	3648	3656	3664	3673	3681	3690	3698	3707	1	2	3	3	4	5	6	7	8
.57	3715	3724	3733	3741	3750	3758	3767	3776	3784	3793	1	2	3	3	4	5	6	7	8
.58	3802	3811	3819	3828	3837	3846	3855	3864	3873	3882	1	2	3	4	4	5	6	7	8
.59	3890	3899	3908	3917	3926	3936	3945	3954	3963	3972	1	2	3	4	5	5	6	7	8
.60	3981	3990	3999	4009	4018	4027	4036	4046	4055	4064	1	2	3	4	5	6	6	7	8
.61	4074	4083	4093	4102	4111	4121	4130	4140	4150	4159	1	2	3	4	5	6	7	8	9
.62	4169	4178	4188	4198	4207	4217	4227	4236	4256	4256	1	2	3	4	5	6	7	8	9
.63	4266	4276	4285	4295	4305	4315	4325	4335	4345	4355	1	2	3	4	5	6	7	8	9
.64	4365	4375	4385	4395	4406	4416	4426	4436	4446	4457	1	2	3	4	5	6	7	8	9
.65	4467	4477	4487	4498	4508	4519	4529	4539	4550	4560	1	2	3	4	5	6	7	8	9
.66	4571	4581	4592	4603	4613	4624	4634	4645	4656	4667	1	2	3	4	5	6	7	9	10
.67	4677	4688	4699	4710	4721	4732	4742	4753	4764	4775	1	2	3	4	5	7	8	9	10
.68	4786	4797	4808	4819	4831	4842	4853	4864	4875	4887	1	2	3	4	6	7	8	9	10
.69	4898	4909	4920	4932	4943	4955	4966	4977	4989	5000	1	2	3	5	6	7	8	9	10
.70	5012	5023	5035	5047	5058	5070	5082	5093	5105	5117	1	2	4	5	6	7	8	9	11
.71	5129	5140	5152	5164	5176	5188	5200	5212	5224	5236	1	2	4	5	6	7	8	10	11
.72	5248	5260	5272	5284	5297	5309	5321	5333	5346	5358	1	2	4	5	6	7	9	10	11
.73	5370	5383	5395	5408	5420	5433	5445	5458	5470	5483	1	3	4	5	6	8	9	10	11
.74	5495	5508	5521	5534	5546	5559	5572	5585	5598	5610	1	3	4	5	6	8	9	10	12
.75	5623	5636	5649	5662	5675	5689	5702	5715	5728	5741	1	3	4	5	7	8	9	10	12
.76	5754	5768	5781	5794	5808	5821	5834	5848	5861	5875	1	3	4	5	7	8	9	11	12
.77	5888	5902	5916	5929	5943	5957	5970	5984	5998	6012	1	3	4	5	7	8	10	11	12
.78	6026	6039	6053	6067	6081	6095	6109	6124	6138	6152	1	3	4	6	7	8	10	11	13
.79	6166	6180	6194	6209	6223	7237	6252	6266	6281	6295	1	3	4	6	7	9	10	11	13
.80	6310	6324	6339	6353	6368	6383	6497	6412	6427	6442	1	3	4	6	7	9	10	12	13
.81	6457	6471	6486	6501	6516	6531	6546	6561	6577	6592	2	3	5	6	8	9	11	12	14
.82	6607	6622	6637	6653	6668	6683	6699	6714	6730	6745	2	3	5	6	8	9	11	12	14
.83	6761	6776	6792	6808	6823	6839	6855	6871	6887	6902	2	3	5	6	8	9	11	13	14
.84	6918	6934	6950	6966	6982	6998	7015	7031	7047	7063	2	3	5	6	8	10	11	13	15
.85	7079	7096	7112	7129	7145	7161	7178	7194	7211	7228	2	3	5	7	8	10	12	13	15
.86	7244	7261	7278	7295	7311	7328	7345	7362	7379	7396	2	3	5	7	8	10	12	13	15
.87	7413	7430	7447	7464	7482	7499	7516	7534	7551	7568	2	3	5	7	9	10	12	14	16
.88	7586	7603	7621	7638	7656	7674	7691	7709	7727	7745	2	4	5	7	9	11	12	14	16
.89	7762	7780	7798	7816	7834	7852	7870	7889	7907	7925	2	4	5	7	9	11	13	14	16
.90	7943	7962	7980	7998	8017	8035	8054	8072	8091	8110	2	4	6	7	9	11	13	15	17
.91	8128	8147	8166	8185	8204	8222	8241	8260	8279	8299	2	4	6	8	9	11	13	15	17
.92	8318	8337	8356	8375	8395	8414	8433	8453	8472	8492	2	4	6	8	10	12	14	15	17
.93	8511	8531	8551	8570	8590	8610	8630	8650	8670	8690	2	4	6	8	10	12	14	16	18
.94	8710	8730	8750	8770	8790	8810	8831	8851	8872	8892	2	4	6	8	10	12	14	16	18
.95	8913	8933	8954	8974	8995	9016	9036	9057	9078	9099	2	4	6	8	10	12	15	17	19
.96	9120	9141	9162	9183	9204	9226	9247	9268	9290	9311	2	4	6	8	11	13	15	17	19
.97	9333	9354	9376	9397	9419	9441	9462	9484	9506	9528	2	4	7	9	11	13	15	17	20
.98	9550	9572	9594	9616	9638	9661	9683	9705	9727	9750	2	4	7	9	11	13	16	18	20
.99	9772	9795	9817	9840	9863	9886	9908	9931	9954	9977	2	5	7	9	11	14	16	18	20

Experiment No.________ Date ________ Page No. ________

Teacher Signature________________

Experiment No.________ Date ________ Page No. ________

Teacher Signature________________

Experiment No.________ Date ________ Page No. ________

Teacher Signature ________________

Experiment No.________ Date ________ Page No. ________

Teacher Signature________________

Experiment No.________ Date ________ Page No. ________

Teacher Signature________________

Experiment No.________ Date ________ Page No. ________

Teacher Signature ________________

Experiment No.________ Date ________ Page No. ________

Teacher Signature ________________

Experiment No.________ Date ________ Page No. ________

Teacher Signature ________________

Experiment No.________ Date ________ Page No. ________

Teacher Signature________________

Experiment No.________ Date ________ Page No. ________

Teacher Signature ________________

Experiment No.________ Date ________ Page No. ________

Teacher Signature________________

Experiment No.________ Date ________ Page No. ________

Teacher Signature________________

Experiment No.________ Date ________ Page No. ________

Teacher Signature________________

Experiment No.________ Date ________ Page No. ________

Teacher Signature________________

Experiment No.________ Date ________ Page No. ________

Teacher Signature________________

Experiment No.________ Date ________ Page No. ________

Teacher Signature ________________

Experiment No.________ Date ________ Page No. ________

Teacher Signature ________________

Experiment No.________ Date ________ Page No. ________

Teacher Signature________________

Experiment No.________ Date ________ Page No. ________

Teacher Signature ________

Experiment No.________ Date ________ Page No. ________

Teacher Signature________________

Experiment No.________ Date ________ Page No. ________

Teacher Signature________________

Experiment No.________ Date ________ Page No. ________

Teacher Signature________________

Experiment No.________ Date ________ Page No. ________

Teacher Signature________________

Experiment No.________ Date ________ Page No. ________

Teacher Signature ____________

Experiment No.________ Date ________ Page No. ________

Teacher Signature________________

Experiment No.________ Date ________ Page No. ________

Teacher Signature________________

Experiment No.________ Date ________ Page No. ________

Teacher Signature________________

Experiment No.________ Date ________ Page No. ________

Teacher Signature ________________

Experiment No.________ Date ________ Page No. ________

Teacher Signature ________________

Experiment No.________ Date ________ Page No. ________

Teacher Signature________________

Experiment No.________ Date ________ Page No. ________

Teacher Signature________________

Experiment No.________ Date ________ Page No. ________

Teacher Signature ________________

Experiment No.________ Date ________ Page No. ________

Teacher Signature________________

Experiment No.________ Date ________ Page No. ________

Teacher Signature ________________

Experiment No.________ Date ________ Page No. ________

Teacher Signature ________________

Experiment No.________ Date ________ Page No. ________

Teacher Signature ________________

Experiment No.________ Date ________ Page No. ________

Teacher Signature________________

Experiment No.________ Date ________ Page No. ________

Teacher Signature________________

Experiment No.________ Date ________ Page No. ________

Teacher Signature________________

Experiment No.________ Date ________ Page No. ________

Teacher Signature ________________

Experiment No.________ Date ________ Page No. ________

Teacher Signature________________

Experiment No.________ Date ________ Page No. ________

Teacher Signature________________

Experiment No.________ Date ________ Page No. ________

Teacher Signature________________

Experiment No.________ Date ________ Page No. ________

Teacher Signature________________

Experiment No.________ Date ________ Page No. ________

Teacher Signature________________

Experiment No.________ Date ________ Page No. ________

Teacher Signature________________

Experiment No.________ Date ________ Page No. ________

Teacher Signature ________________

Experiment No.________ Date ________ Page No. ________

Teacher Signature________________

Experiment No.________ Date ________ Page No. ________

Teacher Signature________________

Experiment No.________ Date ________ Page No. ________

Teacher Signature ________________

Experiment No.________ Date ________ Page No. ________

Teacher Signature________________

Experiment No.________ Date ________ Page No. ________

Teacher Signature______________

Experiment No.________ Date ________ Page No. ________

Teacher Signature ________________

Experiment No.________ Date ________ Page No. ________

Teacher Signature ________________

Experiment No.________ Date ________ Page No. ________

Teacher Signature ________

Experiment No.________ Date ________ Page No. ________

Teacher Signature________________

Experiment No.________ Date ________ Page No. ________

Teacher Signature________________

Experiment No.________ Date ________ Page No. ________

Teacher Signature ________________

Experiment No.________ Date ________ Page No. ________

Teacher Signature________________

Experiment No.________ Date ________ Page No. ________

Teacher Signature________________

Experiment No.________ Date ________ Page No. ________

Teacher Signature________________

Experiment No.________ Date ________ Page No. ________

Teacher Signature ________________

Experiment No.________ Date ________ Page No. ________

Teacher Signature________________

Experiment No.________ Date ________ Page No. ________

Teacher Signature________________

Experiment No.________ Date ________ Page No. ________

Teacher Signature________________

Experiment No.________ Date ________ Page No. ________

Teacher Signature________________

Experiment No.________ Date ________ Page No. ________

Teacher Signature________________

Experiment No.________ Date ________ Page No. ________

Teacher Signature________________

Experiment No.________ Date ________ Page No. ________

Teacher Signature________________

Experiment No.________ Date ________ Page No. ________

Teacher Signature________________

Experiment No.________ Date ________ Page No. ________

Teacher Signature________________

Experiment No.________ Date ________ Page No. ________

Teacher Signature________________

Experiment No.________ Date ________ Page No. ________

Teacher Signature ________________

Experiment No.________ Date ________ Page No. ________

Teacher Signature________________

Experiment No.________ Date ________ Page No. ________

Teacher Signature________________

Experiment No.________ Date ________ Page No. ________

Teacher Signature ________________

Experiment No.________ Date ________ Page No. ________

Teacher Signature ________________

Experiment No.________ Date ________ Page No. ________

Teacher Signature ____________________

Experiment No.________ Date ________ Page No. ________

Teacher Signature________________

Experiment No.________ Date ________ Page No. ________

Teacher Signature ____________________